DATE		

THE DOUBLE LIFE OF
Stephen Crane

Christopher Benfey

THE DOUBLE LIFE OF
Stephen Crane

1992

NEW YORK   ALFRED A. KNOPF

THIS IS A BORZOI BOOK
PUBLISHED BY ALFRED A. KNOPF, INC.

Copyright © 1992 by Christopher Benfey

All rights reserved under International and Pan-American Copyright Conventions. Published in the United States by Alfred A. Knopf, Inc., New York, and simultaneously in Canada by Random House of Canada Limited, Toronto. Distributed by Random House, Inc., New York.

Parts of the "Introduction" appeared in slightly different form in "The Courage of Stephen Crane," *The New York Review of Books* (March 16, 1989).
Part of Chapter One appeared in *Syracuse University Library Associates Courier*, 25/1 (Spring 1990).
Chapter Nine, in slightly different form, appeared in *Pequod*, 32. Reprinted by permission.

Library of Congress Cataloging-in-Publication Data

Benfey, Christopher E. G.
    The double life of Stephen Crane / Christopher Benfey.—1st ed.
        p.   cm.
    Includes bibliographical references and index.
    ISBN 0–394–56864–8
    1. Crane, Stephen, 1871–1900—Biography.   2. Authors,
American—19th century—Biography.   I. Title.
PS1449.C85Z554   1992
813'.4—dc20
[B]   91–36726
                                                                   CIP

Manufactured in the United States of America
First Edition

FOR MICKEY AND THOMAS
my own double life

A whole generation of young people are growing up, to whom solid books are unknown, to whom the great historic names of the past are but a sound, and whose ignorance of the world of fact is poorly compensated by their acquaintance with the world of dreams. . . . In fact, the Cinderella of the old nursery story is the true type of thousands of our novel-readers. They live a sort of double life—one in their own proper persons, and in their real homes; the other as ideal lords and ladies in dream-land. . . . How can the two parts of this double existence harmonize? How is it possible for those whose minds are thus bewildered, and who have formed this inveterate habit of indulging in sentimental reverie, to engage heartily in the performance of commonplace duties? The inevitable result of excessive novel-reading is a distaste, if not an incapacity, for the sober thought and patient effort which are the price of success in every worthy path of life.

J. T. C R A N E , *Popular Amusements* (1869)

CONTENTS

ILLUSTRATIONS

ACKNOWLEDGMENTS

THIS BOOK had its origins and endings in many conversations. Robert Silvers and Barbara Epstein, of the *New York Review of Books*, encouraged me in an early statement of some of the leading ideas for the book. Lee Goerner was my first editor, and talked me through the kind of biography I wanted to write. Harry Ford has been an exemplary editor in every way—gracious, exacting, and as obsessed with Crane as I am. Melanie Jackson, my agent, has pushed and pulled at the right times to get the pages done. Mark Rudman, editor of *Pequod,* and Gwen Robinson, editor of the Syracuse University Library *Courier,* oversaw the previous publication of chapters of the book. I had key discussions along the way with Tom Bender, John Clendenning, Dan Czitrom, Jonathan Galassi, Ann Hulbert, Bill Sharpe, Jean Strouse, and Stanley Wertheim. (That's a short list; I'm sure there are names I've missed.) What I owe to earlier Crane scholars and sleuths should be clear from my references in the text; I am particularly indebted to the work of Michael Fried, Daniel Hoffman, Melvin Schoberlin, Paul Sorrentino, R. W. Stallman, and Stanley Wertheim. The following collections offered friendly help: the Archives of American Art, New York City; Columbia University; Drew University; Mount Holyoke College and its interlibrary loan services; the University of Minnesota; New York University; Syracuse University (with special thanks to Ed Lyon and Kathleen Manwaring). I'm especially grateful for a fellowship from the Guggenheim Foundation, a residency at the MacDowell Colony, and a faculty grant from Mount Holyoke College. The dedication names a debt that can't be repaid.

THE DOUBLE LIFE OF
Stephen Crane

INTRODUCTION

STEPHEN CRANE'S extraordinary career was once the stuff of legend. A hundred years later we are still trying to sort out the facts of his life from the fictions. Crane was the most vivid and innovative writer to emerge in the United States during the 1890s. Today he is remembered mainly as the author of *The Red Badge of Courage*, a novel that is inflicted on high-school students as though it were documentary coverage of the Civil War. It fooled some of Crane's contemporaries too; at least one veteran claimed, "I was with Crane at Antietam."* Crane, who was born in 1871, enjoyed the confusion.

In his time Crane was one of the most visible American writers, and one of the most talked about. As a young reporter of New York slum life he once caused a scandal by defending a prostitute in court against a policeman's charges. Later he was a highly paid war correspondent, covering conflicts in Greece and Cuba for the papers of Pulitzer

*Notes and references will be found at the back of this book, starting on page 273.

3

and Hearst. (They knew his celebrity value; his account of the first major battle of the Spanish-American War carried the headline THE RED BADGE OF COURAGE WAS HIS WIG-WAG FLAG.) During the last year of his life he took refuge, from creditors and hangers-on, in a huge Elizabethan manor house in the south of England. There he lived quietly with his common-law wife, Cora Taylor, the former madam of a Jacksonville brothel called the Hotel de Dream. But shrewd witnesses lived nearby; for his close friends and neighbors in England included Joseph Conrad, Ford Madox Ford, and Henry James.

Crane was twenty-three in the fall of 1895, when *The Red Badge of Courage* was published. An impoverished newspaper reporter living in New York, he watched the machinery of fame that had been perfected by his bosses go to work for him. *The Red Badge* was a bestseller in the United States, and inspired among English critics what H. G. Wells called an "orgy of praise." During the next few years Crane worked as a journalist in New York and England, trying to keep the promise of his early work. "People may just as well discover now," he complained in 1896, "that the high dramatic key of *The Red Badge* cannot be sustained." While he recovered the intensity of *The Red Badge* in at least a dozen dazzling short stories, as well as in some of his cryptic poems, the hectic pace of Crane's life caught up with him. Exhausted from covering the Spanish-American War and claiming to be "disappointed with success," Crane died of tuberculosis in a sanatorium in the Black Forest on June 5, 1900. He had managed to see the new century—just, though he had not yet reached his twenty-ninth birthday.

To his contemporaries Crane's short life had some of the allure of pulp fiction; "he actually lived what his average countrymen collectively dreamed," J. C. Levenson has written. If the lives of writers tend to be conspicuous for their lack of outward event (one thinks of the quiet lives of Hawthorne or Dickinson or Wallace Stevens), Crane's life sometimes seems nothing but outward event—one wonders when he found the time to write.

The shape of Crane's career has a peculiar fascination for the biographer. If most writers tend to write about their experience, however disguised, Crane did the reverse: he tried to live what he'd already written. *Maggie*, his first, and affecting, novel about a "girl of the streets," shows more curiosity than knowledge; a few years after writing it Crane fell in love with a real-life madam. His acquaintance with conflict was limited to football when he wrote *The Red Badge of Courage*; he became a war correspondent in Cuba and Greece to see, he told Joseph Conrad, whether *The Red Badge* was accurate. He wrote several shipwreck narratives before he managed to find himself aboard a foundering steamer. Even in his newspaper work he sometimes lacked the patience to wait for something to happen. On one occasion he "covered" in great detail a fire in the Bowery, and was much praised for his vivid account; he'd made it all up.

The biographer's major task, in making sense of Stephen Crane, is not the tedious and often unconvincing effort to tie the work, however tenuously, to possible models in the life, tracing every fictional mother to the novelist's mother, and every artist to the novelist-in-disguise. The challenge, instead, is to make sense of Crane's fascinating attempts to live his fictions, to make his life an analogue of his work.

For Crane lived his life backwards, or rather he wrote it forwards. While Crane's case is particularly extreme (and all the more visible for being so literal—no metaphorical shipwrecks for him), I suspect that this pattern is more common among writers than might be supposed. Indeed, one might push the generalization further. We are mistaken when, in trying to understand an author's career, we take the "real life" for granted, and look for its imprint in the "imaginary life" of the subject's writings. For surely this is the wrong way around; what solidity, and givenness, there

5

is in a writer's life exists first in the writings. The problem is to see how the work of art shaped the writer's life.

In a further turn of the screw, some of Crane's best-known works are about people who try—usually in vain—to live according to the shapes of their own previously imagined stories, stories that are in turn often based on the popular culture of the nineteenth century. Maggie believes a knight will come to her rescue, as so often happens in the melodramas she sees on stage; Henry Fleming assumes the Civil War will correspond to his own fantasies of heroism, drawn from epics and soldiers' yarns; the Swede who visits the Blue Hotel is convinced that he'll die in the manner of gunmen in dime westerns. In Crane's world, written narratives tend to precede experience, rather than the reverse.

This doesn't mean that we can dispense with psychological explanations in making sense of Crane's life and work. On the contrary, we must deal with a psyche so powerful that it shaped events according to its own, mainly literary, patterns. Crane probably came to this practice early, growing up in a religious household devoted to the written word, and found it confirmed in a newspaper world that emphasized getting the story even if one had to foment it.

To some extent, of course, we all try to live our fantasies. But the sheer extremity of Crane's write-it-then-live-it procedures deserves special attention. John Berryman said of Crane's hunger for danger: "after imagining it for a masterpiece he needed to feel [it], and to see what he would do with it." Or, as Crane himself remarked in one of his sketches, "when a man gets the ant of desire-to-see-what-it's-like stirring in his heart, he will wallow out to sea in a pail."

Crane's ancestry did not promise a life of adventure. He was born in Newark, New Jersey, in 1871, the youngest of fourteen children, of whom nine survived infancy. On his mother's side of the family, Crane wrote, "everybody as

soon as he could walk became a Methodist clergyman—of
the old ambling-nag, saddlebag, exhorting kind." His
mother married a minister of the same faith, who wrote reformist tracts on the dangers of dancing and drinking. He
died when Crane was eight, a loss crucial to the child's
growing sense of his world. Crane's industrious but overex-
tended mother wrote for Methodist journals to support the
family and lectured for the New Jersey Woman's Christian
Temperance Union. Thus, Crane's parents were both writers; he grew up in a world in which words were powerful.
Biographers have tended to dismiss Crane's parents as
slightly comical characters. One aim of this book is to re-
unite, so to speak, the prodigal son and his parents.

Like the careers of other highly visible and self-
dramatizing writers, Crane's has seemed to crystallize
around a series of near-legendary incidents. During the
years between his arrival in New York City in 1891 at the
age of nineteen and his death nine years later, his life (like
his novels) was curiously *episodic*, as though he were inten-
tionally living a narrative plot. The chapters of his life—
from scandal to shipwreck to love and war—tend to have
clear beginnings and endings.

Crane's life was at once so productive and so short that
it's easy to forget that he could have been a twentieth-
century writer. He was born in 1871, the same year as
Dreiser. Willa Cather, Gertrude Stein, and Robert Frost
were born during the following three years. Only Crane's
amazing precocity makes us think of him as belonging to
the generation that preceded theirs.

But for a writer of Crane's proximity to our own time
(had he lived to be seventy he would have died in 1941), we
know remarkably little about his day-to-day existence; indeed, we know even less than earlier students of Crane's life
thought they did. The astonishing fact is that for seven decades much of the scholarship on Crane's life and work has
been based on a fraud. The single greatest bar to a right
understanding of Stephen Crane's life is the work of his first

7

biographer, Thomas Beer, on whose vivid and remarkable book all later biographers have depended heavily. In the writing of biography, invention is supposed to play a subsidiary role; in Beer's *Stephen Crane* (1923) it was primary. Beer was never quite above suspicion; doubts were raised early on—especially during the 1950s—about this detail or that one: Was the singer Helen Trent (of whose existence no evidence has come to light) really one of his first loves? Had Crane really counted the great painter Albert Pinkham Ryder among his drinking buddies? Did he really write a story, the manuscript of which has been lost, called "Vashti in the Dark," about a Methodist minister who finds that his wife has been raped by a black man, and kills himself in grief?

But the extent of Beer's invention has only quite recently been clarified, thanks to the detective work of Stanley Wertheim and Paul Sorrentino, who edited Crane's correspondence, and the analysis of John Clendenning. Beer's book on Crane, it now seems fair to say, is a tissue of lies, a forgery through and through. But having discovered so much, we find that we know far less than we thought we did about the enigmatic Crane, and especially about his childhood and early youth. For with regard to those years, Beer was the major, almost the only, source. As for the extraordinary letters Beer quotes at length, containing some of Crane's most bracing, and most often quoted, literary and philosophical opinions, they too are apparently forgeries— brilliant forgeries, one feels compelled to add. (Beer's drafts of these letters have come to light, allowing us to appreciate his mastery of the forger's art.) We must now forget that Crane claimed he got his artistic education on the Bowery, that he thought *War and Peace* went on and on like Texas, that he said that while Robert Louis Stevenson had passed away, he hadn't passed away far enough.

Half the clues to Crane's life have gone up in smoke. Under such circumstances, to try to make sense anew of Crane's career is particularly challenging. The disappearance of so much biographical detail shifts the balance—the documentary balance, so to speak—back toward Crane's writings, where of course it should have been all along.

"Each generation has something different at which they are all looking," Gertrude Stein observed. The generation that came of age during the 1890s—the generation of both Stein and Crane—shared Crane's mania for risk. The usual diagnosis is that prosperity resulting from industrialization removed the monied classes from the immediacy of life. ("Secular and religious education had effaced the throat-grappling instinct," Crane wrote in *The Red Badge,* "or else firm finance held in check the passions.") How much earlier this immediacy of life was present was much debated, as the vogue shifted from medieval knighthood to the equally chivalrous cowboys in Owen Wister's *The Virginian* and Frederic Remington's illustrations. Wister's friend Theodore Roosevelt (who admired Crane) offered a cure with his cult of "strenuousness," and William James looked for a "moral equivalent of war" in peacetime. There was widespread fear that the lower classes, still exposed to the vivifying diet of risk, were getting stronger and the ruling classes weaker—a dangerous situation in the eyes of establishment figures like Roosevelt and Remington.

While Crane shared this sense of malaise, he also questioned it. One of his early poems is a shrewd critique of the strenuous ethic, as well as an anxious meditation on his own action-obsessed life:

THERE WAS A MAN WHO LIVED A LIFE OF FIRE.
EVEN UPON THE FABRIC OF TIME,
WHERE PURPLE BECOMES ORANGE
AND ORANGE PURPLE,
THIS LIFE GLOWED,
A DIRE RED STAIN, INDELIBLE;

9

YET WHEN HE WAS DEAD,
HE SAW THAT HE HAD NOT LIVED

(*The Black Riders,* LXII)

The fear expressed in the last line would seem more appropriate when voiced, as it is in Henry James's *The Ambassadors,* by a provincial like Lambert Strether; it sounds odd from Crane, whose life was packed with those intensities that Strether was afraid he'd miss. The indelible red stain is, presumably, Crane's own written works, including *The Red Badge of Courage,* as though his writing somehow canceled out his life.

What Crane is reacting to is his suspicion that "real life" had itself become unreal by the 1890s. The strenuous life of the West, as portrayed by Wister, Remington, and Roosevelt, already seemed conventionalized, sentimentalized, lost to real experience. Crane's obsessive search throughout the 1890s was to find a way to become absorbed in the actual lives of the people he wrote about without lapsing into artifice and theatricality. Crane's stated allegiance to William Dean Howells's variety of literary realism was always less an aesthetic conviction than a commitment to intense experience. While he dutifully concurred in Howells's ambition to "picture the daily life in the most exact terms possible," the lives that interested Crane were those of people caught in extreme situations, too absorbed in their difficulties to indulge in hypocrisy and selfishness.

It was ultimately *inner* experience that Crane was after; the fear in his poem is that of an inner life lost. But it is precisely Crane's psyche that has proved baffling and unavailable, not least because he indulged in none of those apparent revelations of private life so dear to biographers: diaries, journals, intimate letters, memoirs, autobiographies. As a result of this paucity of self-exposure, we're in the dark about some of the most basic things about Crane. His feelings about his parents, for example, and his childhood in general are virtually a blank. The precise tenor of his relations with Cora remain an enigma; their letters have never come to light. We don't know, for example, whether they ever considered having children, or were capable of having them. We don't know when Crane contracted tuberculosis, or when he knew he was dying of it. And there are months in his life when we have virtually no idea where he was or what he was doing. One is faced with these mysteries in addition to the usual cruxes, such as how this boy, recently escaped from college, managed to write the greatest war novel by an American.

Stephen Crane comes across, nearly a hundred years later, as a figure of extraordinary personal magnetism. This pull comes partly from the surface of his own writings—those flashing, ironic, crystalline constructions that have so successfully resisted the clumsy advances of academic criticism. And part of the magnetism comes from the man himself, as he appears (and disappears) in the distorting mirrors of personal reminiscence and anecdote. Crane was talked about almost from the beginning of his career, and written about from the end. This elusive, angular, underweight, physically unobtrusive figure was singularly blessed, and cursed, with the gift of being noticed.

Crane was aware of his mercurial existence; he seemed almost to revel in it. "I cannot help vanishing and disappearing and dissolving," he told an editor in 1897. "It is my foremost trait." The lack of conventional biographical "material"—other than his own extensive published works—is worth thinking about. For Crane was a man who, in peculiar ways, vanished into his own fictions. He once excused himself for not writing long descriptions home of what he saw and did in England: "I write myself so completely out . . . that an attempt of the sort would be absurd."

Equally absurd is the frequent tendency, by Crane's biographers and critics, to slide over our ignorance and pretend that we know more about this enigmatic life than we do. In this book I have tried instead to preserve the mystery, to highlight what we don't know, while at the same time providing a key for what we know.

That key is a simple one, though complex in its application. For Crane's double life was not so much duplicitous as strangely *duplicate*. His fictions were not retrospective; they were eerily predictive. The question is why he felt it necessary to try to live what he had already so masterfully imagined. He planned his life; he seemed to plan his death. It was the most deliberate life imaginable.

Jessie's Dream

THE NIGHT before the summons to Dover, on May 15, 1900, Jessie Conrad had a vivid dream. She dreamed that a stretcher was placed in a horse-drawn ambulance, and that on the stretcher lay the body of Stephen Crane. Two nurses attended, along with Cora Crane, and the ambulance was driven to the coast as quickly as possible. The dream was particularly strange, for the Conrads, close friends of the Cranes, had heard nothing of Stephen for several months, and had no idea that he was desperately ill. Jessie told the dream to her husband, the novelist Joseph Conrad, the next morning.

> When the post arrived an hour later [she recalled] a letter told us the exact substance of my dream and begged us to go that morning to the "Lord Warden" in Dover, where the poor fellow lay awaiting a calm sea to cross and try to reach the Black Forest in search of health.

By the time the Conrads arrived at the hotel, on May 16, it was clear that this was to be their last visit with Crane. "It is the end Jess," Conrad remarked. "He knows it is all useless. He goes only to please Cora, and he would rather have died at home!"

The twenty-eight-year-old writer who had spent much of his adult life chronicling the ravages of the human body in war, in books like *The Red Badge of Courage* and *Wounds in the Rain*, was now himself little more than a living wound: his lungs incapacitated by tuberculosis, an abscess festering in his rectum, and fever, perhaps from malaria contracted in Cuba, making his hands and torso shake. The doctors had done what they could with Crane, which wasn't much. With the usual manic-depressive responses of the medical profession to tubercular symptoms at the turn of the century—announcing now that Crane was "out of the woods," a few days later that he had a month or two to live— they had merely confused Crane's friends and family.

But the hideous facts of the disease were not allowed to intrude on the scene in the upper room of the elegant Lord Warden, where Crane lay with a view of the sea. The doctors were done, and the novelists took over as a parade of visitors—the distinguished neighbors Crane had befriended during his months living in Sussex: Conrad, H. G. Wells, Ford Madox Ford—tried to fit the scene in the bedroom into a larger, inevitably euphemistic narrative.

Wells, five years older than Crane but just beginning his own career, set the tone after a visit on the fifteenth:

> If you would figure him as I saw him, you must think of him as a face of a type very typically American, long and spare, with very straight hair and straight features and long, quiet hands and hollow eyes, moving slowly, smiling and speaking slowly, and with that deliberate New Jersey manner he had, and lapsing from speech again into a quiet contemplation of his ancient enemy. For it was the sea that had

taken his strength, the same sea that now shone,
level waters beyond level waters, with here and there
a minute, shining ship, warm and tranquil beneath
the tranquil evening sky.

Here all is peace and decorum; contemplating this death-
bed scene we're allowed to forget that Crane was waiting for
the weather to calm down. Conrad, writing twenty years
after the event and probably using Wells's account as a
source, also remembered Crane "staring wistfully out of the
window at the sails of a cutter yacht that glided slowly across
the frame, like a dim shadow against the grey sky."

Was the sea indeed Crane's "ancient enemy"? We cannot be as certain as Wells that Crane's last encounter with
it, in a shipwreck off the Florida coast three years earlier,
had started the disintegration of his body. Perhaps the decline began earlier, during his years of living hand to mouth
as a journalist in New York, or earlier still, during his
"sickly" childhood in New Jersey and upstate New York. In
any case the return to the sea gave a satisfying shape to his
life, while the ships trailing across the evening sky served
Conrad and Wells as typical late-Victorian symbols for the
final journey of the soul. Henry James, another of Crane's
Sussex neighbors, had planned to arrive in Dover on the
twenty-first, but the sudden arrival of page proofs requiring
his immediate attention prevented the trip—we are seldom
allowed to forget, in these final encounters, that these were
men of letters, whose primary allegiance was to their
printed words.

The euphemistic haze surrounding the facts of Crane's
illness is rarely dissipated, by his visitors then or his biographers now. H. G. Wells, who had had tuberculosis in his
youth, knew better than to slight its effects. A month earlier,
when the prognosis of Crane's tubercular lungs looked
good, Wells joked in a letter to Crane about how he was not
"the hectic sort of person."

> As an expert in haemorrhages I would be prepared
> to bet you any reasonable sum ... that haemor-
> rhages aren't the way you will take out of this terres-
> trial Tumult. From any point of view it's a bloody
> way of dying. . . . I know few, more infernally dis-
> agreeable.

Cora took one look at the letter and hid it away.

For two years Crane had written almost unceasingly, for
money to keep up his and Cora's extravagant mode of life.
They rented a huge, partially furnished manor house,
called Brede Place, as open to damp drafts as to freeloading
visitors. For his final Christmas the Cranes had thrown an
enormous party, the centerpiece of which was a play written
by Crane called *The Ghost.* Its gothic plot seems in retro-
spect his way of announcing his own impending death. The
party dragged into New Year's, the end of one century and
the start of another, when it was abruptly interrupted by a
severe hemorrhage in Crane's lungs. But during the following weeks Crane, patched up and lightly doped, went on
writing, writing, as though, Scheherazade-like, to ward off
the arrival of death by the sheer vivacity of his stories.

Even as he lay in the Lord Warden Hotel, Crane was
sketching the final chapters of a Three Musketeers–like romance titled *The O'Ruddy,* with an Irish hero who has pic-
aresque adventures in England. Crane extracted from his
friend Robert Barr, an American hack writer and the last of
his visitors in Dover, a promise to finish the novel. Barr
couldn't imagine "anything more ghastly than the dying
man, lying by an open window overlooking the English
channel, relating in a sepulchral whisper the comic situations of his humorous hero so that I might take up the
thread of his story."

Barr would finish the tale, efficiently enough, but he ignored in his closing chapters a hidden theme Crane had set
going—one unnoticed as well by critics since. For strangely
enough the story has, as its protagonists, a hero called

16

"O'Ruddy" and a tubercular English lord called "Strepp." Crane, perhaps unconsciously, was spinning an allegory of his own illness, with the ruddy foreigner risking corruption in the damp and infectious hallways of England. The story concludes, as Crane specified to Barr, in the tomblike chambers of Brede Place itself.

Crane had entertained various possibilities of flight—he was especially drawn to the idea of a ranch in Texas—as a means of restoring his health. A magic mountain in the Black Forest was not among his fantasies. And besides, there were sanatoria in England offering the same cure as the German and Swiss resorts. But Cora, ever attentive to the ways of the rich, wanted Crane to die in the most decorous and fashionable way.

So Crane and his unwieldy entourage—Cora, two nurses, a doctor, a butler, one of Crane's nieces, and his dog, Sponge—crossed the channel on May 24 and boarded a train at Calais bound for Basel. The journey ended on the twenty-seventh or twenty-eighth (details of the trip are scant), and by the time Crane arrived at Badenweiler he was too sick to take part in the fresh-air rituals of the "Nordrach" treatment, with its chaise longues wheeled out into the sun, its cod-liver oil and bracing mountain air. Crane was carried into a second-floor bedroom in the Villa Eberhardt, rented by the distinguished lung specialist Dr. Albert Fraenkel for his private patients. On June 3 Crane was delirious. "My husband's brain is never at rest," Cora wrote. "He lives over everything in dreams and talks aloud constantly. It is too awful to hear him try to change places in the 'Open Boat.' "

Fraenkel injected morphine, and Crane lapsed into a coma. He died on June 5 at 3:00 a.m.

And then the corpse was made to retrace the journey, back to Basel, back across the channel to Dover, for a brief sojourn in London, where friends could pay their respects.

17

"There was a glass let in the lid of the coffin," Jessie Conrad remembered, "and people were allowed to take a last look at poor Stephen." Again Henry James stayed away, but his note to Cora, on hearing of Crane's death, shows the shock of the news and the depth of his grief:

> What a brutal needless extinction—what an unmitigated, unredeemed catastrophe! I think of him with such a sense of possibilities & powers! Not that one would have drawn out long these last cruel weeks—! . . . Shall you come back—for any time at all—to Brede Place? You will of course hate to—but it occurs to me you may have things to do there, or possessions to collect. What a strange, pathetic, memorable chapter his short—so troubled, yet also so peaceful—passage there!

Once more the novelist's hand takes over, as James puns on the two meanings of "passage"—in the "memorable chapter" and in the journey of life. He thinks of Crane's life as betraying a particular pattern, modeled by the book.

But the corpse's journey wasn't over. As though by some strange curse, it had to revisit the places that had figured in Crane's life. Cora wanted the body buried in America, so it traveled to New York in the hold of a ship, to the city where Crane had started his writing career as a newspaperman.

And there, such are the twists of fate, another fledgling reporter with a great career before him was sent to cover the funeral. Wallace Stevens, fresh from Harvard and trying his hand at journalism before settling on the law, was assigned the job by the New York *Tribune* (the same paper that had hired Crane eight years before). Stevens dutifully described the eulogy; the Reverend Dr. James M. Buckley, a friend of the Crane family, "spoke of the life of Mr. Crane and of the inheritance of many of the traits of character of his father." Stevens added his own, rather gratuitous, view of the shortcomings of Crane's work: "If he saw life clearly upon occasion he never saw it steadily; he never saw it whole. A sense of proportion was missing from his equipment."

Stevens's private journal, for June 28, 1900, gives a franker account.

> This morning I went to the funeral of Stephen Crane at the Central Metropolitan Temple on Seventh Avenue near Fourteenth Street. The church is a small one and was about [a] third full. Most of the people were of the lower classes and had dropped in apparently to pass away the time. There was a sprinkling of men and women who looked literary, but they were a wretched, rag, tag, and bob-tail. . . . The whole thing was frightful.

Stevens noted that the prayers were "perfunctory, the choir worse than perfunctory, with the exception of its hymn 'Nearer My God to Thee' which is the only appropriate hymn for funerals I ever heard. The address was absurd. The man kept me tittering from the time he began till the time he ended." The minister managed to work in mention of Goethe, Shelley ("on the line of premature death"), and Hawthorne—incongruous company for the rough-edged Crane, Stevens felt.

> A few of the figures to appear that day flashed through my head—and poor Crane looked ridiculous among them. But he lived a brave, aspiring, hard-working life. Certainly he deserved something better than this absolutely common-place, bare, silly service I have just come from. As the hearse rattled up the street over the cobbles, in the stifling heat of the sun, with not a single person paying the least attention to it and with only four or five carriages behind it at a distance I realized much that I had doubtingly suspected before—There are few hero-worshipers.

19

Stevens, approaching a crossroads in his own career, seems to be weighing the ambiguous rewards of the writer's life.

Crane's corpse, meanwhile, had one more stop on its travels. It was fated to return to the part of New Jersey that curls around Manhattan like a protective hand, where Crane had been born and come of age in his "oyster-like family." And there the body was finally buried, in Hillside Cemetery, a few miles from where Crane's journey, twenty-eight years earlier, had begun.

ONE

Holiness

How did the author of *Maggie* and *The Red Badge of Courage* have *those* parents, who seem to have stepped from the pages of a novel: the minister opposed to dancing and the reading of fiction; and his wife, the lecturer and pamphleteer for the Woman's Christian Temperance Union? As forebears they seem predestined to provide comic relief in the hero's life, foils for his triumphs. And such is their role in many accounts of Stephen Crane's career. In more sober versions they are enlisted to define a conveniently narrow world for Crane to "rebel against." Thus, Jonathan Townley Crane is portrayed as a mild and otherworldly divine, while M. Helen Crane appears as a tireless Christian soldier.

The Methodist Church and the Woman's Christian Temperance Union (it is undignified to use the initials, Helen Crane insisted) have come to seem to many people, especially after the early decades of this century, somewhat ridiculous entities. The first step toward making sense of Crane's parents is to gauge the gravity of those institutions during the 1870s and 1880s and to understand the significant and controversial contributions that the Cranes made to them. We must consign Stephen to the margins for a few years, in the interest of letting his parents stand on their own, and speak for themselves.

Ambition isn't necessarily hereditary: successful parents may foster nothing better in their children than a smug complacency. But thwarted ambition is often handed down, as a later generation struggles to avoid and avenge the humiliations of its forebears. Stephen Crane was the son and grandson of prominent Methodist ministers, and it is often assumed that his colorful life of excess and adventure was an understandable rejection of that legacy. But his father's prominence during Crane's childhood was tinged with something close to scandal, and what the son rejected is not entirely clear. Indeed, Crane the novelist seems to have inherited certain traits of character from Crane the minister—tenacity of purpose, intellectual integrity, iconoclastic fearlessness—and adapted them to his own ends.

At a critical moment in Jonathan Townley Crane's life, his promising career went into abrupt eclipse. He resigned the prestigious position of presiding elder in the Elizabeth (New Jersey) district of the Methodist Episcopal church, in 1876, and returned to the far less prestigious itinerant ministry. This decision has never been adequately explained. The reasons for J. T. Crane's professional decline turn out to have some bearing on the reputed differences between the conceptions of God held by the two sides of Stephen Crane's family, and on his own obsessive search for intense experience. This momentous and hitherto unsuspected episode in J. T. Crane's life may also help to convey the troubled atmosphere in the Crane household during the years when Stephen, born in 1871, was growing up. At precisely the time when Stephen was most in need of paternal strength—the years of early childhood—his father was apparently least able to provide it.

Jonathan Townley Crane's strange fate was to find himself in the midst of one of those awakenings of religious fervor that erupt periodically in American history. His life during the years of Stephen Crane's childhood must be seen in relation to what was known as the "Holiness Movement," which convulsed the Methodist church in the United States, and especially its New Jersey wing, during the 1870s. As one chronicler of the movement grandly proclaimed in 1873, "It was in the divine order that New Jersey should be the place where this advance movement of the times should be made." J. T. Crane's intellectual integrity was such that amid the doctrinal controversies that ensued he consistently took positions opposed to those of his influential in-laws, the Reverends George and Jesse T. Peck, his wife's father and uncle, respectively.

J. T. Crane paid for his courage. From being the presiding elder of the Elizabeth district in 1876, a position of great responsibility and adequate pay, he was demoted to the itinerant ministry. By the time of his death from heart failure in 1880, he was living in virtual exile in the backwater of Port Jervis, New York, still trying to convince his opponents of the superiority of his views. The first eight years of Stephen Crane's life corresponded to his father's professional and financial humiliation. It is not unreasonable to imagine that the effects of his father's clouded last years lingered on in the family circle, to be discussed in whatever terms— shame, anger, desire to redress (we can never know)—in front of the growing boy.

Jonathan Townley Crane was born in 1819 to Presbyterian parents on a farm in what is now Union, New Jersey, and orphaned at thirteen. His own religious conversion five years later was apparently more intellectual than emotional.

23

1. *Jonathan Townley Crane, Stephen Crane's father.*

Repelled like many of his generation by the Calvinist doc-
trine of infant damnation, he converted to the kinder creed
of Methodism. To pay his way through the College of New
Jersey (the Presbyterian forerunner of Princeton University), he worked in a Newark trunk factory. The Methodist
ministry had had no educational requirements in the first
half of the century, and its unlettered, plain-speaking
preachers appealed to the heterogeneous population of the
American West, where Methodism had spread rapidly. Pe-
ter Cartwright (1785–1872), a famous itinerant preacher
known as "the Methodist bulldog," wrote with scorn in his
Autobiography of learned ministers of other denominations,
boasting that "illiterate Methodist preachers set the world
on fire while they [the others] were lighting their matches!"

But J. T. Crane was a minister of the new stamp. Well
educated, bookish, respectable in every way, Crane was of
the generation of Methodist ministers who brought the
post–Civil War church much closer to the other Protestant
denominations. If, as Stephen Crane's friend Harold Frederic was to say of these ministers, "they were not the men
their forbears had been," they were nonetheless proud of
having brought Methodism up to date. By the 1870s the old
Methodist "campgrounds," where histrionic conversions
took place under the trees, had become summer resorts
where respectable Methodists vacationed together. (Two
such resorts in New Jersey, Asbury Park and Ocean Grove,
figured prominently in Stephen Crane's life.) Having
purged Methodism of its ruder aspects, J. T. Crane and his
colleagues had made their faith competitive in the civilized
Northeast, a part of the country where its appeal had tradi-
tionally been weakest.

To all appearances, J. T. Crane married strategically,
only to learn that an alliance of love and ambition can have
its own intrinsic constraints. Mary Helen Peck was the only
daughter of the Reverend George Peck, editor of the influential *Christian Advocate* of New York; author of several
much-admired books, including an autobiography; and

presiding elder of the large Wyoming (Pennsylvania) Conference of the Methodist church. Peck's four brothers were all ministers, among them the imposing Jesse T. Peck—he weighed three hundred pounds—whose career was to be even more illustrious than his brother George's, culminating in his rise to the rank of bishop. (He was also one of the founders of Syracuse University, an important connection when his wayward grandnephew was looking for a college.) These Pecks, who were much in demand as speakers, assembled yearly for family reunions, where they prayed together and listened to one another preach.

J. T. Crane first caught the attention of the Methodist leadership with his "An Essay on Dancing" (1849), published the year after his marriage banns. In the preface to this joyless and puritanical attack, Crane revealed (and reveled in) the narrowness of his own experience: "The author is constrained to admit the charge of being wholly unacquainted, *experimentally*, with his theme." He resorted perforce to a scholarly treatment, in which he established that dancing had declined in grace and morality since biblical times:

> Our dances are performed by males and females mingled together, and arranged in pairs; that of the [ancient] Hebrews was performed by a band of maidens and women alone. The modern dance is regulated by the senseless whine of a violin, while that of the Hebrews was accompanied by a noble anthem of praise.

Crane worried about the effects of dancing on domestic order: "Young lady, by imbibing a love for the dance, you will almost necessarily acquire a distaste for the duties of everyday life." His readers would appreciate the delicacy of his implication that "imbibing" a taste for dance might be as dangerous as drinking hard liquor.

Crane's concern for the morals of youth won him appointment to the Methodist seminary at Pennington, New

Jersey, where he served as principal for ten pleasant years before returning, in 1858, to the active ministry. The expanding Crane household at Pennington seems to have been a cozy refuge for sentimental piety. His mother-in-law, Mary Peck, visiting at Pennington to care for her daughter's latest baby, described the scene to her husband, George. One of the grandchildren, having spent the afternoon playing in the sand,

> was saying his prayers to his Mother [i.e., M. Helen Crane] one evening after which he asked her whether the Lord would take care of him down here or up yonder she said she thought he would take care of him down here but asked him if he would like to go up into the sky and be a little Angel. He replied that he would rather be a little Angel down here in the dirt.

Though Crane, like other northern ministers, opposed slavery he suggested that a period of serfdom "on the Russian model" might ease the morally treacherous transition from bondage to freedom, and prevent a civil war. The idea, however naive, so appealed to Crane's audience that his sermon on slavery was published and widely distributed.

After the war Crane turned his attention to social issues. Two of his books, *Popular Amusements* (1869) and *Arts of Intoxication* (1870), departed in no significant way from Methodist orthodoxy; the latter was noticed in the religious press primarily for its "captivating style" and "true eloquence." What struck his contemporaries as graceful and scholarly sounds merely pedantic today. He liked to mix scientific expertise with the narrowest fundamentalism; he defended Noah's intemperance, for example, as a regrettable but not damnable lapse:

> The Scriptures tell us that Noah planted a vineyard and on one occasion drank of the wine until he was drunken. Very possibly the process of fermentation

27

had not before been noticed, the results were not known, and the consequences in this case were wholly unexpected.

Crane's anxious promotion of temperance and of healthy forms of recreation—he admitted, characteristically, that he'd never even smoked a cigarette—reflects a change in the preoccupations of post–Civil War Methodism. The emotional and physical trauma of backwoods revivals had begun to yield to an emphasis on social reform. This taming of Methodism's "heroic" energies—part of the process that Ann Douglas has called the "feminization" of American culture in the nineteenth century—led to a diminished stress on individual religious experience. One searches in vain through J. T. Crane's writings for a sense of religion as intense experience and finds instead a great deal about religion as social control.

A countermovement was perhaps to be expected, especially after the American wing of the Methodist church celebrated its centenary, in 1866, amid a widely felt mood of spiritual torpor. Observers at the time blamed the malaise on the "demoralizing influence of our civil war," and some ventured sociological explanations for the church's declining influence:

> Many of her members went forth to the sanguinary field. Removal from elevating home-influences and from sanctuary privileges had a tendency to loosen, and often to sunder, the bonds of fervent piety.

To reawaken that fervor was the explicit goal of the group of prominent ministers who met at Vineland, New Jersey, in 1867 and formed the National Association for the Promotion of Holiness.

The Holiness Movement followed the pattern of other religious renewals by clothing its program for change in a conservative rhetoric that demanded a return to earlier values. Among the innovations its adherents condemned were

Gothic architecture in church buildings; the new "operatic" style of church music; and modern sermons, with their "ornate" style and references to "science, philosophy, polite literature, poetry, and even *antique fables*"—an adequate description of the kind of sermons that J. T. Crane, with his fondness for examples from Homer and folklore, preached.

Promoters of Holiness called for a return to "the primitive simplicity and power of Christianity" and for the revival of camp meetings; tabernacles in the woods would replace Gothic churches and become scenes of violent conversion—the campsites were referred to as "battlegrounds"—and of that further spiritual cleansing they called "entire sanctification." Much emphasis was put on this "second blessing," which Jesse T. Peck had discussed at length in his popular tract *The Central Idea of Christianity* (1865, revised 1876), while his brother, George, described his own experience of it in his autobiography of 1874. Despite its conservative rhetoric, the Holiness Movement, with its rejection of outer ritual and insistence on individual religious experience, found itself spiritually in step with such progressive denominations as the Society of Friends.

Given his family ties, J. T. Crane's open hostility to the Holiness Movement, as expressed in his book *Holiness the Birthright of All God's Children* (1874), was impolitic, to say the least. Two traits of Crane's temperament are evident in his opposition to the promoters of Holiness, however: his compassion and his cautiousness, especially with regard to intense experience. He thought that the movement's insistence on a second stage of religious experience diminished the gravity of the first conversion, or "justification," of the regenerate sinner. He was offended by the corollary claim that there lingered after conversion a "residue of depravity," which put the convert right back to the risk of damnation at any moment. This view sounded cruel and Calvinistic to Crane, and challenged his reasons for embracing Methodism in the first place. In what constituted something of a compromise, he preferred a gradual "groaning" toward perfection, usually unattainable in this life, to the "instantaneous" experience of sanctity.

It did not escape the attention of Crane's fellow ministers that with the publication of his book he had in effect launched a public attack on the most cherished beliefs of his own father-in-law. One must assume a measure of détente within the family; certainly there is evidence for it in the fact that an advertisement for J. T. Crane's *Holiness* appeared at the end of Peck's *The Life and Times of Rev. George Peck* (1874), a book that advanced contrary ideas. Furthermore, J. T. Crane had dutifully delivered a eulogy at his father-in-law's golden-anniversary celebration four years earlier. But such civility was not to be found in all segments of the Peck camp. The Reverend Anthony Atwood of Philadelphia, a Peck associate and one of the original organizers of the National Association for the Promotion of Holiness, published a particularly vicious, book-length response to Crane's arguments, adding the gratuitous observation that Crane's "natural manner" as a preacher was "dry and devoid of sympathy or feeling." Atwood quotes at some length from a Holiness tract by George Peck and concludes:

> Dr. George Peck, here quoted, is the venerable father-in-law (still living) of Dr. Crane. The father is sound, Methodistic [i.e., his arguments correspond to John Wesley's, a view disputed by Crane, who found Wesley's positions inconsistent] and scriptural; the son-in-law is neither. . . . The blessed Master said that "the father would be against the son, and the son against the father." Herein is this prediction fulfilled.

There was, in fact, a vigorous and well-organized effort to suppress Crane's book and end his career in the upper ranks of the Methodist hierarchy. The editor of the *Methodist Quarterly Review*, a magazine that had serialized Crane's temperance tract the previous year, ran a mildly critical review of *Holiness the Birthright*, only to find himself attacked for refusing "to join in a purpose to personally victimize Dr. Crane." The editor explained,

> By letter and by interview, we had been made to understand that Dr. C. had now destroyed "all his hopes of ecclesiastical preferment," and we were urged to "speak out," so that he should be put down reputationally and officially.

One reviewer quoted in the article had announced that he "felt so cheated by the book that after a careful reading *I put it into the stove*, where I was sure it would do no harm" (his emphasis), while another referred to it as a "poisonous reptile."

George Peck was indeed still living in 1874, as Atwood had remarked, though he did not live for much longer. He died within two years, in 1876—the same year that J. T. Crane was compelled to return (perhaps no longer protected by Peck family ties) to the itinerant ministry, and sent first to Paterson, New Jersey, then to Port Jervis. He spent the last four years of his life fretting about the controversial ideas he had advanced. "He was rewriting [*Holiness the Birthright*] when he died," his widow recalled, "and he expressed the hope that he would be able to 're-state his views in a manner that would commend them to those who differed from him theoretically.'"

Oddly enough, arguments similar to J. T. Crane's eventually triumphed in the Methodist church, but so long after his death that his own expression of them was forgotten. The idea of a "second blessing" (and sometimes a third, accompanied by speaking in tongues) took refuge in the various Holiness sects, such as the Assemblies of God, that split off from Methodism after the 1890s to flourish in the twentieth century. The reasons for schism were complex and involved issues of administration and ordination irrelevant to the difficulties of J. T. Crane. But he seems to have understood, twenty years earlier, that the future of Methodism in the cities would require a tamer, more social-minded set of religious practices than those offered by the Holiness Movement.

Crane's doctrinal arguments, interestingly, have won a measure of recent respect. The historian J. L. Peters, in his account of the controversies surrounding the concept of Christian holiness in American churches, offers an appreciative analysis of J. T. Crane's ideas. Peters suggests that Crane was ahead of his time, and that his attempt at a "general synthesis"—of conversion followed by gradual growth in spiritual awareness—"was not heeded by an age absorbed wholly with thesis and antithesis." A re-evaluation of Crane as one of the major Methodist thinkers of the last century, while suggested in recent scholarship, seems best left to the future. But it would be a noteworthy reversal if the father of Stephen Crane, hitherto viewed as an intellectually timid and unworldly divine, came to be seen as a path-breaking innovator, someone who, like his son, relied on his writings to shock and provoke.

If Stephen Crane's childhood was a time of professional exile and humiliation for his father, it was precisely the opposite for his mother. During the early 1870s her childbearing and rearing finally came to a close, and her vocation became clear. Paternal failure and maternal success probably had the same result for Stephen: less attention from his distracted parents. Whatever feelings of abandonment he felt could only have increased when his father died in 1880. Crane's adolescence was marked by a further, perhaps more disturbing, loss, when his mother suffered from mental illness. Of the members of Crane's family, M. Helen Crane has proved the most difficult to understand. Her madness suggests that she was apparently a mystery to herself as well.

M. Helen Crane was forty-five when her son Stephen was born in 1871; whether he was "wanted" or not, his con-

2. *Mary Helen Peck Crane, Stephen Crane's mother.*

ception must have been a surprise. The four children immediately preceding him had all died in infancy; the Cranes, who had eight living children, may have hoped for a last child to help ease the memory of those early deaths. But having borne fourteen children in twenty years, Helen Crane was becoming interested in things other than babies during the early 1870s, and there may be some truth to the gossip of Newark neighbors that "she spent so much time doing good work outside her home that her children and the house were not as well looked after as they should have been."

The neighbors saw little enough of the Cranes in any case. J. T. Crane's duties as presiding elder kept him on the road much of the time. During the pivotal year of 1873, while her husband was entering the Holiness controversy, M. Helen Crane became involved in the major women's movement of her time. Thomas Beer records J. T. Crane's dismay when "four ladies from Ohio" visited his wife that year to discuss temperance. "Mrs. Crane is much impressed by this project," J. T. Crane wrote, according to Beer. "I do not think it exactly practical . . . but they mean very well. Little Stephen has a bad cold this week."

Beer is an unreliable source, as usual. He says that the women were members of "the Christian Temperance Union League," but no organization of that name existed in 1873. The Women's Crusade for temperance did indeed begin in Ohio in the fall of 1873, however, largely as a spontaneous movement to protect women from the dangers posed by the drunken behavior of men, in the house and in the streets.

But Helen Crane had reasons closer to home for taking an interest in temperance: there was a case of alcoholism in her own straitlaced, evangelical family. Two of her brothers were ministers, but a third, Wilbur F. Peck, was an alcoholic who had dropped out of New York University and had trouble holding onto a job. In 1869 he had written to his father on the subject of Holiness, expressing his longing for "a progressive work of grace in my heart, to the uprooting and turning out [of] all sin. I am not satisfied with what I am yet long and hope to be better." He took the pledge in Newark on June 30, 1873, with his father, George Peck, and J. T. Crane serving as witnesses, "not [to] use as a beverage or habit any intoxicating drink whatever, for the term of three years." The signed pledge remained among his father's papers. Wilbur was apparently visiting the Cranes at the time, who had named one of their sons after him. Under the circumstances, Helen Crane's interest in the Ohio crusade would not be surprising, nor would her enthusiastic involvement in the Woman's Christian Temperance Union, the new organization founded in the fall of 1874.

The WCTU left its members a great deal of freedom to deal with local problems as they saw fit. By 1878, Helen Crane had defined her own approach to the problem of alcohol abuse. In a series of lectures delivered in Port Jervis, with her children serving as assistants, she focused on the effects of alcohol on the body. Her technical apparatus was apparently persuasive, if newspaper accounts are to be trusted:

> The room was filled to its utmost capacity, and it is estimated that over 100 persons were unable to gain admittance. Her subject was "The effects of alcohol upon the organs and tissues of the body." Illustrations in crayon, executed by her self and daughter [Mary Helen], showed the effect of introducing liquor into the system, advanced stages being represented by different drawings.

A week later she demonstrated the effect of alcohol on the brain "by breaking into a glass the white of an egg, upon which was poured a small quantity of the liquid. The result was the albumen of the egg became transformed into a solid mass, much resembling the state of being cooked."

The Cranes were involved in other schemes for social uplift in Port Jervis, including a Sunday school in the poor district of town, which they hoped, to the dismay of some of

35

the townspeople, would help "the colored people of the vicinity." (This school may well have provided Stephen with his first experience of black people, which he drew on for his later, "Whilomville," stories.) But J. T. Crane's sudden death from heart seizure in 1880 forced Helen Crane to make a living, and her lectures and other WCTU work became the center of her life. The WCTU, meanwhile, was changing, under the dynamic leadership of Frances Willard, who was elected president in 1879. Under Willard's "do-everything policy" during the 1880s, the organization broadened its concerns to include such related issues as women's suffrage and organization of labor.

In 1883 Helen Crane moved her family to the Methodist resort of Asbury Park, New Jersey, and was elected president, soon after her arrival, of the Asbury park and Ocean Grove chapter of the WCTU. She repeated her series of talks on the effects of alcohol on the body, with a new emphasis on the beneficial effects of water (the shortage of clean water in urban slums was a recurring subject among urban reformers like Jacob Riis). She had chosen Asbury Park partly because her son Townley ran a summer news agency on the Jersey shore. Soon she was contributing reports on religious events to his agency, and used Stephen as a runner. She seems to have thought of herself as a force for reform within the press. At the annual temperance convention in Ocean Grove in 1889, she delivered a paper on "press work," the result of which was an angry gathering of women protesting the ratio of sports to religious coverage in the newspapers. "A New York paper had nearly two pages about the [Sullivan] fight," one woman complained, "and there was not a line about temperance in the paper."

Maybe she worked too hard, or maybe there was a recurring instability in her mind, but M. Helen Crane suffered some sort of mental breakdown in 1886, when she was fifty-nine. The Asbury Park *Shore News* of March 11 reported that she was "now suffering from a temporary aberration of the mind and is in a critical condition." Two days later the Asbury Park *Journal* stated that "though her mind is yet feeble it is hoped with returning strength her mental troubles will disappear." These vague diagnoses are frustrating, but the symptoms were clearly alarming. One wonders especially about the effect of the crisis on her youngest son, but there is no record of his feelings in his letters. Crane's biographers, oddly, have ignored the whole issue of his mother's mental illness, as though it had no bearing on Crane's coming of age.

Helen Crane evidently recovered, sufficiently at least to resume her WCTU work. She published a letter in the Asbury Park *New Jersey Tribune* in February 1887 that provides a rare opportunity to hear her public voice. Mrs. Crane is reporting her visit to a temperance meeting in Jersey City: "Judging by the attendance at that meeting temperance sentiment is not very strong in that rum-ridden city," she writes. "Scarcely enough to save it from the fate of Sodom." (Is this meant to be hyperbolically witty, one wonders, or merely matter-of-fact?) She turns to the subject of labor strikes, frequent events in the last quarter of the century:

> During my stay in Jersey City I had the privilege of sitting at meat a number of times with a dozen of laboring men of different nationalities and of different occupations, and during the worst days of the [railroad] strikes . . . I heard but one opinion of the strikes and the originators thereof. That was that strikes were fomented by the idle and the vicious, and that the drinking habits of the working classes were largely if not entirely the cause of the distress among them.

One of the men was an unemployed Irishman whose teetotalism, she remarked, "may account for the fact of his having a bank account."

Such reactionary views, especially the facile assumption that the problems of the poor are all caused by liquor, were

37

quite far from those of the socialist-leaning Frances Willard. But it is on this slightly hysterical note that M. Helen Crane falls silent for us, her voice no longer audible except as it enters, transposed and disguised, the fictitious characters of her youngest son.

She died on December 7, 1891, in Paterson, New Jersey, having been admitted to the hospital two months earlier with a tumor in her neck. We don't know whether this illness was a further eruption or intensification of the earlier one, with its mental disturbances. The Crane family was silent about the hospitalization in 1886 (we know of it because of newspaper reports); if Mrs. Crane's mind remained off-kilter for the next five years, it is precisely the kind of secret the family would have desired kept. And if so, Stephen Crane's orphanhood began when he was fourteen, and not when he was twenty.

But now we have to shift our perspective from the distracted parents to the absorbed child. For within this household of the humiliated minister and the mentally unbalanced agitator, a boy was growing up. He found himself in a place where language was paramount, and at the same time perilously ambiguous. For words had brought his father to prominence and plunged him into controversy and despair. Words had helped his mother survive and keep the family together; they had also, apparently, contributed to the unhinging of her mind. Out of the words he heard around him, Stephen Crane was slowly fashioning his own distinctive idiom, with its own economy of scandal and survival.

TWO

Acquiring a Language

A BABY BOY was born on the first of November, All Saints' Day, in 1871. His parents, the Reverend and Mrs. Jonathan Townley Crane, named the child Stephen Crane, having run out of middle names, perhaps, on the thirteen children who had preceded him. He was born and baptized in the Methodist parsonage on the fashionable street of Mulberry Place, in Newark, New Jersey. The three-story, red-brick parsonage, like many of the buildings in which Stephen Crane passed his early years, is gone now, and we are left to imagine what might have occurred in its narrow but high-ceilinged rooms. It was, we may be sure, a place of daily rituals and quiet pastimes—especially the godly ones recommended in J. T. Crane's *Popular Amusements*. First among the rituals was the one that J. T. Crane took most seriously: the daily prayers, with the whole family gathered round, and on their knees, reading aloud from the King James Bible.

Crane was born into a straitened world in which certain words were spoken and read several times a day in reverence. He heard familiar passages of the Bible over and over again, at home and at church (twice on Sunday, once on Wednesday). It would be hard to overestimate the importance of this ritual—the book, the words, the respectful decorum—on the baby and the growing boy. In this world, words were powerful, utterly serious.

Like many children with a gift for words (one thinks of Flaubert and Henry James), Crane was apparently slow to win control of them. Throughout his life he wrote slowly and spoke slowly. He didn't begin attending school until he was eight or so, and there is no evidence that he knew how to read before that time. We can risk a hypothesis. When his father died, in 1880, Stephen Crane had just learned to read. When his mother died eleven years later, he learned to write—for *Maggie*, his first novel, was written in 1891. It is tempting to view the first twenty years of Crane's life as taking shape around these losses, these attainments. For Crane, almost from the start, language and mourning were inseparable. Words filled a space where people once breathed.

It was, furthermore, a family of writers, wordsmiths, scribblers. J. T. Crane wrote his sermons and his books. Helen Crane began contributing, after her husband's death, to Methodist journals. One son, Townley, was a reporter for New York and New Jersey papers, while a daughter, Agnes, wrote fictional sketches and dreamed, in her diary, of becoming a successful writer. In such a family, writing defined one's identity; one wrote oneself into existence.

Not surprisingly, Stephen Crane was drawn early on to the mystique of writing. As his brother Edmund remembered:

When he [Stephen] was about three years old, an older brother, Townley, was a cub reporter on one of the Newark dailies . . . and when writing his stories at home would often call on his Mother for the correct spelling of a word. Stevie was making wierd [*sic*] marks on a paper with a lead pencil one day and in

40

3. *Stephen Crane as a baby, around age two.*

the exact tone of one, absorbed in composition, and coming to the surface only for a moment of needed information, called to his mother, "Ma, how do you spell 'O'?", this happening to be a letter he had just become acquainted with.

It's a charming story, but certain details are also talismanic of Crane's enduring relation to language: writing as something strange and "weird"; the intense absorption in the act of writing; the idea that letters are like friends one "becomes acquainted with," especially when other intimacies are lacking. And the faintly ominous choice of the letter *O*, with its kinship to zero, its aura of absence.

The first fact of Crane's childhood is that we know so little about it; the second is that he apparently wished this to be so. "I go through the world unexplained," he said, as though warning his future biographers. And again: "I cannot help vanishing and disappearing and dissolving. It is my foremost trait." The first ten years of his life have all but vanished.

Thomas Beer, Crane's first chronicler, invented a childhood for his subject by lifting details from Crane's fictional tales about children, especially the late *Whilomville Stories.* He filled Crane's closet with boots and mittens and a big handkerchief—bright red to prefigure *The Red Badge of Courage.* He jazzed up Crane's early years with terrifying encounters and nightmares. In May of 1884, according to Beer, Stephen "saw a white girl stabbed by her negro lover on the edge of a roadmaker's camp" near Asbury Park, and was so frightened he told no one about it. Who told Thomas Beer?

Beer's account of Crane's adult years is notoriously full of inaccuracies and fabrications, but his fanciful version of Crane's childhood, in the absence of other material or contradicting evidence, has been eagerly pilfered, first and extensively by John Berryman, and then by the more skeptical R. W. Stallman. After all, what kind of biography begins in adolescence?

There are in fact only two reasonably reliable witnesses of Crane's childhood. His sister Agnes, fifteen years his senior, kept a diary during the early 1870s. His older brother Edmund wrote a memoir, in 1921 or so, about the star of the family. Also a few pages of J. T. Crane's diary, during the period when Stephen was a child, have come to light. The rest is hearsay, invention, extrapolation, lies.

Every childhood is in certain predictable ways unhappy; to grow up means to learn, slowly and painfully, that all our wishes cannot be granted. But there is more direct evidence of neglect in Crane's case. In Agnes's diary of 1874, Stephen's third year, Mrs. Crane is often "away," attending sessions, one assumes, of the WCTU and the state legislature. At one point Agnes apparently refers to "my baby"—the word, alas, is partially obscured—suggesting that she may have served as a sort of surrogate mother for baby Stephen. If so, she must have been a depressing mother. Her diary records a continual round of prayer meetings and complaints about her loneliness. Here are some representative entries just before and after Stephen's third birthday; they are quoted in their entirety:

> *Sunday Oct. 30th* [1874]
> Went with Clara and joined Dr. Sims bible class. Eve. Went to St. Pauls with Miss Cooke.
>
> *Monday Dec. 1st*
> Went to Dr. Sims lecture "Mindmarks of the Century."
>
> *Saturday 6th*
> Swept.
>
> *Sunday 7th*
> Was out only to the Bible class.

43

4. *Agnes Elizabeth Crane, Stephen Crane's sister.*

Thursday 11th
Looked for [i.e., waited for the return of] Ma all day
but it stormed.

In the light of such evidence, one is tempted to agree with
Lillian Gilkes, biographer of Cora Crane, when she specu-
lates that "Stephen, the fourteenth child, had known little
of that refuge of mother love."

Crane as a child was sickly and frail, perhaps already
showing tubercular symptoms or susceptibilities. "He had
always been delicate," Edmund Crane remembered, "and
was not sent to school until the fall before his eighth birthday." One pauses to note that Crane's learning to read, that
fall of 1879, was immediately followed by his father's death
on February 16, 1880. So Crane's formal education began
with the death of his father. He soon came to see his real
education as a repudiation of his father's learning and
writing.

Stephen Crane was J. T. Crane's last chance to have a
minister among his children. The date of Stephen's birth
must have seemed auspicious. Not only was he born on All
Saints' Day (classmates later teased him for having the
name of the first Christian martyr), he was also born one
hundred years almost to the day after Bishop Asbury—the
first bishop of the American church—had arrived in America to establish the Methodist church in the New World. The
Cranes might have noted too that Stephen was born seventy
years after the pivotal meeting at Cane Ridge (August 6,
1801), the great camp meeting that has been called "a
watershed in American church history." Does the son's
gnawing guilt in Crane's third novel, *George's Mother,* with
its portraits of a feckless alcoholic and his pious mother,
have something to do with J. T. and Helen Crane's dashed
hopes that Stephen would attend to these propitious dates
and follow the long Peck line into the ministry?

45

The void left in Crane's life by his father's death in 1880 must have been immense. No letters or reliable testimony survive from this period, but Crane's works are notable for their absent fathers, their harassed and difficult mothers. The move from Port Jervis to Asbury Park, New Jersey, in 1883, brought Helen Crane closer to the Methodist papers and organizations that employed her, but it uprooted Stephen from whatever friendships he left behind. William Crane, seventeen years older than Stephen, stayed in Port Jervis, where he continued to practice law; he remained an anchor and a sort of paterfamilias throughout Stephen's life. For twelve-year-old Stephen, the Jersey shore, with its resorts strung like beads along the coast, must have had its own attractions. The sea, one assumes, began to impinge on his imagination at this time. Ships ran afoul of the dangerous rocks offshore, and there were daring rescues along the beach. The Methodist festivities at Ocean Grove were surely interesting, if less vivid than the more secular amusements of neighboring Asbury Park.

In 1884 Crane suffered another loss, when Agnes, the depressed older sister who was apparently Stephen's closest companion, died of meningitis at the age of twenty-eight. Two years later his brother Luther, employed by the Erie Railroad, was crushed to death between two freight cars. Again, there is no record of Stephen's response to these deaths.

Crane was to see his genealogy as consisting of two distinct lines, one ministerial and the other martial, that had become joined in the generation previous to his own. His education, and to some extent his writing, swung between these two estates, these two roads not quite taken. Crane's years at the Pennington Seminary, from September 1885 to December 1887, were merely an extension of his late father's influence. For this was the school that J. T. Crane had created, developed, molded to his own ideals. It was the right place for a young man bound for the ministry. But from childhood Crane had dreamed of becoming a soldier instead, and retained the ambition for the rest of his life. His biographers have played down his military aspirations, perhaps out of the dubious but curiously widespread conviction that *The Red Badge of Courage* is somehow an antiwar novel.

Crane's transfer to Claverack College and Hudson River Institute, in the spring of 1888, marked an abrupt shift of direction. For Claverack, a leisurely and co-educational military academy in upstate New York, was as martial as Pennington was ministerial. Crane called his two years there "the happiest period of my life." He had the rank of first lieutenant in the military regiment of the school, and enjoyed drilling his squad, surely the source of some of the fantasies of leadership that made their way into *The Red Badge of Courage.*

Still, one looks in vain through these years of schooling for remarkable events, signs of the prodigy soon to step forth on the world's stage. As Crane drifted from school to school, no one seems to have taken special notice of this inconspicuous student.

As it turned out, Crane was no more destined to be a soldier than a minister. His older brother William, arguing that the United States was unlikely to fight a war during Stephen's lifetime, persuaded him to attend a civilian college rather than West Point. So Stephen enrolled at Lafayette College, in Pennsylvania, as uncertain of his plans as most freshmen are. Nothing he did there made his future seem any more certain. "I went to Lafayette College but did not graduate," he later reported. "I found mining-engineering not at all to my taste. I preferred base-ball."

A major ritual at Lafayette, as at other colleges, was the hazing of freshmen. In this exercise, according to one report, Crane responded decisively. A group of sophomores

47

5. *Stephen Crane as a cadet, second from the left, with his Claverack company, c. 1889. "The happiest period of my life,"* Crane later said.

knocked at Crane's dormitory room one night. When he didn't answer they broke down the door. Ernest Smith, who was one of the invaders, described what happened next:

> An oil lamp burning in the room indicated plainly . . . the figure of Crane backed into a corner with a revolver in hand. He was ghastly white . . . and extremely nervous. There was no time to escape what might have proved a real tragedy until Crane unexpectedly seemed to wilt limply in place and the loaded revolver dropped harmlessly to the floor.

The anecdote, if it is accurate, suggests Crane's precocious sense of drama, and prefigures his later habit of inserting himself into the midst of conflict. But of course the sense of drama may have been Smith's own; the burning lamp, the "ghastly" face, the "real tragedy" averted—all suggest an imagination working up partially remembered details.

After one semester at Lafayette, where he flunked five of his seven classes, Crane transferred to Syracuse as a special student. His mother's uncle, Jesse Peck, had been one of the founders of Syracuse. The family tie must have eased Crane's admission to the school, as did the fact that he was a prime prospect for the Syracuse baseball team, on which he starred as a catcher and shortstop. He wrote for the school paper as well; using his summer connections, he sent a few workmanlike dispatches to the New York *Tribune*. But the only real sign of things to come was Crane's decision— apparently opposed by no one—to quit school and move to New York, in June 1891.

Report cards tell us little of what school meant to Crane. Here is his own summary of his college education:

> I did little work at school, but confined my abilities, such as they were, to the diamond. Not that I disliked books, but the cut-and-dried curriculum of the college did not appeal to me. Humanity was a much more interesting study. When I ought to have been

49

6. *Crane and his teammates from the Syracuse baseball team, spring 1891.*

at recitations I was studying faces on the streets, and when I ought to have been studying my next day's lessons I was watching the trains roll in and out of the Central Station. So, you see, I had, first of all, to recover from college.

Faces and baseball—the rest was a disease he had to overcome. His real education, as he well knew, was elsewhere. Books were fine, but better to write them than read them. (Crane's spotty familiarity with major works of literature, aside from such popular contemporaries as Kipling, has remained something of a scandal among scholarly critics of his work.) Crane's formal schooling had begun late and ended early. There is no indication that he ever regretted his decision to abandon it.

When he was older, and starting to have some success with his writing, Crane remade his background to fit his own newly conceived identity. His contemporaries, who were as curious and in the dark as we are, often asked him about his childhood. He responded with elaborate—and generally accurate—genealogies, assertions of impressive ancestry rather than memories of a personal past. Crane used such genealogies as much to conceal as to reveal. "I am not much versed in talking about myself," he wrote the journalist John Northern Hilliard in January 1896, and went on to talk about his name, as though that were the same thing:

> Occasionally, interested acquaintances have asked me if "Stephen Crane" was a nom de guerre but it is my own name. In childhood, I was bitterly ashamed of it and now when I sometimes see it in print, it strikes me as being the homliest [*sic*] name in created things.

But this homely name turns out to have a distinguished pedigree. The rest of the extraordinary letter to Hilliard,

51

which is often quoted but never given sustained attention, reads like a researched and memorized self-justification, a record of dynastic promise and challenge.

> The first Stephen Crane to appear in America, arrived in Massachusetts from England in 1635. His son Stephen Crane settled in Connecticut and the Stephen Crane of the third American generation settled in New Jersey on lands that now hold the cities of Newark and Elizabeth. When the troubles with England came, he was president of both Colonial Assemblies that met in New York. Then he was sent by New Jersey to the Continental Congress and he served in that body until just about a week before the Declaration was signed, when the Tories made such trouble in New Jersey that he was obliged to return and serve as speaker in the colony's assembly.

That detail, "until just about a week before the Declaration was signed," remains an aching missed opportunity for Crane; his name might have been among the most famous signatures in American history, and instead was lost among the "trouble." In his early twenties, according to some reports, Crane "sometimes for hours when he was not working . . . would sit writing his name—Stephen Crane—Stephen Crane—Stephen Crane—on the books, magazines, and loose sheets of paper about the studio."

The rest of Crane's pedigree abounds in military men. The eldest son of the president of the Colonial Assemblies "commanded the 6th New Jersey infantry during the Revolution and ultimately died the ranking Major-general in the regular army from an old wound received in the expedition to Quebec." Another son was a commodore in the navy "at a time when the title of admiral was unknown," while a third, on his way to his father's deathbed,

> was captured by some Hessians and upon his refusing to tell the road by which they intended to sur-

prise a certain American out-post, they beat him with their muskets and then having stabbed him with their bayonets, they left him dead in the road. In those old times the family did it's [*sic*] duty.

During his adolescence Crane sometimes used the middle initial "T" to make his name sound more impressive, but by the end of this ritual recitation, the homely name of "Stephen Crane" seems nothing to be ashamed of. By his count, Crane is Stephen Crane IV, and "nom de guerre" takes on a more heroic meaning in this martial genealogy. It should be noted, by the way, that in this string of paternal Cranes, he has not yet mentioned his own father.

"In those old times the family did it's duty." The implication is that there has been a falling off in the meantime. Before Crane mentions his father, he finds it appropriate to make a detour through his maternal line, starting with a bit of slapstick: "Upon my mother's side, everybody as soon as he could walk, became a Methodist clergyman—of the old ambling-nag, saddle-bag, exhorting kind." But the Pecks were as impressive, in their way, as the Cranes: "My uncle, Jesse T. Peck, D.D., L.L.D., was a bishop in the Methodist Church." At this point Crane is finally ready to talk about his own father:

> My father was also a clergyman of that church, author of numerous works of theology, an editor of various periodicals of the church. He graduated at Princeton. He was a great, fine, simple mind.

Crane's father, then, has become an afterthought on his mother's side. Not part of the heroic line of soldier-patriot Cranes, he is merely "also a clergyman of that church" to which Crane's maternal ancestors belong. And while those ancestors are partly an occasion for comedy—"the old ambling-nag, saddle-bag, exhorting kind"—Crane is consciously evoking the earlier heroic period of itinerant Methodist circuit riders and camp meetings. The implied point is that Crane's own father is the newer kind of Methodist minister—respectable, educated, rooted in his community, dull. There is a palpable diminuendo in the triad of adjectives: "great, fine, simple." Stephen Crane's ambition, as he left Syracuse bound for New York City, was somehow to restore the heroic dimension to his family.

THREE

Mean Streets

T HE REMARKABLE convergence of three major events—the death of his mother, the drafting of his first novel, and his arrival in New York City—all in the brief space of a few months during the fall and winter of 1891, decisively affected Stephen Crane's career. We have seen how his childhood was laced with language and mourning, words filling the absences opened by death. When M. Helen Crane died, Crane was close by, at his brother Edmund's house in Lake View, New Jersey, but only Townley was at the deathbed. There is no record of Crane's reaction, at this time or later, to the loss of his mother, but he did claim to have written *Maggie* in one "intensive spurt" after her death. Scholars have disputed the dating, but accuracy is less important here than what Crane meant by his assertion. The point is that he saw the closest relation between the death of his mother and the birth of his fictional Maggie, as though one event allowed for, or called for, the other.

Maggie served another purpose as well. This vivid novel

of New York slum life was apparently sketched *before* Crane had had any direct experience of the metropolis. As such, it was a sort of declaration of intent, a college-boy's challenge to the city to meet his expectations. Moreover, in the character of Maggie, he created a dreamer like himself, who tries to fit her experience to her melodramatic imaginings.

By the summer of 1891, Crane knew that he wanted to be a writer. He was less certain what he wanted to write about. During that summer (and the five to follow), Crane spent a few weeks with friends in the woods surrounding Port Jervis, hunting and fishing. As yet he knew nothing much of the city, but he did know something of the vacation world of shore and mountain. The mountains had their own traditions of tale telling, mainly masculine boasts of prowess and proven courage. The tall tale, the fishing yarn, the ghost story—these kindled a laugh around the campfire and stoked Crane's nineteen-year-old imagination. The first of Crane's writings that count for anything are the odd sketches—"little grotesque tales of the woods," Crane later called them—that he wrote between the fall of 1891 and the following spring.

The so-called Sullivan County sketches are as rustic as *Maggie* is urban—it's hard to keep in mind that they were written concurrently. Still, the woods and the slums were both regions of danger and mystery for Crane, and there is a good deal of continuity of style and technique between the sketchy novel and the innovative sketches. The best of the latter—for example, "Killing His Bear" and "The Mesmeric Mountain"—have an eerie, Poe-like aura. The opening lines of "Killing His Bear" call up an alien world potent with animistic wildness:

> In a field of snow some green pines huddled together and sang in quavers as the wind whirled among the gullies and ridges. Icicles dangled from

the trees' beards, and fine dusts of snow lay upon their brows. On the ridge-top a dismal choir of hemlocks crooned over one that had fallen. The dying sun created a dim purple and flame-colored tumult on the horizon's edge and then sank until level crimson beams struck the trees. As the red rays retreated, armies of shadows stole forward. A gray, ponderous stillness came heavily in the steps of the sun. A little man stood under the quavering pines. He was muffled to the nose in fur and wool, and a hideous cap was pulled tightly over his ears. His cold and impatient feet had stamped a small platform of hard snow beneath him. A black-barrelled rifle lay in the hollow of his arm. . . . The shadows crept about his feet until he was merely a blurred blackness, with keen eyes.

In such passages, the human presence pales in its furiously alive surroundings, just as Maggie is lost among the personified buildings of New York City. And this little man, like Crane's other heroes and anti-heroes, harbors expectations that are destined for disillusionment: "Swift pictures of himself in a thousand attitudes under a thousand combinations of circumstances, killing a thousand bears, passed panoramically through him." Crane points up the irony still further in his closing image of the small-minded man, drunk with his preconceived heroics, oblivious to the reality of the bear's sufferings:

"Hit!" he yelled, and ran on. Some hundreds of yards forward he came to a dead bear with his nose in the snow. Blood was oozing slowly from a wound under the shoulder, and the snow about was sprinkled with blood. A mad froth lay in the animal's open mouth and his limbs were twisted from agony.
The little man yelled again and sprang forward, waving his hat as if he were leading the cheering of thousands. He ran up and kicked the ribs of the

bear. Upon his face was the smile of the successful lover.

That last sentence, in its cruel irony, prefigures Crane's later writing. This rib-kicking hunter is only a lover in the Wildean sense that you always kill the thing you love.

At a certain point a writer knows what kind of education he needs, and Crane's instincts, that fall of 1891, drew him toward New York City. Even earlier, his orbit—from Newark to Paterson, up to Port Jervis and down to the Jersey shore—seemed a cautious circling of the metropolis. The pull of the American publishing center must have been formidable: not only had Crane's parents and two of his siblings (his sister Agnes and his brother Townley) found a market for their writing there, but he himself had sent some dispatches from Syracuse to the New York *Tribune.* Crane tested the waters, though, before diving in. His home base was his brother Edmund's house in Lake View (now part of Paterson), where he could count on a meal, a bed, and a writing table after his forays into the New York slums. It wasn't until a year later that Crane took his first residence in New York, a room in a cheap boardinghouse on Avenue A (now Sutton Place) on the East Side.

Why was New York City during the early 1890s a place where a young writer interested in studying faces might sojourn? Why not go out West, say, or eastward to Europe? One answer is that the West by the 1890s was no longer very wild. Six years later Crane wrote his own elegy, for the passing of the frontier, "The Bride Comes to Yellow Sky." In 1893, the historian Frederick Jackson Turner advanced his "frontier thesis," and the implication was that having settled the continent the United States would have to look elsewhere for new frontiers, which it found, soon enough, in Cuba and the Philippines. As for Europe, it seemed overcivilized to the younger American writers, who wanted adventure and "real life." And in any case, many Europeans—Italians, Irish, Germans, Russians—had re-settled in neighborhoods in lower Manhattan, joining Asians, freed Blacks, Hasidic Jews. Nowhere else, perhaps, was there a greater diversity, in so small an expanse, of faces to study.

It was this urban frontier—as close as Fourteenth Street—that needed to be opened, scouted, mapped, and named. Guides appeared on the scene, Kit Carsons of the tenements. None was more famous than the reformist jour-nalist and photographer Jacob Riis, author of *How the Other Half Lives* (1890), whom Crane as a teenager had heard lecture on the Jersey shore. For Riis, the city was stratified like Dante's universe, and lower Manhattan was Hell.

> Leaving the Elevated Railroad where it dives under the Brooklyn Bridge at Franklin Square, scarce a dozen steps will take us where we wish to go. With its rush and roar echoing yet in our ears, we have turned the corner from prosperity to pov-erty. We stand upon the domain of the tenement. In the shadow of the great stone abutments the old Knickerbocker houses linger like ghosts of a de-parted day. . . . Dirt and desolation reign in the wide hallway, and danger lurks on the stairs. . . . A horde of dirty children play about the dripping hy-drant. . . . These are the children of the tenements, the growing generation of the slums; this their home.

Such details, named and codified by Riis—the sense of a great city already in ruins, haunted by its former grandeur; dangerous interiors; children playing in the mean streets— were repeated in hundreds of stories and newspaper sketches of the 1890s. There was enormous imaginative ap-peal in the idea of a dangerous underworld bordering the complacent neighborhoods to the north.

59

Crane was, like his father the minister, an avid student of urban vice. Inspired by Riis and others, he began roaming the theater districts and immigrant neighborhoods of the Bowery and the Lower East Side for material. This was his primary beat as a freelancer for the following three years or so. In the sketches he began publishing during the summer of 1892 for the New York *Press* and other papers, which he rightly considered among his finest work, Crane consistently saw the modern city as a place of dissimulation and disguise. No special vision was needed to pierce the appearances of Manhattan architecture during the Gilded Age, when luxurious façades announced industrial and commercial success. Americans returning from study and travel abroad advertised their newly acquired good taste by erecting French châteaux on Fifth Avenue, schools that looked like Gothic cloisters, and department stores dressed up like the Doge's palace. Like many of his contemporaries, Crane was amused by this cacophony of styles, but he also detected something sinister in the looming façades, as though America was hiding something behind its false fronts. He studied façades as well as faces, probing the physiognomy of New York to find what was hidden within.

Crane increasingly tried to expose himself to the intensities of the modern city. For a sketch called "Experiment in Misery," published in the *Press* in the depression year of 1894, he dressed up as a tramp and spent the night in a flophouse. He was convinced that "you can tell nothing of [how a homeless man feels] unless you are in that condition yourself." For Crane, the landscape of "misery" is a dark underworld. He enlists for his journey the services of a Virgil-like guide, in tattered garments, who "appeared like an assassin steeped in crimes performed awkwardly." This man accompanies Crane through the "gloom-shrouded corridor" of the shelter for the homeless, leading him to its "dark and secret places." Crane's description of his companions has a nightmare vividness, strikingly similar to that of the carnage in *The Red Badge of Courage:*

60

And all through the room could be seen the tawny hues of naked flesh, limbs thrust into the darkness, projecting beyond the cots; up-reared knees; arms hanging, long and thin, over the cot edges. For the most part they were statuesque, carven, dead. With the curious lockers standing all about like tombstones there was a strange effect of a graveyard, where bodies were merely flung.

Crane conceives of these bodies the way a sculptor might—limb by carven limb—and then tops them off with metaphorical tombstones. Later, pursuing his experiments in stupor, he tried opium as part of his research for a sketch on opium dens. "When a man arises from his first trial of the pipe," he reported, "the nausea that clutches him is something that can give cards and spades and big casino to seasickness. If he had swallowed a live chimney-sweep he could not feel more like dying."

Crane set his first novel, *Maggie: A Girl of the Streets*, in the grim neighborhoods of lower Manhattan. We don't know exactly when he began work on the novel, nor do we know much about the circumstances of its composition. This uncertainty has not prevented scholars from treating *Maggie* as the result of Crane's experiments in the slums of New York. This tempting notion neatly fits our view of Crane's generation—Frank Norris, Dreiser, Jack London, and the rest—as "naturalists," assiduously at work in the laboratory of suffering humanity. But Crane, as usual, confounds such orderly schemes. For *Maggie* was less the result of Crane's experiments than their cause.

The external evidence, scrappy as it is, suggests that *Maggie* was well under way by the fall of 1891. Classmates at Syracuse remembered that Crane liked to watch suspects being booked at the local courthouse. He may already have been learning the physiognomy of crime—studying "faces

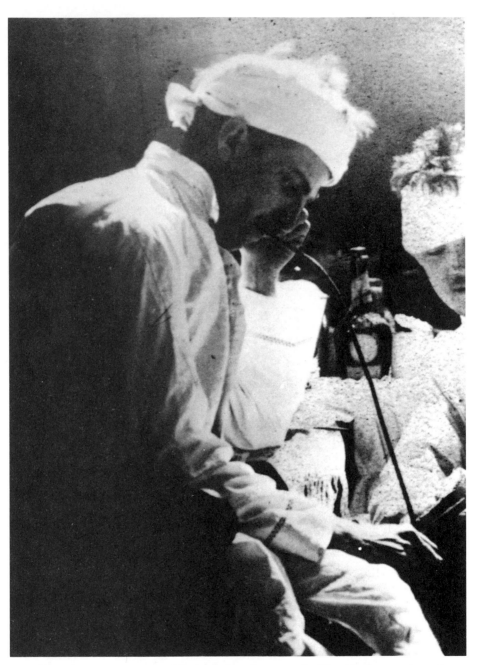

7. *Crane experimenting with the bohemian arts, in New York, c. spring 1893.*

on the street" instead of books, as we noted earlier—in preparation for his novel. One of his college friends, Frank Noxon, saw manuscript pages of *Maggie* at Syracuse the previous spring; the newspaper editor Willis Johnson reported seeing a "first draft" during the summer; and Crane himself claimed to have finished the novel just after his mother's death in December. In the face of such evidence it's hard not to believe that some version of *Maggie* was written before Crane arrived in New York, though he probably rewrote and revised it, drawing on his New York experience, before its publication in 1893.

There is internal evidence as well for its early conception, for *Maggie* hardly reads like a researched and documented novel. What urban texture the novel manages to muster is borrowed from Riis and from Methodist tracts about the evils of the modern city. The rest of the novel, and the best of it, is all hypothesis, speculation, dream. *Maggie* apparently served as a preliminary sketch for what Crane expected to find in the city. His newspaper sketches—"The Men in the Storm," "Experiment in Misery," and the like—flesh out *Maggie*, rather than the reverse. The novel's influence on the course of Crane's life extended still further. For in his idealized portrait of a prostitute he was already imagining the kind of fallen women whom he later sought out, first in the streets of New York, and then in the aptly named Hotel de Dream.

Maggie is experimental in another sense as well. It takes risks with a familiar subject, boldly cutting new patterns out of old cloth. Crane chose a theme that invited sentimentality—the fall of an innocent slum girl into prostitution and suicide. The challenge was to play a new song on this battered instrument, handed from author to author in the nineteenth century, discarded by Zola, taken up by the English writer Arthur Morrison in his book *Tales of Mean*

Streets, and now making the rounds of American writers of reformist and sentimental fiction.

Crane probably thought his material would prove more innovative and shocking than it did. After all, he had spent far more time among the novel-burning Methodists of the Jersey shore than among world-weary New Yorkers. He may even have feared prosecution for writing pornography when he had the novel published in 1893, at his own expense, under the deliberately colorless and relatively untraceable pseudonym "Johnston Smith." But reviewers were quick to point out that Crane's characters were already, as the novelist Frank Norris noted, "old acquaintances in the world of fiction." The hackneyed plot, to be sure, is simple enough. Maggie and Jimmie grow up in the slums. Their father dies and their mother drinks. Maggie is seduced by Jimmie's friend Pete. He ditches her and she becomes a prostitute. Jimmie and her mother kick her out of the house. She dies in the river.

Perhaps the very familiarity of the material appealed to Crane, though not from some modernist drive to "make it new." It would be more accurate to say that Crane made these materials *old.* Like a jazz musician toying with a "standard," he seems confident that we know the tune. He slows down some passages, takes others in cut time, and still others—like the exact circumstances of Maggie's death—he leaves out altogether. To contemporary reviewers the book seemed unfinished. But this sketchlike quality is ultimately part of Crane's argument. The lives he describes are fragmentary, built up of discordant parts, caught in a city that refuses to hold together.

Crane often seems to be building rather than simply observing his urban world; he makes it up as he goes, out of walls and stairs and fire escapes. It is fitting that his opening scene, when Maggie is a child, takes place on a heap of gravel—dumped there, presumably, to make or repair a street. And Maggie, we are told, "blossomed in a mudpuddle"—as much a product of the street as her brother,

Jimmie. For these children, the streets are safer than the buildings that line them. The tenements are not, like the uptown brownstones of Edith Wharton or Henry James, refuges of domestic privacy. They are dangerous "dark regions," sites of incessant violence and rampage.

The street is an appropriate stage for all Jimmie's roles. The king-of-the-mountain game that opens the book has an almost comic energy. Jimmie is fighting for the "honor of Rum Alley"—his street identity. Crane describes this battle as a primitive rite, the children swearing "in barbaric trebles" and "fighting in the modes of four thousand years ago." It is as though the patrician wish for a "strenuous" life in the 1890s, which Teddy Roosevelt and his friend Frederic Remington imagined in the West, were available right here, a trolley-car ride away. The political anxiety among the uptown classes was that these urban warriors would rise up and take American society by force from the flabby aristocrats. It was in this context that Frederick Law Olmsted conceived of Central Park as a way to defuse urban hostilities.

Like the dangerous roughs that Olmsted and other reformers worried about, the teen-aged Jimmie begins hanging out on street corners.

> He menaced mankind at the intersections of streets.
> On the corners he was in life and of life. The world was going on and he was there to perceive it.

Not content to be a spectator, he soon takes a job as a truck driver, a lord of the streets who despises mere "foot passengers" and yields only to the sublime color and noise of fire trucks. And the women Jimmie favors are of course women of the street, whom he can treat with the same bullying disdain that he accords pedestrians.

A major theme in *Maggie* is the different status of "boys of the street," like Jimmie, and "girls of the street," like his sister. A young man hanging out on street corners is a spectator, a *flâneur*, taking in the passing scene, while a woman doing the same thing is something altogether different. As long as Jimmie's friend Pete, the seductive bartender, accompanies Maggie through the streets, appearances are preserved. But once she wanders the streets alone she becomes fair game for any passing man.

As Crane depicts him, Pete is nothing but appearance: he is the embodiment of the city-as-disguise. He's a slick talker and a slicker dresser, with "his blue double-breasted coat, edged with black braid, buttoned close to a red puff tie." The bar where he works is a little shrine to fakery and illusion.

> The interior of the place was papered in olive and bronze tints of imitation leather. A shining bar of counterfeit massiveness extended down the side of the room. Behind it a great mahogany-appearing sideboard reached the ceiling. Upon its shelves rested pyramids of shimmering glasses that were never disturbed. Mirrors set in the face of the sideboard multiplied them.

Maggie, once she has emerged from her childhood "disguise of dirt," is of course taken in by all of Pete's fakery, and her destiny is to become herself a person of illusion and façade, "one of the painted cohorts of the city." When she turns to a minister for help, she finds that he too is concerned only with façades, with "saving his own respectability" instead of her soul.

Jimmie, using the alienating argot Crane assigns his low-life characters, offers his sister a choice: "Yeh've edder got teh go teh hell or go teh work!" Experience soon teaches her that this is no choice at all: for a poor girl in New York City during the 1890s work is hell and hell is work. In the collar-and-cuff factory where she has her first job, the endless repetition of mechanical gestures slowly turns the workers into machines:

> She knew she was gradually and surely shrivelling in the hot, stuffy room. The begrimed windows rat-

tled incessantly from the passing of elevated trains. . . . She wondered as she regarded some of the grizzled women in the room, mere mechanical contrivances sewing seams. . . .

The silly melodramas Pete takes her to see offer an illusory alternative to this punishing world of machinery. For a brief moment she really believes that he is the "hero with the beautiful sentiments" who has come to rescue her from poverty and bondage. As she leaves the theater, she wonders whether the "culture and refinement" of the rescued heroine might be "acquired by a girl who lived in a tenement house and worked in a shirt factory."

She lives by the book, so to speak, until her "ruin" forces her to resort to what Jimmie calls "hell." Then she finds to her horror that it's hard work to read the faces of strangers, accost them in the street, strike a deal, deliver the goods. And Crane invites the parallel of work and hell by making the "fat foreigner" with the "oily beard" who owns the collar factory resemble Maggie's last customer, the "huge fat man in torn and greasy garments" who stares with her at the river, where a "hidden factory" lights up the waters "lapping oilily against the timbers." These hideous men who loom over Maggie's fate make it almost irrelevant whether she dies by murder or suicide. She's doomed in any case.

Crane withheld from Maggie the sexual confidence and swagger of the Parisian courtesan. Unlike Zola's Nana, she never learns to convert her allure into power. Nana's relative independence, social and financial, is at the farthest extreme from Maggie's forlorn dependence. The whole alternative social hierarchy that Zola—and, for that matter, Balzac and Maupassant—constructed is missing in Crane's narrower world. Something of Crane's own Methodist upbringing seems to color his portrait of moral furtiveness; it is as though Maggie paints her face more to hide her shame than to heighten her beauty. She wanders the streets as a diffident beggar, rather than a seductress, and no one is charitable enough to have her. One customer turns away after discerning that she is "neither new, Parisian, nor theatrical."

Even Maggie's suicide—if it is a suicide—is strangely passive. She is absorbed by her surroundings, extinguished like a last city light in the gathering darkness:

> She went into the blackness of the final block. The shutters of the tall buildings were closed like grim lips. The structures seemed to have eyes that looked over her, beyond her, at other things.

She approaches the East River, past personified buildings that seem more alive than she is:

> The river appeared a deathly black hue. Some hidden factory sent up a yellow glare, that lit for a moment the waters lapping oilily against timbers. The varied sounds of life, made joyous by distance and seeming unapproachableness, came faintly and died away to silence.

In the morning they pull her body from the river.

If work is hellish for Maggie, what about play, the round of theaters, museums, amusement spots that Pete introduces her to? Pete takes Maggie to three different music halls, and each for her is a further descent into tawdriness and dependency. They have their first date at a "great hall" of cheerful families and sentimental patriotism, where the working man brings his wife and kids to see cheap versions of uptown variety shows. Maggie is so curious and eager to take it all in that she's a bit bewildered when Pete implies that she owes him something for "treating" her. A few weeks later, after Pete has "ruined" Maggie, he takes her for a cheaper night out. Her prospects have shrunk with the shape of the hall, which is now twisted and "irregular," a dingy place of male fantasy. Clinging to Pete and oblivious to the stripper on the stage, Maggie wonders why the men in the place look at her with such knowing leers. The third hall, where Pete and Maggie encounter Pete's old friend Nellie, has "dim monstrosities" painted on the walls. It is an undisguised place of assignation, where there are twenty-eight subsidized prostitutes sitting at twenty-eight tables.

At times Crane seems to want us to turn as innocent an eye as Maggie's on this city and its pleasures. Watching a dancer flip up her skirts, all Maggie notices is how fine the skirts are—the sexual meaning of the cancan is lost on her. Listening to a ventriloquist, she asks, "Do those little men talk?" Pete, himself the master of deceit, explains that "it's all some damn fake." At such demoralizing moments, Crane risks making Maggie more pathetic than sympathetic. We want her to rally her forces and somehow strike back at her tawdry surroundings. But Crane leaves her little room.

It is in the pace of these scenes, however, that Crane most asserts his artistry. He describes the orchestras as though he's devising a sound track for his story line. The first is relatively elegant, composed of "yellow silk women and bald-headed men" playing waltzes. The second, mirroring Maggie, is "submissive" to its frowsy but well-dressed conductor. The third looks as though its players "had just happened in." The music of the orchestras echoes Maggie's fate, accompanying it, so to speak, from the hopeful waltz to the sexy ballad to the frenetic music of the third hall. Here Crane encourages us to see that he is accelerating Maggie's fate as well:

> The chief element in the music of the orchestra was speed. The musicians played in intent fury. A woman was singing and smiling upon the stage, but no one took notice of her. The rate at which the piano, cornet and violins were going, seemed to impart wildness to the half-drunken crowd. Beer glasses were emptied at a gulp and conversation be-

came a rapid chatter. The smoke eddied and swirled like a shadowy river hurrying toward some unseen falls. Pete and Maggie entered the hall. . . .

This scene establishes the staccato rhythm of Maggie's life, as it jolts and shifts out of control. Pete abandons her, the family refuses to take her back, she walks the streets—all these things happen in a few short pages. The culminating sequence is the amazing seventeenth chapter, which veers ineluctably towards that "shadowy river."

Frank Norris had noted that "the impression left with the reader [of *Maggie*] is one of hurry." To Crane, this sense of speed was central to city life during the 1890s. He wanted to suggest that city life had somehow sped everything up, that people had lost control of their own fates. To quote Norris once more:

> The picture he makes is not a single carefully composed painting, serious, finished, scrupulously studied, but rather scores and scores of tiny flashlight photographs, instantaneous, caught, as it were, on the run. Of a necessity, then, the movement of his tale must be rapid, brief, very hurried, hardly more than a glimpse.

On closing *Maggie* we feel that we have caught a glimpse of this overwhelming city and its furtive inhabitants, this world of faces and façades, gravel heaps and mud puddles, boys and girls of the street.

If the contours of Crane's imaginary city were in place before he arrived in New York, an unanticipated event seems to have colored his view of the actual city. When he insisted that he'd completed *Maggie* soon after his mother's death, on December 7, 1891, he was hinting that part of the meaning of the novel resided in its tie to maternity. But if *Maggie* can indeed be read as a requiem for Helen Crane, and for motherhood in general, the interpretation cannot be a literal one. It's difficult to match the hard-working promoter of the New Jersey WCTU with the furniture-bashing harridan of *Maggie.* Crane's grief is disguised and displaced in the novel. Its setting in the slums of lower Manhattan is typical of this displacement; for Crane, economic deprivation is a metaphor for its emotional counterpart. His mother's death left him feeling bereft and in need of appropriate language to express his loss.

The last scene of *Maggie* is famous for its savage irony; as she holds her dead daughter's faded baby shoes in her hand, Mrs. Johnson manages to scream, after much coaxing, "Oh, yes, I'll fergive her! I'll fergive her!" One would have thought that Maggie's mother was the greater sinner, more in need of forgiveness than her hapless daughter. But Maggie herself is the dominant maternal presence in the novel, and the figure upon whom Crane's own feelings and yearnings crystallize. She is often portrayed as a potential mother, her path repeatedly crossed by the threat of pregnancy and by actual babies. We first see her as "a small ragged girl dragg[ing] a red, bawling infant along the crowded ways." After she grows up—or in the novel's words, "blossoms in a mud-puddle"—she continually runs the risk of "ruin" at the hands of men. When her boyfriend, Pete, seduces her, she drifts into prostitution, and Crane obliquely suggests that she is pregnant when she dies. Her condition is hinted at by the ubiquity of babies in the scene when Maggie returns to her mother's house after her "ruin." Neighbors stare at Maggie, "nodding their heads with airs of profound philosophy."

> A baby, overcome with curiosity concerning this object at which all were looking, sidled forward and touched her dress, cautiously, as if investigating a red-hot stove.

Maggie is hounded from the house, her brother's "repelling hands express[ing] horror of contamination."

> The crowd at the door fell back precipitately. A baby falling down in front of the door, wrenched a scream like a wounded animal from its mother. Another woman sprang forward and picked it up.

This jerky scene suggests a nightmare vision of childbirth—the mother's labor pains; the baby falling into the hands of others; the sense of pregnancy and childbirth as contaminating, taboo. The baby is meant to signal recognition; there may be a hint as well, in the stove metaphor, that something is cooking inside Maggie.

The figures Maggie meets in her final march to the river also seem like babies, as seen in the distorting mirror of a dream: first, the "man with blotched features" who refuses her advances; then, the "huge fat man" whose "small, bleared eyes, sparkling from amidst great rolls of red fat, swept eagerly over the girl's upturned face." Maggie's date with the river repeats the familiar tale—chronicled by Jacob Riis and other reformers—of the fallen woman whose unwanted pregnancy is terminated by suicide. For Crane, however, the story commemorates and disguises his own mother's death, but not without a certain remainder left over: a weight of private mourning encoded within the texture of the tale.

Thus, the uncanny paragraphs that end the third chapter allow Crane to mourn his mother's passing. After one of her fits of furniture smashing, Mrs. Johnson collapses, and Maggie and Jimmie hold a sort of wake for their sleeping mother:

> The eyes of both were drawn, by some force, to stare at the woman's face, for they thought she need only to awake and all fiends would come from below.
>
> They crouched until the ghost-mists of dawn appeared at the window, drawing close to the panes, and looking in at the prostrate heaving body of the mother.

The passage has a posthumous feel to it, with its ghostlike mists and hellish fiends. The mother's body is never more palpable than when the spirit has temporarily departed from it.

A year after Crane had *Maggie* published privately, he wrote a second slum novel, as a sort of sequel to the first. In *George's Mother*, with its explicit maternal theme, Crane again associated his arrival in New York City with the madness and death of his mother. This neglected work feels at times like the most openly confessional of Crane's books, and it is the one example of his writing in which autobiographical material seems imperfectly assimilated. Indeed, its claustrophobic evocation of the intense relationship between pious mother and backsliding son seems to dare us *not* to read it as autobiography. "I have read George's Mother since I received your letter," wrote Stephen Crane's niece Edith F. Crane to Thomas Beer, in 1922, "in order to compare the mother's character with my mother's knowledge of my grandmother's. My mother [who apparently did not read the book herself] says that she can see no connection at all. Grandmother was a religious woman. My mother says she never scolded or nagged."

But Helen Crane, as her letters of the late 1880s make clear, was quite capable of scolding and nagging. Two possible explanations come to mind. First, there may have been a considerable gap between Mrs. Crane's public and private personae. Second, she may have changed after her mental collapse, becoming less tolerant of the sins of others, at a time when Edith's mother had little contact with her. In any case, Crane drew his portrait of *George's Mother* "after" his own mother in several obvious respects.

In the novel, George Kelcey lives alone with his pious mother in a tenement in New York City. The only way for him to escape her cloying demands—she expects him to "beau" her to weekly prayer meetings—is to join the unemployed "gang" at the corner bar. The narrative is built around the opposite worlds of chapel and barroom: the feminine society of clergymen and temperance agitators and the masculine rites of alcoholic camaraderie and failure. George becomes precisely the kind of rowdy drunk his mother despises. In the final chapter, he's called away from his buddies who have gathered to drink in a vacant lot, and led home to "the chamber of death," where his mother, who doesn't recognize him, is dying. A clergyman is there to preside over the final moments of her life. Thus, both *George's Mother* and *Maggie* end with the death of a maternal figure.

Like Crane, George is the last son in his mother's house: "Outa five boys you're th' on'y one she's got left," his drinking buddy Jones, who knew the Kelceys before their move from a small town, tells him.

> "How is th' ol' lady anyhow?" continued Jones. "Th' last time I remember she was as spry as a little ol' cricket, an' was helpeltin' aroun' th' country lecturin' before W.C.T.U.'s an' one thing an' another."

The role of WCTU lecturer doesn't fit the poor tenement dweller we meet in the novel, though, and Crane remains vague about the circumstances of the Kelceys' move to the city, except to say that Mr. Kelcey died in a fall from a scaffold.

But in the exuberant and experimental second chapter, in which we're given our first view of Mrs. Kelcey, Crane may have found a way to respond to his mother's mental illness. Mrs. Kelcey is obsessively cleaning an apartment that is already clean. "It was a picture of indomitable courage," Crane writes ironically. "And as she went on her way her voice was often raised in a long cry, a strange war-chant, a shout of battle and defiance, that rose and fell in harsh screams." The real enemy, however, isn't the dust within but the threat of pollution outside. She looks out the window:

> In the distance an enormous brewery towered over the other buildings. Great gilt letters advertised a brand of beer. Thick smoke came from funnels

and spread near it like vast and powerful wings. The structure seemed a great bird, flying. The letters of the sign made a chain of gold hanging from its neck.

This powerful winged image of liberation, with its ambiguous suggestion that the promised freedom may be illusory—the letters are gilt and the bird is chained—is an apt one for George's circumscribed existence. But Crane is also describing a madwoman, possessed by the kind of paranoid intensity that may have led to his mother's breakdown eight years earlier.

A novel is more than the psychological "working through" of what Freud called the novelist's family romance, and no weight of fictive evidence can prove what Crane's relations with his parents were "really like." Such relationships are dynamic in any case, everchanging rather than static. The novelist's aim is to make something new out of the most vivid materials at his command. But it is striking that Crane's imagined world is repeatedly one of absent fathers and vulnerable mothers, where children as a consequence are continually at risk. Exposure is the dominant condition in all Crane's imaginary landscapes: the bear-filled woods of Sullivan County, the streets of New York, the battlefield. Surely one can be pardoned for wondering where Crane's imagination for disaster came from.

Such landscapes probably had their shadowy origins in lonely and distracted encounters in the Methodist parsonage. For what we have seen in the lives of Crane's parents is an intensity of engagement—with the Holiness Movement and with the WCTU—that their son may have found disturbing on two counts: first, because the elder Cranes' moral commitments shut out too many of life's intensities; and second, because one thing that was shut out of their attentions was Stephen Crane himself. Again we find ourselves, in the absence of sufficient documentation, groping in the dark. If *Maggie* and *George's Mother* did indeed allow Crane to make sense of one part of his life—his childhood

75

losses—even as he embarked on another, the life of a professional writer, it's that later life we turn to now, with a brief stopover on the Jersey shore.

Crane's education on the streets of New York gave him a fresh perspective on the beaches of New Jersey. After his discouraging months of freelancing, he returned in the summer of 1892 to his old job with his brother Townley's Asbury Park news bureau. Crane joined other "shore reporters" in chronicling the visits of important families and flamboyant shysters to the various resorts along the boardwalk, from the "Methodist Mecca" of Ocean Grove to the "Irish Riviera" at Spring Lake. Crane's writing had acquired a new edge in the city, and he soon revealed a more sophisticated sense of what news was made of than his job required. With three paragraphs of prose Crane managed to turn a humdrum annual event into a newsmaking scandal, with political repercussions. He lost his job as a result, and compromised that of his brother.

Townley probably assumed that nothing much could be done with the annual parade of the Junior Order of United American Mechanics on August 17, 1892. He himself had covered the parade of this right-wing brotherhood in previous years and apparently delegated the job to his younger brother and took the day off. But Stephen, alert to street spectacles like the "Broken-Down Van" he'd just described in the *Tribune* on July 10, used the parade as a peg for toying with multiple perspectives on an event in the street. His report, featured in the Sunday edition of the *Tribune* on August 21, begins:

> The parade of the Junior Order of United American Mechanics here on Wednesday afternoon was a deeply impressive one to some persons. There were hundreds of the members of the order, and they wound through the streets to the music of enough

brass bands to make furious discords. It probably was the most awkward, ungainly, uncut and un-carved procession that ever raised clouds of dust on sun-beaten streets.

The reader is invited to think that Crane is simply going to knock the marchers, but the sting in the tail of the first sentence is the key to the piece: in unpacking the phrases "some persons" and "deeply impressive," Crane managed to offend just about everyone involved in the event.

Discord is the effect Crane is after, and with one of those mercurial shifts that are the chief delight of his newspaper work, he turns the self-satisfied spectators of Asbury Park, presumably sharing his amusement at the marchers, into the entertainment: "Nevertheless, the spectacle of an Asbury Park crowd confronting such an aggregation was an interesting sight to a few people." The comfortable "some people" of the opening has shrunk to a more discerning "few," as Crane undercuts the snooty perspective he had previously invited:

> Asbury Park creates nothing. It does not make; it merely amuses. There is a factory where nightshirts are manufactured, but it is some miles from town. This is a resort of wealth and leisure, of women and considerable wine.

Now we're invited to scorn the spectators as mere consumers, who have banished productivity to the outskirts of town. Oblivious to the making of clothes, they are in fact mere clotheshorses themselves:

> The throng along the line of march was composed of summer gowns, lace parasols, tennis trousers, straw hats and indifferent smiles. The procession was composed of men, bronzed, slope-shouldered, uncouth and begrimed with dust.

Clothes versus men, the distinction seems clear enough. But the sequence of adjectives has, like the shoulders, a

77

downward slope, and Crane the former drillmaster is soon attacking the marchers for having "no idea of marching . . . not seeming quite to understand." Nor is he done with the spectators:

> The bona fide Asbury Parker is a man to whom a dollar, when held close to his eye, often shuts out any impression he may have that other people possess rights. He is apt to consider that men and women, especially city men and women, were created to be mulcted by him. Hence the tan-colored, sun-beaten honesty in the faces of the members of the Junior Order of United American Mechanics is expected to have a very staggering effect upon them.

The whole piece is a delicate balancing act, of shifting scorn and viewpoint, and delicacy was not what the readers of the Sunday *Tribune* were attuned to. No Asbury Parkers complained, as it turned out, but the Junior Mechanics did, claiming the article was an insult to their principles—principles that were, roughly, opposition to immigration and to "sectarian" (i.e., Catholic and Jewish) influences in the public schools, promotion of "Americanism" (all members of the order were American-born), and a commitment to "honor and protect our country and to vow allegiance to the Stars and Stripes."

The owner of the New York *Tribune* was Whitelaw Reid, who also happened to be, in the summer of the election year of 1892, the Republican candidate for vice president of the United States. He couldn't afford to alienate the working man's vote, and the *Tribune*, in a retraction, came down hard on the three paragraphs, while a local paper in Asbury Park attacked Crane: "This young man has a hankering for razzledazzle style and has a great future before him if, unlike the good, he fails to die young." Townley was apparently fired by the *Tribune* for sending in the offending article, and Crane's career as a shore reporter was over.

We see in this episode something characteristic of

Crane's best journalism. When he set out to cover such stock muckraking subjects as conditions in Pennsylvania coal mines or drought-ridden Nebraska farms, the results, despite patches of vivid writing, were predictably flat. But when he felt his way into an ambiguous situation like the Asbury Park parade, worrying the fault lines and not knowing quite what to expect, the results were improvisatory and vivid. If the political agenda of such work is not clear, this is because Crane was experimenting with a treatment of events that embraced multiple points of view. He remained purposefully noncommittal, preferring angles to arguments. And if conflicting perspectives were his quarry, surely no more ambiguous circumstances were available to his imagination than those of war. Crane found himself, during the following year, ready to turn his attention to another kind of marching men.

FOUR

Ominous Babies

DURING THE SPRING of 1893, when the twenty-one-year-old Crane was living in New York City and trying to make a living as a freelance newspaperman, he wrote a series of stories about the adventures of a baby who wanders through the city streets. No one has shown much curiosity about these stories. They have seemed, at most, a sideshow to the main event Crane was working on at the time: his study of the mind of a private in the American Civil War. Surely their scale partly explains the neglect. They are small, like their subject, and they seem fairly clear about their meanings. But that very clarity—which invites a political, or at least social, interpretation—has distracted readers from what is truly interesting in these stories. The interest is in the babies, who, like real babies, have more to tell us than we may at first suspect.

The stories I have in mind are the so-called baby sketches: "An Ominous Baby," "A Great Mistake," and "A Dark-Brown Dog." Some manuscript material found by Crane's friend and sometime roommate, the illustrator Corwin Knapp Linson, identifies the unnamed protagonist of these stories as Maggie's baby brother, Tommie, who dies in the fourth chapter of *Maggie: A Girl of the Streets*. This fact alone should command our attention; for Crane's interest in the psychology of babies is the bridge between his earlier slum novel and the war novel he had begun writing. What is more, the baby sketches, read correctly, constitute Crane's clearest statement regarding the sources of his art.

What was it about babies that fascinated Stephen Crane, and made him "put them under a detached observation and play with them by the hour," as Thomas Beer remarked? Beer himself suggested a reason: "[Crane] loved babies, horses, oceans or anything that offered an enigmatic surface to his thought." It sounds like the start of a long list. But Crane's curiosity was more specific. Like several of his famous, turn-of-the-century contemporaries, he wondered what babies think about, and how one might deduce their thoughts, so to speak, from their surfaces. In 1895 Crane was reading a volume of essays by Henry James and ran across some Kantian ideas that bothered him. "What, though, does the man mean by disinterested contemplation?" Crane asked in a letter quoted by Beer.

> It won't wash. If you care enough about a thing to study it, you are interested and have stopped being disinterested. That's so, is it not? Well, Q.E.D. It clamours in my skull that there is no such thing as disinterested contemplation except that empty as a beerpail look that a babe turns on you and shrivels you to grass with. Does anybody know how a child thinks? The horrible thing about a kid is that it makes no excuses, none at all. They are much like breakers on a beach. They do something and that is all there is in it.

While there's considerable doubt about the authenticity of this and other letters quoted by Beer, witnesses confirm

Crane's fascination with how children think. Crane's friend C. K. Linson recalled that their conversation "warmed" when it involved "the processes of a child's mind"; and Joseph Conrad, who frankly admitted that he himself detested babies, remembered Crane "stretched full length and sustained on his elbows on a grass plot, in order to gaze" at five-week-old Borys Conrad. "I might say that I never heard him laugh," Conrad added, "except in connection with the baby."

Some of Crane's most intense writing about babies concerns the children of the poor. His habitual skepticism about our access to the minds of children recurs in his description of a baby from a Mexican slum, whom he encountered during a trip west in 1895. He paused to watch while the baby, "brown as a water-jar and of the shape of an alderman, paraded the bank in utter indifference or ignorance or defiance." The portrayal of indigent children was a familiar enough subject during the 1890s, when Crane did all his work. Jacob Riis's chapters on children in *How the Other Half Lives*, with shocking statistics about infant mortality and "unauthorized babies," had first appeared in 1890, and Riis followed up that reformist success two years later with *The Children of the Poor*. At about the same time, the psychologist G. Stanley Hall was pursuing research for his study on "The Contents of Children's Minds on Entering School." Hall, who was William James's first graduate student and an early proponent of psychoanalysis in America (as president of Clark University, he invited Freud and Jung to lecture there in 1908), shared both of Crane's interests in babies: what they think about and how poor children differ from rich ones.

But it is not widely known that Crane explored the realm of infant experience in a rich and critically neglected area of his writing, and succeeded in probing more deeply than Riis's tear-jerking portraits or Hall's positivistic enumeration of mental "contents." Indeed, it is not an exaggeration to say that Crane, in three vivid sketches, anticipated some of the most interesting twentieth-century thinking about children's minds.

The plots of the baby sketches are simple enough. In "A Great Mistake" the baby snatches a lemon from the fruit stand of an Italian vendor. He steals a toy fire engine from a rich child in "An Ominous Baby." In the third story he befriends a "dark-brown dog" that follows him home, only to be thrown out of the fifth-floor window by the boy's drunken father.

Crane recognized that a political message of some kind could be drawn from these plots, though he may have hit on the political angle as an afterthought, when he was looking for a market for work already completed. "An Ominous Baby" was published in B. O. Flower's left-wing *Arena* magazine—a pioneer in muckraking journalism—in May 1894, and Linson was hired to provide illustrations. "Have you finished the 'Ominous Baby' story yet?" Crane wrote impatiently to Linson, in the depression summer of 1893. "At the present time—during these labor troubles—is the best time to dispose of it." There's a certain cynicism in Crane's words, deepened by the grim—and perhaps unconscious—punning on "labor troubles" and "disposing" of the baby. (Crane didn't want his work to be stillborn.)

These stories were read at the time as political allegories, and that is how they are still read—when they are read at all. But they have certain odd features in common, specific details in the representation of the baby that go beyond any explicit concern with class conflict. I want to suggest a line of interpretation that allows a wider sense for the theme of deprivation that these stories explore. This is not a matter of slighting "political" concerns in favor of "aesthetic" ones; it would be more accurate to say that Crane broadens the realm of the political to cover infant experience as well, specifically the earliest experiences of possession and ownership.

83

But before I turn to the baby sketches themselves, an examination of the baby Tommie's first appearance in Crane's writing will give clues to Crane's later development of the character. In the second chapter of *Maggie*, Maggie's father drags her brother Jimmie home after Jimmie has gotten into a fight with some neighborhood kids. The chapter begins with the often-quoted sentence: "Eventually they entered a dark region where, from a careening building, a dozen gruesome doorways gave up loads of babies to the street and the gutter." One of the babies produced by this womblike region is Maggie's brother, Tommie, who first appears in her arms:

> A small ragged girl dragged a red, bawling infant along the crowded ways. He was hanging back, babylike, bracing his wrinkled, bare legs. The little girl cried out: "Ah, Tommie, come ahn. Dere's Jimmie and fader. Don't be a-pullin' me back."
>
> She jerked the baby's arm impatiently. He fell on his face, roaring. With a second jerk she pulled him to his feet, and they went on. With the obstinacy of his order, he protested against being dragged in a chosen direction. He made heroic endeavors to keep on his legs, denounced his sister, and consumed a bit of orange peeling which he chewed between the times of his infantile orations.

Crane is alert to the possibilities of this furiously alive baby. We can already see a political discourse emerging in Tommie's rebelliousness. The "obstinacy of his order" suggests that infancy is a distinct social class, as does his tendency, like dissatisfied workers, to "protest," "denounce," and deliver "orations." But in giving special attention to the baby, Crane also manages to mark Maggie as a potential mother, a "daughter of the tenements" who could be "ruined" if she isn't careful, or lucky. Tommie's real mother is at home, drunk. The scandal of babies inadequately tended by immature girls is stock material in reform literature of the 1880s and 1890s; Riis, for example, gives it full play.

There are other insistent details, however, whose purpose is not so clear. There is, for example, the verb that is regularly associated with Tommie: Maggie "dragged" him, a word reinforced by its proximity to "ragged." He protests "against being *dragged*"; half a page later he is "protesting with great violence. During his sister's hasty manoeuvres he was *dragged* by the arm." And then there are the objects that Crane places in Tommie's hands and mouth: the "bit of orange peeling" he chews on, the "old quilt of faded red and green grandeur" that he clutches "with his fists doubled."

But Crane brings this complicated baby to life only to dispose of him, in the opening sentence of the fourth chapter:

> The babe, Tommie, died. He went away in an insignificant coffin, his small waxen hand clutching a flower that the girl, Maggie, had stolen from an Italian.

Again the details are arresting. The theft is especially surprising, not at all in keeping with Maggie's otherwise immaculate behavior. But the stolen flower clutched in the baby's hand—as well as the earlier emphasis on "dragging" and on bits of things in the hand and mouth—will begin to make more sense if we look closely at the three baby sketches in which Tommie, now a year or two older, is given a continuing life.

In the first of the sketches, "A Great Mistake," Crane reassembles some of the furniture from *Maggie*: a baby, an Italian vendor, a piece of fruit for the baby to grasp. The sketch is brief, barely two pages in the Library of America edition, yet the action is so simple and the writing so rich that the story gives an impression of amplitude and grandeur, like a Persian miniature. Crane takes his time as he develops the two parts of the tale: first, the baby's worship of the Italian's fruit stand; second, his theft of a lemon, thus

desecrating the temple. Crane introduces his antagonists by
their placement amid the movement of the city.

> An Italian kept a fruit stand on a corner where he
> had good aim at the people who came down from
> the elevated station and at those who went along two
> thronged streets. He sat most of the day in a backless
> chair that was placed strategically.
>
> There was a babe living hard by, up five flights of
> stairs, who regarded this Italian as a tremendous
> being. The babe had investigated this fruit stand. It
> had thrilled him as few things he had met with in his
> travels had thrilled him.

Crane insists on the religious intensity of the baby's regard for the "tremendous being" and his fruit stand:

> his eyes raised to the vendor's face were filled with
> deep respect, worship, as if he saw omnipotence. . . .
> He was fascinated by the tranquility of the vendor,
> the majesty of power and possession. . . .The
> breathless spectator moved across the sidewalk until
> his small face almost touched the vendor's sleeve.
> His fingers were gripped in a fold of his dress.

Everything is fixed in the baby's eyes. We are told that he
was "so engrossed in his contemplation that people, hurrying, had to use care to avoid bumping him down."

But with the mention of the baby's gripping fingers the
second phase of the story is set in motion: "For a time he
was a simple worshipper at this golden shrine. Then tumul-
tuous desires began to shake him. His dreams were of con-
quest. His lips moved." (We will want to remember that
shaking body and those moving lips.) In the remainder of
the story, as the Italian reads his newspaper, Crane shifts
our attention from the baby's contemplative eyes to his exploring hand, a hand that seems eerily separate and autonomous: "From the tattered skirt came slowly his small dirty
hand." The inversion of subject and predicate as well as the

86

placement of the adverb increase the impression of the hand's agency. "It was moved with supreme caution toward the fruit. The fingers were bent, claw-like, in the manner of great heart-shaking greed." He's caught in the act, of course, and the story abruptly concludes: "The Italian howled. He sprang to his feet, and with three steps overtook the babe. He whirled him fiercely and took from the little fingers a lemon."

For his famous "Experiment in Misery" Crane disguised himself as a bum and wandered downtown, like Jacob Riis, to see how the other half lived. In "An Ominous Baby," the second of the baby sketches, he imagines the journey in reverse, and without the disguise.

> A baby was wandering in a strange country. He was a tattered child with a frowsled wealth of yellow hair. His dress, of a checked stuff, was soiled and showed the marks of many conflicts like the chain-shirt of a warrior. His suntanned knees shone above wrinkled stockings which he pulled up occasionally with an impatient movement when they entangled his feet. From a gaping shoe there appeared an array of tiny toes.
> He was toddling along an avenue between rows of stolid, brown houses. He went slowly, with a look of absorbed interest on his small, flushed face.

Crane's attention to the baby's appearance is as intensely absorbed as the baby's own look. He slowly scans the small body from head to toe; the sequence is hair, dress, knees, stockings, feet, toes. He artfully introduces the theme of inequality in the opposition of "*tattered* child" and "frowsled *wealth* of yellow hair." (In this neighborhood even the light suggests metallic wealth: "High up, near the roofs, glancing sun-rays changed cornices to blazing gold and silvered the fronts of windows.")

87

But it is the baby's capacity for concentration—his "look of absorbed interest" and, a page later, the "small, absorbed figure in the middle of the sidewalk"—that draws Crane most, and makes us wonder just what this "strange country" is that the baby is wandering in. As in "A Great Mistake," the child's fixity in the midst of movement particularly interests Crane.

In this scene, Crane's baby happens to support one of G. Stanley Hall's hypotheses about the differences between city and country children. Hall concluded that motion was critical to the city child's choice of objects:

> It is things that live and, as it were, detach themselves from their background by moving that catch the eye and with it the attention, and the subjects which occupy and interest the city child are mainly in motion and therefore transient, while the country child comes to know objects at rest better.

Crane also contrasts city and country—"The people and houses struck [the baby] with interest as would flowers and trees"—and his urban baby notices things in motion:

> His blue eyes stared curiously. Carriages went with a musical rumble over the smooth asphalt. A man with a chrysanthemum was going up steps. Two nursery maids chatted as they walked slowly. . . .

As in "A Great Mistake," Crane is careful to draw our attention to what the child is holding: "He gazed at [one nursemaid] with infant tranquillity for a moment and then went slowly off, dragging behind him a bit of rope he had acquired in another street." Finally his attention settles on "a pretty child in fine clothes playing with a toy," a tiny fire engine whose "wheels rattled as its small owner dragged it uproariously about by means of a string. The boy with his bit of rope trailing behind him paused and regarded the child and the toy." (We might pause ourselves for a moment to note how such material fed Crane's imagination as he wrote *The Red Badge*: "There was something curious in this little intent pause of the lieutenant. He was like a babe which, having wept its fill, raises its eyes and fixes upon a distant toy. He was engrossed in this contemplation, and the soft under lip quivered from self-whispered words."

Each child, then, *drags* something about. The baby abandons the piece of rope and asks the child to let him play with the fire engine. The rich child refuses, so "the child in tatters gave a supreme tug and wrenched the string from the other's hand." The dispossessed child chases the thief. At the end of the sketch, "the little vandal turned and vanished down a dark street as into a swallowing cavern."

But what of the "bit of rope"? The baby in tatters forgets it, but Crane does not. When the baby first approaches the fire engine, "his bit of rope, now forgotten, dropped at his feet." A few lines later, after the rich child refuses to share his toy, "the wanderer retreated to the curb. He failed to notice the bit of rope, once treasured." In fact, what Crane emphasizes is not the difference between the two objects but their similarities: they are both "dragged about"; one is a bit of rope, one is attached to a string. Four times in the course of his brief tale Crane specifies that the tattered child's toy is a "bit of rope." (We might note, in passing, that the word *bit* comes from *bite* and that the rich boy says the fire engine is his because "my ma-ma buyed it." These oral/maternal associations are completed in the last words of the tale, when the child in tatters vanishes into the "swallowing cavern" of the street.)

The third of the baby sketches, "A Dark-Brown Dog," was never published during Crane's life, although, as John Berryman remarks, "it was to look well enough in various collections of 'Great Short Stories of the World' thirty years later." One can see why it was popular; its theme of child-

hood devotion and subsequent loss is perfectly geared to
elicit tears. This time the child is absorbed at the outset, in
the midst of movement:

> A child was standing on a street-corner. He
> leaned with one shoulder against a high board-
> fence and swayed the other to and fro, the while
> kicking carelessly at the gravel.
> Sunshine beat upon the cobbles, and a lazy sum-
> mer wind raised yellow dust which trailed in clouds
> down the avenue. Clattering trucks moved with in-
> distinctness through it. The child stood dreamily
> gazing.

The rhythmical swaying and kicking, and the dreamlike
gaze, will require our attention in a moment. The baby is
ready for an object for his attention to settle on, and such an
object appears:

> After a time, a little dark-brown dog came trot-
> ting with an intent air down the sidewalk. A short
> rope was dragging from his neck. Occasionally he
> trod upon the end of it and stumbled.

We have seen that bit of dragging rope before, of course,
in the ominous baby's bit of rope and in the string attached
to the toy fire engine. It consistently marks the fact of possession in these stories. Here it shows that the dog has already been a possession (the rope is presumably the remains
of a leash, or a retainer of some sort), while at the same time
providing the child with a way of taking possession of
the dog.
Crane gives a great deal of attention to the ways in
which boy and dog begin to communicate, from mutual
(and mirror-like) regarding, to tail wagging, to patting, to
"gleeful caperings" that "threatened to overturn the child,
whereupon the child lifted his hand and struck the dog a
blow upon the head." The consequences of this blow must
be negotiated; the dog pleads, the child ignores him, and

this pattern continues as the child wanders homeward, "stopping at times to investigate various matters." But at a crucial moment the rope reappears:

> When the child reached his door-step, the dog was industriously ambling a few yards in the rear. He became so agitated with shame when he again confronted the child that he forgot the dragging rope. He tripped upon it and fell forward.
>
> The child sat down on the step and the two had another interview. During it the dog greatly exerted himself to please the child. He performed a few gambols with such abandon that the child suddenly saw him to be a valuable thing. He made a swift, avaricious charge and seized the rope.
>
> He dragged his captive into a hall and up many long stairways in a dark tenement.

This is not the last mention of "dragging" in the tale: in this and the following paragraph we are told, "In [the dog's] mind he was being dragged toward a grim unknown"; after a struggle the child "dragged his acquirement to the door of his house. . . ." Indeed, Crane's use of the verb is so insistent that one is tempted to see a play on the word *drag*, a sort of buried anagram, in the title of the story, "A Dark-Brown Dog."

The rest of the tale specifies the closeness of boy and dog: "So it came to pass that the dog was a member of the household. He and the child were associated together at all times"; "His devotion to the child grew until it was a sublime thing." Crane makes interesting efforts to represent the inner life of the dog ("Deep down in the mystic, hidden fields of his little dog-soul bloomed flowers of love and fidelity and perfect faith").

This intimacy is interrupted by sporadic violence, however. Unspecified members of the child's family throw things at the dog. ("He could force three or four people armed with brooms, sticks and handfuls of coal, to use all their ingenuity to get in a blow.") And we learn, to our surprise, that "sometimes, too, the child himself used to beat the dog, although it is not known that he ever had what could be truly called a just cause. The dog always accepted these thrashings with an air of admitted guilt. He was too much of a dog to try to look to be a martyr or to plot revenge." One day, though, the father gets drunk. "He came home and held carnival with the cooking utensils, the furniture and his wife." He decides it might be fun to throw the dog out the window. The child climbs down the five flights of stairs to find "the body of his dark-brown friend": "It took him a long time to reach the alley, because his size compelled him to go downstairs backward, one step at a time, and holding with both hands to the step above."

It's time to say something about the choice of objects Crane's ominous babies drag around with them, and about the "strange country" they wander in. I believe that Crane in his baby sketches is investigating the same territory mapped out in the child psychologist D. W. Winnicott's classic paper "Transitional Objects and Transitional Phenomena" (1953). Those bits of orange peel, rope, and string, and the faded old quilt (marked, so to speak, by recurring words like *bit* and *drag*), are examples of what Winnicott calls "transitional objects," his term for the comforting things, neither entirely subjective nor objective, that ease the child's journey from dependence on the mother to independence. They constitute the earliest phase of "reality testing," when the child is playing with the uses of illusion. (It should be said that Winnicott, like Freud, repeatedly acknowledged that his insights had been anticipated by artists and writers; on the nature of transitional objects he explicitly mentioned A. A. Milne and Charles Schultz.)

Winnicott identifies a whole realm of "transitional phenomena" as the infant progresses from thumb sucking and other physical substitutions for the mother's breast to what he calls "the handling of truly 'not-me' objects," or "first possessions"—"the intermediate area of experience between the thumb and the teddy bear." Winnicott also mentions as transitional the sort of rhythmical swaying we encountered in "A Dark-Brown Dog," as well as various mouthing sounds, such as those performed by the baby in "A Great Mistake." Winnicott concludes:

> All these things I am calling *transitional phenomena.* Also, out of all this (if we study any one infant) there may emerge some thing or some phenomenon—perhaps a bundle of wool or the corner of a blanket or ciderdown, or a word or tune, or a mannerism—that becomes vitally important to the infant . . . and is a defense against anxiety.

I would suggest that the "strange country" the ominous baby is wandering in is precisely that "third part of the life of a human being . . . an intermediate area of experiencing" between inner and outer, that Winnicott calls "transitional."

Winnicott relates this area of experience, where the child's task is one of "keeping inner and outer reality separate yet interrelated," to such later activities as artistic creativity, religion, dreaming, and (interestingly) stealing and drug addiction. It is in this context that the peculiar combination of religious awe and grasping covetousness, explored by Crane in "A Great Mistake" and in Maggie's stolen flower, makes most sense.

What Crane shows us, in each of the baby sketches, is the process by which the child finds, becomes absorbed in, and adopts an object. There is, moreover, a progression among the objects in the three sketches: from the inert but still captivating lemon, to the more interesting piece of rope (Winnicott has a whole analysis of a patient who is fixated on the relational possibilities of string), to the fully alive dog. We seem to be moving along the continuum Winnicott traces from full identification with the mother, through "holding," and on to "communication." Crane's infants, it

93

should be noted, are never accompanied by their mothers; no mother is mentioned in the first two sketches, while the baby's mother in "A Dark-Brown Dog" is only referred to once, in passing, as the father's wife. The babies are thereby forced, unlike the rich kids with their protective nurse-maids, to address in an unmediated way the world of "not-me" objects, while at the same time they are allowed undistracted absorption in the objects that attract their attention. Surely this is one reason for Crane's choice of *poor* children as his protagonists.

Winnicott also helps to interpret the recurrent violence in these sketches (especially marked in "A Dark-Brown Dog"), a degree of violence that has baffled critics. James Colvert calls "A Dark-Brown Dog" "a perfectly detached account of senseless cruelty," thus putting the emphasis on the killing of the dog at the end. R. W. Stallman remarks rather mysteriously that the "young urchin becomes friends with a dark brown dog, mainly by beating him with a stick." Berryman, who considers the tale "one of the perfectly imagined American stories," notes the "relation of tyranny and adoration" between the baby and dog, thus suggesting a political allegory. Crane's own description of the relationship suggests profound ambivalence:

> When misfortune came upon the child, and his troubles overwhelmed him, he would often crawl under the table and lay his small distressed head on the dog's back. The dog was ever sympathetic. It is not to be supposed that at such times he took occasion to refer to the unjust beatings his friend, when provoked, had administered to him.

Winnicott says of a transitional object that "it must seem to the infant to give warmth, or to move, or to have texture, or to do something that seems to show it has vitality or reality of its own"—all demands easily fulfilled by the dark-brown dog. Of course a dog, unlike the typical objects Winnicott lists, is animate; but Crane describes it, interestingly, as "a small rug of a dog" that has "the air of a footpad," while giving special attention, as we have seen, to the rope dragging behind. But the transitional object must also serve as a target of violence. Winnicott specifies that "the object is affectionately cuddled as well as excitedly loved and mutilated," and that "it must survive instinctual loving, and also hating and, if it be a feature, pure aggression." The dark-brown dog does survive these things, as long as they come from the child. But the moral of the tale—a moral that goes beyond Winnicott's speculations—might be taken to be that animate objects are particularly unreliable as object choices, for the simple reason that they are mortal.

"The mother's eventual task," Winnicott says, "is gradually to disillusion the infant"—and it is not difficult to find traces of frustration and disappointment in Stephen Crane's early years. The relation between his own childhood and the deprived children of his stories cannot, however, be a simple causal one; wouldn't a deprived child be just as likely to imagine compensatory satisfactions as to repeat, in his art, the fact of disappointment? What engages our curiosity—and perhaps our suspicion as well—in Crane's case is the peculiarly close fit of what we have been told of his early years and the fantasies worked out in his stories. Consider the following:

> He took cold with regularity and his first appearances in the solid society of Mulberry Place [in Newark] were made as an attachment to a monstrous red handkerchief which he liked immensely as a plaything and dropped into the aisle of his father's church, cutting the drift of a sermon with wails until somebody brought it back and his parent could go on talking slowly of the necessity of foreign missions and the danger of frivolous amusements to the youth of his sect.

This is Beer, reporting a common choice of "transitional object." But when he mentions in the following pages the baby's fascination with a girl's red skirt and his pleasure in having "mittens of the brightest red . . . and red topped boots," we see what he's driving at. It's the *red*—not the handkerchief, boots, and mittens—that we're meant to register, and keep in mind when we encounter the red badge of courage. The three objects are all lifted from Crane's fictions. The Italian vendor in "A Great Mistake" polishes oranges with "a red pocket-handkerchief"; the boots Scratchy Wilson wears in Crane's imaginary town of "Yellow Sky" have "red tops with gilded imprints, of the kind beloved in winter by little sledding boys on the hillsides of New England"; and it should come as no surprise that "His New Mittens," in Crane's late story of that title, are red. Since Beer is the only source for these luminous objects of Crane's infancy, one may assume that he is inventing the biography from the work.

Crane's babies wander the city streets by themselves, and our questions about Crane's own experience of deprivation center on his sense of separation from his mother. Here again the evidence is scanty. Does Crane's persistent orality, noted by many of his friends, deserve analysis? "He must have something to fondle," Beer notes, "or he wasn't comfortable. Smoking seemed to mean just an object between his fingers" (more tactile than oral, perhaps). There is Crane's attack on tradition in a poem in which he says it is "for suckling children," but concludes, "we all are babes." And there is the weight of oral reference in the baby sketches themselves—though here we run the risk of merely repeating Beer's tendency to invent the life from the work. Crane's accuracy in representing deprived babies is no more a proof of his own deprivation than is Winnicott's or Freud's.

More suggestive are two other details. First, Crane consistently associated the writing of *Maggie*—and thus the in-

8. *Crane at the "ominous" age of five or six.*

vention of the baby Tommie—with the death of his own mother. And second, there is some evidence of an early separation of Crane and his mother. From Freud's classic "Analysis of a Phobia in a Five-Year-Old Boy" to Winnicott's *The Piggle*, a child's most acute anxiety about separation from the mother generally coincides with the arrival of a new sibling. Stephen Crane was the baby of the family, but something may have happened to change his status. Here is Beer quoting from Crane:

> My mother was a very religious woman but I don't think that she was as narrow as most of her friends or her family. . . . My brothers tell me that she got herself into trouble before I was old enough to follow proceedings by taking care of a girl who had an accidental baby. Inopportune babies are not part of Methodist ritual but mother was always more of a Christian than a Methodist and she kept this girl at our house in Asbury until she found a home elsewhere.

This may be Beer's invention as well, but it seems possible that he did get wind of some such story as this, perhaps from one of Crane's brothers who were still living when Beer's book was published (they raised no objections to this anecdote, though they did to others). What is more, there is a mysterious entry in Crane's sister Agnes's diary for December 4, 1873: "Amy had a spell Ma at New York all day." Melvin Schoberlin, in his draft for a Crane biography, identified this Amy with the accidental baby reported by Crane in Beer's account. But if it is the same girl, then Crane, as Paul Sorrentino points out, "must have meant 'Newark' when he said 'Asbury.'"

There may have been a period, then, when Crane was not the only baby in the house. It is particularly interesting that Crane claims that he doesn't remember "the proceedings." Did he repress them? The episode would help explain the peculiar convergence of his mother's death and the writing of a novel about a deprived girl of the slums, whose baby brother dies.

Finally I want to call attention, with more curiosity than conviction, to another connection between the early chapters of *Maggie* and the baby sketches. In several of his stories Crane conceives of cities as capable of turning at any moment into theaters. Windows provide an immediate audience for anything out of the ordinary. Crane assembles such an audience when the baby's father flings the "dark-brown dog" out the window.

> The soaring dog created a surprise in the block. A woman watering plants in an opposite window gave an involuntary shout and dropped a flower pot. A man in another window leaned perilously out to watch the flight of the dog. A woman, who had been hanging out clothes in a yard, began to caper wildly. Her mouth was filled with clothes-pins, but her arms gave vent to a sort of exclamation. In appearance she was like a gagged prisoner. Children ran whooping.

It seems random enough—a clever way to slow down the flight of the dog, to give duration to his five-story plunge. Indeed, Crane is *aiming* for an impression of randomness: no matter what people were up to at the time, they stopped, dropped (in one case, literally) whatever they were doing, and looked at the flying dog. (It's the opposite of the business-as-usual scene in Auden's "Musée des Beaux Arts.")

Still, we may wonder about the specific gestures of these women: the "involuntary shout" of one, as she drops a flowerpot, the wild caper of another, with her arms giving "vent to a sort of exclamation." Especially interesting is the latter's "mouth . . . filled with clothes-pins . . . like a gagged prisoner." We may be even more interested when we turn to

99

a very similar paragraph on the first page of *Maggie*. Jimmie is losing his fight to the urchins of Devil's Row.

> From a window of an apartment house that upreared its form from amid squat, ignorant stables, there leaned a curious woman. Some laborers, unloading a scow at a dock at the river, paused for a moment and regarded the fight. The engineer of a passive tugboat hung lazily to a railing and watched. Over on the Island, a worm of yellow convicts came from the shadow of a grey ominous building and crawled slowly along the river's bank.

I want to suggest, without insisting, that one thing these passages are about is pregnancy and childbirth. We have seen the link of "ominous"—here ascribed to a building—and "laborers" before, in Crane's letter to Linson about "An Ominous Baby." The themes of filling up and unloading (as in the woman's mouth filled with clothespins or the "laborers, unloading a scow"), so clearly linked to childbearing by Freud's five-year-old Little Hans, seem to have the same referent here. A couple of pages later in *Maggie*, Crane describes a building that "gave up *loads of babies* to the street and gutter." (Linson found a fragment of a further baby sketch, "evidently a sequel to 'An Ominous Baby,'" that included this sentence: "He avoided with care some men who were unloading some boxes from a truck. . . .") Some of the odd diction in the passage—the "worm" of convicts coming out of the "ominous building" that "crawled slowly"; the "*squat.* . . . stables"; the "*passive* tugboat"—seems easily interpretable as related to pregnancy and childbirth.

Finally there is the strange presence of prisoners in both passages; the simile about the "gagged prisoner" in the first paragraph becomes real enough in the second. If we assume that the "Island" is Blackwell's (now Roosevelt) Island, visible from Crane's lodging near the East River, the prisoners are from the women's penitentiary there. Even if we don't assume this, and Crane doesn't specify it, the two passages are nonetheless densely populated with women. I would suggest that the prisoner theme is related to the notion of *confinement*, though I would not insist that Crane was conscious of the pun.

FIVE

The Private War

T HE STRANGE RHYTHM of Stephen Crane's career—his obsessive attempt to shape his life to the patterns and plots of his own stories—is nowhere more striking than in his experience of war. His direct knowledge of conflict was limited to football and baseball when he wrote *The Red Badge of Courage*—"I never smelled even the powder of a sham battle," he told a reviewer. The origins of *The Red Badge*, which he began drafting in the spring of 1893, remain, like much else in Crane's life, in shadow. To be sure, as scholars tirelessly point out, he had drilled his company at Claverack, one or two of his teachers there had fought in the war, his brother Edmund was a Civil War buff, and so on. But thousands of other American boys, some of them writers, had had similar "influences." Despite attempts to explain—or explain away—its genesis, the greatest war novel written by an American still seems, in essential ways, to come out of nowhere.

The wonder of its creation extended to Crane himself, especially when it became clear that editors expected more of the same. He dutifully cobbled together more tales of the Civil War, but he knew the life had gone out of the material. "I used myself up," he later wrote ruefully, "in the accursed 'Red Badge.' " It is often said that the marvel of *The Red Badge* is that someone so inexperienced could have written it, the implication being that had Crane been a veteran, the book would have been even better. This is absurd, like saying *Madame Bovary* would have been better if Flaubert had been born a woman. *The Red Badge* is compelling because of its speculative feel, not despite it.

But once Crane had written the novel, he made every effort to experience real war—to exchange lines of words for lines of fire—first, and fruitlessly, in Cuba, and then, successfully, as a war correspondent in Greece. He wanted to see, he later told his friend Joseph Conrad, whether *The Red Badge of Courage* was "all right."

Maggie: A Girl of the Streets, published at Crane's own expense in January 1893, had drawn the somewhat guarded encouragement of William Dean Howells, to whom Crane had sent a copy. While publicly supporting Howells's version of realism, Crane commented with his characteristic vagueness on matters of literary practice. "I decided that the nearer a writer gets to life the greater he becomes as an artist," he wrote in 1895, "and most of my prose writings have been toward the goal partially described by the misunderstood and abused word *realism.*" The lives Crane wanted to get nearer to, however, were not the sort one encountered in Howells's novels. Extremity and shock were Crane's goals, not the patient portrayal of the mores of contemporary society.

But *Maggie* had failed to cause the stir Crane had anticipated. "My first great disappointment," he recalled later, "was in the reception of 'Maggie, a Girl of the Streets.' I remember how I looked forward to its publication, and pictured the sensation I thought it would make. It fell flat.

Nobody seemed to notice it or care for it." After this humiliation, he was determined to make a splash, and he turned
from one popular genre, the slum novel, to another, the
novel of men at war. He began his research by examining
eyewitness reports of the gruesome and protracted
battle of Chancellorsville, where the battle lines were never
clearly drawn, and Stonewall Jackson was accidentally
killed by one of his own men. Veterans' accounts disappointed him, however: "I wonder that *some* of these fellows
don't tell how they *felt* in those scraps!" he remarked, putting aside a batch of *Century* magazines with a popular series on "Battles and Leaders of the Civil War." "They spout
eternally of what they *did*, but they are as emotionless as
rocks!"

Crane began drafting his own "psychological portrayal
of fear," as he called *The Red Badge*, in late March or early
April of 1893, in the cramped quarters of the former Art
Students League building on East Twenty-third Street. In
one of the gloomy old studios, Crane and two of his artist
friends shared a double bed, while a fourth slept on a cot.
Under these barracks-like conditions, he worked steadily at
the novel; six months or so later he was done with the book.
During the summer weeks, he worked in the more comfortable rooms of Hartwood, his brother William's wilderness
lodge in Sullivan County outside Port Jervis.

Some of the structural balance of the book seems to
arise from these contrasting places: the crowded city and
the sheltering woods. Crane remarked to his friend C. K.
Linson that "The sense of a city is war," and *The Red Badge*
is nowhere more intense than when Crane's hero, afraid of
his own thoughts concerning his capacity for cowardice, is
looking for a place to hide from the prying eyes of his com-
rades. Life in the army, he feels, exposes him to "a society
that probes pitilessly at secrets until all is apparent." He
looks for safety in the wilderness surrounding the field of
battle, a wilderness described with such specificity that it's

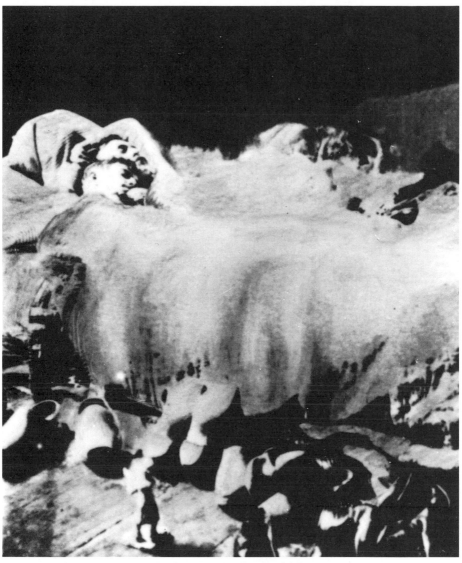

9. *Crane sharing a bed in the Art Students' League, 1893 or 1894.
In a letter of 1933 Crane's niece, Edith Crane, explained
that friends had piled up all the shoes they could find, and
a statuette, next to the sleepers, and taken the picture.*

easy to imagine Crane working up such scenes in the relative privacy of his Sullivan County retreat.

But what lingered most in Crane's mind from his months among artists in the Twenty-third Street building was more a mood than a memory. He had found, scrawled in chalk on an old beam in a top-floor studio, a quotation attributed—perhaps falsely, for its provenance has never been traced—to Emerson: "Congratulate yourselves if you have done something strange and extravagant and broken the monotony of a decorous age." Strangeness and extravagance were what Crane was after in *The Red Badge of Courage*: he wanted to shock and surprise. To feel that surprise, we in turn must resist judging the novel according to some naive standard of the realistic portrayal of war and try to follow, instead, the strange turns of Crane's highly idiosyncratic vision.

The hero of *The Red Badge,* a moody farmboy called Henry Fleming, shares Crane's own impulse to move from imagined to real war: "He had read of marches, sieges, conflicts, and he had longed to see it all." Despite his mother's pleas, Fleming enlists in the Union Army after having

> dreamed of battles all his life—of vague and bloody conflicts that had thrilled him with their sweep and fire. In visions he had seen himself in many struggles. He had imagined peoples secure in the shadow of his eagle-eyed prowess.

Private Fleming, like his creator, sets out to live his literary fantasies, but real war refuses to conform to them. Instead of discipline, prowess, and heroism, he finds chaos, incompetence, and fear.

The plot of the book is deceptively simple, consisting of a series of episodes during two days in the life of the new recruit—episodes ranging from tedium to terror, after

106

which Fleming is changed forever. He holds up bravely during the enemy's first charge but panics after the second, and tries to justify his cowardice by telling himself that he "had fled with discretion and dignity." Amid the confusion of retreat, a Union soldier whom he asks for help hits him on the head with a rifle, and Fleming allows the scar to be mistaken for a bullet wound—hence the "red badge" of the novel's ironic title. In a charge the following day Fleming is conspicuously, if somewhat frantically, brave in capturing the enemy flag. During the "frenzy made from this furious rush," Crane is careful to note, there is a "temporary but sublime absence of selfishness" among the other soldiers— the fierce absorption that drew Crane to war.

Crane's battle scenes were so convincingly chaotic that one confused veteran was moved to claim that he had been with Crane at Antietam. Crane was especially attuned to the contrasting points of view—and especially the mutual scorn—that separates the officers and their men. For the officers, the men are nothing but "mule drivers" ripe for sacrifice, while in Fleming's view the Union Army is "generaled by a lot 'a lunkheads."

The ambiguous ending to the novel has provoked much debate, however, especially because Crane left two versions of it, as well as of several other passages. His manuscript, indeed, is about two thousand words longer than the published version of 1895, and some academic readers have argued strenuously that the manuscript should be regarded as the "authoritative" text, embodying Crane's final intentions before his editors mucked around with it. Such a view depends, however, on a rather idealized notion of how books come into being, for a book—at least the kind of book Crane wrote—is the result of writing *and* editing. Furthermore, Crane never complained about the published version of *The Red Badge,* so it must be regarded, for better or worse, as the authoritative text. The manuscript is interesting, precisely to the degree that any significant writer's drafts are interesting, and especially because it casts a somewhat colder eye on Henry Fleming's illusions than does the published version. But a manuscript is not a book.

In American high schools *The Red Badge* is often, like Faulkner's "The Bear," used to illustrate a boy's initiation into manhood, and much has been made of four sentences in the final chapter, in which Fleming reflects on his two days of bewildering warfare.

> He felt a quiet manhood, nonassertive but of sturdy and strong blood. He knew that he would no more quail before his guides wherever they should point. He had been to touch the great death, and found that, after all, it was but the great death. He was a man.

Elsewhere, and intermittently, Crane treats Fleming with such savage irony that "He was a man" can be read as gently mocking. Fleming's pompousness seems clearer in the manuscript, where Crane first wrote, "it was but the great death and was for others"—as though Fleming himself were immune.

In any case, readers have tended to be more disturbed by what isn't in *The Red Badge* than by what is. It's true that Crane shows notoriously little interest in the causes—in both senses of the word—of the Civil War. "Negroes and Lincoln and hospitals and prisons are not to be found in Crane's theatre," as Daniel Aaron has remarked. But Crane's theater is far from empty, and maybe what is in it is more disturbing than readers have generally thought.

The Red Badge of Courage is indeed about an initiation, though not necessarily into manhood. What Crane tried to imagine in *The Red Badge*, and what repeatedly captured his attention when he came to experience real war, was the fate of the body in human conflict. To put it another way, Crane found no better place than war to show the alarming

fact—alarming to him and to his hero Henry Fleming—
that human beings have bodies, and are therefore mortal.
(Perhaps it's worth remembering here that the household in
which Crane grew up was a place of physical denial—no
dancing, smoking, or drinking.) This may seem like a small
or self-evident or peculiar discovery to make on the battle-
ground—one made more easily and pleasantly on the play-
ground. And indeed Crane did often compare his vision of
war with his experience in sports, telling one correspondent
soon after the publication of the novel that "I have never
been in a battle, but I believe that I got my sense of the rage
of conflict on the football field." But war presented obvious
opportunities for opening up the human body for explora-
tion. *The Red Badge of Courage* can be read as a series of
confrontations, of increasing intensity, with human corporeality, as Henry Fleming is awakened to the fact of his own
physical existence.

The novel begins with an army that is all body and a
private who is all mind: the task of Crane's narrative is to
unite them. The famous opening paragraph envisions the
army as itself a great body in the process of awakening.

> The cold passed reluctantly from the earth, and
> the retiring fogs revealed an army stretched out on
> the hills, resting. As the landscape changed from
> brown to green, the army awakened, and began to
> tremble with eagerness at the noise of rumors. It cast
> its eyes upon the roads, which were growing from
> long troughs of liquid mud to proper thoroughfares.
> A river, amber-tinted in the shadow of its banks,
> purled at the army's feet; and at night, when the
> stream had become of a sorrowful blackness, one
> could see across it the red, eyelike gleam of hostile
> camp-fires set in the low brows of distant hills.

The first two sentences establish the pattern for how Crane
will divide his episodes throughout the novel. It is by means
of fade-ins and fade-outs, dissipating fogs and gathering

haze, that Crane makes his transitions. The equally famous and often maligned last sentence of the novel—it doesn't occur in the manuscript, and may have been an editor's suggestion—has seemed to some critics to strike a major note of cheer in what should be a minor ending. In fact it merely completes the pattern: "Over the river a golden ray of sun came through the hosts of leaden rain clouds." Such verbal alchemy, gold out of lead, is typical of the high polish of Crane's prose, as he steers his private through a series of baffling scenes. The fogs and hazes often seem as much inner as outer weather, for Fleming is constantly trying to clear his head to make sense of what is happening to him.

It is often said that Crane's novel takes the perspective of an ordinary soldier, an observation that has been made repeatedly in recent comparisons of *The Red Badge* to various films based on the Vietnam War. But Henry Fleming is not ordinary. Crane introduces him as a sort of budding intellectual who spends much of his time lying on his bunk or on the ground thinking. Amid the confusing rumors and predictions in the opening scene, the "youthful private" wants above all a quiet place in which to reflect.

> After receiving a fill of discussions concerning marches and attacks, he went through his hut and crawled through an intricate hole that served it as a door. He wished to be alone with some new thoughts that had lately come to him.

It is privacy that Fleming is after, and Crane's preliminary title for the novel was *"Private* Fleming / His various battles."

In the opening scenes, Private Fleming is a disembodied mind consumed by thinking. He doesn't conceive of war as involving wounding and dying. Instead, he thinks of it as an abstract sequence of doubts, demonstrations, and proofs. He lies in his bunk pondering his "serious problem": "He tried to mathematically prove to himself that he would not run from a battle." Fleming's greatest fear is of humiliation.

The Red Badge of Courage.
An Episode of the American Civil War.
By Stephen Crane.

The cold passed reluctantly from the earth and the retiring fogs, revealed an army stretched out on the hills, resting. As the landscape changed from brown to green the army awakened and began to tremble with eagerness at the noise of rumors. It cast its eyes upon the roads which were growing from long ~~troughs~~ troughs of liquid mud to proper thoroughfares. A river, amber-tinted in the shadow of its banks, purled at the army's feet and at night when the stream had become of a sorrowful blackness one could see across the red eye-like gleam of hostile camp-fires set in the low brows of distant hills.

Once, ~~Jim Conklin~~ a certain soldier, developed virtues and went resolutely to wash a shirt. He came flying back from a brook waving his garment banner-like. He was swelled with a tale he had heard from a reliable friend who had heard it from a ~~reliable~~ truthful cavalryman who had heard it from his trust-worthy brother, one of the orderlies at division head-quarters. He adopted the important air of a herald in red and gold.

"We're goin' t' move t' morrah - sure," he said

10. *The first page of the manuscript of* The Red Badge of Courage. *The original title, "Private Fleming/ His various battles," has been canceled.*

He's not afraid that he'll go forward to his death, but backwards to his shame.

But the fear of shame and the fear of death are of course related, the one in effect masking the other. For what Fleming at the outset of the novel is afraid of is to own—or to own up to—his own body. To be embodied is to carry your own death around with you. Only when Fleming has been initiated into this mystery can he show true courage. The physicality of the title points to this lesson, for the red badge is a wound, and courage is, as the root of the word suggests, a matter of the organ that pumps the blood.

Fleming's need for convincing proof of his own courage can only be satisfied by a wound. This association of wounds with doubt and verification has a long foreground in Western culture. Jacob's wounding in the Old Testament indicates the existence of an unseen God. Christ's wounds on the cross verify his mortality, just as his wounds after the resurrection prove, to doubting Thomas, his divinity. Crane invokes biblical scenes of verification-by-wounding at several key points in the novel.

Crane orchestrates Fleming's progress in and out of battle as an education in wounds and corpses. Accounts of the novel, in their attention to its "psychological truth," tend to overlook how physical the novel is in its focus, how minutely concerned with details of the fate of the body in war—its characteristic gestures, its gait, its pervasive vulnerability, its contorted positions in death. As in other war writings, the first view of a corpse, as the army marches toward the battlefield, is a critical moment, and Crane lingers over it.

Once the line encountered the body of a dead soldier. He lay upon his back staring at the sky. He was dressed in an awkward suit of yellowish brown. The youth could see that the soles of his shoes had been worn to the thinness of writing paper, and from a great rent in one the dead foot projected piteously.

> And it was as if fate had betrayed the soldier. In
> death it exposed to his enemies that poverty which
> in life he had perhaps concealed from his friends.

Death is here conceived of as the ultimate violation of privacy, as though the rending of the body reveals the mind's secrets.

> The youth looked keenly at the ashen face. The
> wind raised the tawny beard. It moved as if a hand
> were stroking it. He vaguely desired to walk around
> and around the body and stare; the impulse of the
> living to try to read in dead eyes the answer to the
> Question.

As Henry continues to wrestle with his problem, he encounters a series of wounded men, as though to find out by what processes men are turned into corpses.

Henry's regiment eventually reaches the battlefield and is involved in intense fighting. Many of the soldiers flee in panic, including Henry. After this ignoble retreat, the earlier sequence of an encounter with a corpse followed by a parade of wounded men is repeated, but this time with far greater intensity. In one of the most celebrated and uncanny scenes in the novel, Henry stumbles through the woods until he reaches "a place where the high, arching boughs made a chapel." What follows is a sort of sacred rite, an initiation into the mysteries.

> He softly pushed the green doors aside and entered.
> Pine needles were a gentle brown carpet. There was
> a religious half light.
>   Near the threshold he stopped, horror-stricken
> at the sight of a thing.
>   He was being looked at by a dead man who was
> seated with his back against a columnlike tree. The
> corpse was dressed in a uniform that once had been
> blue, but was now faded to a melancholy shade of
> green. The eyes, staring at the youth, had changed

113

to the dull hue to be seen on the side of a dead fish. The mouth was open. Its red had changed to an appalling yellow. Over the gray skin of the face ran little ants. One was trundling some sort of a bundle along the upper lip.

Each detail—the faded, green uniform, the dull hue of the eyes, the busy ants—draws this corpse back into the natural landscape, as if to prove that the body returns to dust.

> The youth gave a shriek as he confronted the thing. He was for moments turned to stone before it. He remained staring into the liquid-looking eyes. The dead man and the living man exchanged a long look. Then the youth cautiously put one hand behind him and brought it against a tree. Leaning upon this he retreated, step by step, with his face still toward the thing. He feared that if he turned his back the body might spring up and stealthily pursue him.

The sense here of a man looking into a mirror is palpable, from the long look exchanged with the liquid-like eyes to the reflected gesture of leaning against a tree. The passage gains in intensity from the eerie stasis of the scene, with the "religious half light" of the chapel and the Medusa-like power of the corpse to turn its confronter to stone. The mystery into which Henry Fleming is being initiated is the fact of his own embodiedness. The real lesson to be learned in this chapel is not the lesson of courage but the lesson of corporeality—and thence mortality.

Like doubting Thomas, Fleming longs to touch the corpse, to experience the fact of the body: "His unguided feet . . . caught aggravatingly in brambles; and with it all he received a subtle suggestion to touch the corpse. As he thought of his hand upon it he shuddered profoundly." After the scene in the wooded chapel, Henry experiences "the steady current of the maimed" with greater intensity, and a deeper understanding of how "the torn bodies expressed the awful machinery in which the men had been entangled."

And now occurs one of the strangest sections of the novel, for Henry, unhurt himself but burdened with the new knowledge of the chapel, begins to envy the wounded. His own intact body becomes an embarrassment to him, and in his new awareness of his body he thinks his shame is visible. "Where yeh hit?" asks one of the wounded men, a "tattered soldier."

> "Why," began the youth, "I—I—that is—why—I—"
>
> He turned away suddenly and slid through the crowd. His brow was heavily flushed, and his fingers were picking nervously at one of his buttons.

His body has become the expression of his soul, and from blushing he progresses to a fantasy of his body as a legible text.

> But he was amid wounds. The mob of men was bleeding. Because of the tattered soldier's question he now felt that his shame could be viewed. He was continually casting sidelong glances to see if the men were contemplating the letters of guilt he felt burned into his brow.
>
> At times he regarded the wounded soldiers in an envious way. He conceived persons with torn bodies to be peculiarly happy. He wished that he, too, had a wound, a red badge of courage.

Two more scenes complete Fleming's initiation into the fate of the body in war. The parade of the wounded culminates in Fleming's encounter with his old friend Jim Conklin, who is severely wounded in the side and about to die. The whole passage is shockingly physical, with Conklin behaving like "a devotee of a mad religion, blood-sucking, muscle-wrenching, bone-crushing." Henry finds himself miming each of Conklin's agonies, as though he's learning about his own body and its capacity for pain:

> Turning his head swiftly, the youth saw his friend running in a staggering and stumbling way toward a little clump of bushes. His heart seemed to wrench itself almost free from his body at this sight. He made a noise of pain.

A moment later, Conklin begins to have trouble breathing.

> The chest of the doomed soldier began to heave with a strained motion. It increased in violence until it was as if an animal was within and was kicking and tumbling furiously to be free.
>
> This spectacle of gradual strangulation made the youth writhe, and once as his friend rolled his eyes, he saw something in them that made him sink wailing to the ground.

Finally, Conklin collapses:

> A swift muscular contortion made the left shoulder strike the ground first.
>
> The body seemed to bounce a little way from the earth. . . .
>
> The youth had watched, spellbound, this ceremony at the place of meeting. His face had been twisted into an expression of every agony he had imagined for his friend.
>
> He now sprang to his feet and, going closer, gazed upon the pastelike face. The mouth was open and the teeth showed in a laugh.
>
> As the flap of the blue jacket fell away from the body, he could see that the side looked as if it had been chewed by wolves.

That last detail, borrowed perhaps from a story by Ambrose Bierce, where the wolves are not metaphorical, could hardly stress more starkly the physical ravages of war.

As Fleming mirrors in his own gestures the contortions of his friend's body, he is learning about his own capacity for pain and death. As J. Glenn Gray has observed in *The Warriors*, his memoir and meditation on men in battle,

> When the belief in one's indestructibility is due to a defect of imagination, other experiences than being wounded may suffice to waken the soldier to his situation. It may be the death of an acquaintance in his arms, where the transition between life and death is made imaginatively visible for the first time. . . .

Such is the strange logic of Henry's initiation that when he does receive his wound, his "red badge of courage," the ironic circumstances seem almost beside the point. The scene is a vivid, if somewhat disguised, reworking of Jacob wrestling with the angel/man at Peniel—one of the central biblical scenes of wounding as verification. Henry clutches one of the retreating Union soldiers by the arm, and they swing around "face to face." "Why—why—" Fleming stammers as the man screams, "Let go me! Let go me!" Instead of a blessing, the man gives Fleming a blow to the head, and he stumbles about "like a babe trying to walk." He is inundated by a rush of intensely physical memories, "certain meals his mother had cooked at home," and "how he and his companions used to go from the school-house to the bank of a shaded pool":

> He saw his clothes in disorderly array upon the grass
> of the bank. He felt the swash of the fragrant water
> upon his body.

Finally a fatherly soldier turns up who cheerily questions Fleming "like one manipulating the mind of a child," and he drops Fleming off at the campsite of his regiment.

The succession of scenes has a hallucinatory quality, and yet an inescapable logic. The recurring themes, especially in the last two scenes, suggest a religious meditation, by this son of a Methodist minister, on God the Father who

117

won't answer "Why?" and perhaps a personal memory as well, on the death of his own father. But the lost child searching for a safe haven is also part of a thread running through Crane's work and life: the search for a private refuge from various kinds of exposure.

We are made to feel that Fleming has undergone a profound change between his flight from battle in the first part of the book and his conspicuous heroism in the second. The scenes of initiation have worked this transformation. If there is a letdown in imaginative vividness in the last third of the book, as I believe there is, it may be because Henry's education about the body is at an end.

But at the conclusion of the book, Crane turns once more to the fate of the body. As he moves his private out of battle, Crane's biblical phrasing lingers for a moment on the healing scars.

> So it came to pass that as he trudged from the place of blood and wrath his soul changed. He came from hot plowshares to prospects of clover tranquilly, and it was as if hot plowshares were not. Scars faded as flowers.
>
> It rained. The procession of weary soldiers became a bedraggled train, despondent and muttering, marching with churning effort in a trough of liquid brown mud under a low, wretched sky. Yet the youth smiled, for he saw that the world was a world for him, though many discovered it to be made of oaths and walking sticks. He had rid himself of the red sickness of battle. The sultry nightmare was in the past. He had been an animal blistered and sweating in the heat and pain of war. He turned now with a lover's thirst to images of tranquil skies, fresh meadows, cool brooks—an existence of soft and eternal peace.
>
> Over the river a golden ray of sun came through the hosts of leaden rain clouds.

By treating Fleming's emergence from battle as the recovery from disease, Crane uses the most intensely physical metaphor he can think of. Fleming's wish for tranquility in the closing sentences has sometimes been taken to be Crane's ironic summing up of Fleming's naive hopes. But it also reads, perhaps unconsciously, as a longing for death— what the poet James Merrill has called "the country of a thousand years of peace." The enigmatic sentence "Scars faded as flowers" moves in two directions: to be like a flower is to live in beauty, but a fading flower is rapidly approaching death. To be fully at home in the body is to find "that the world is a world for [us]" and one that we can love with "a lover's thirst." But it is also to acknowledge that our lives are, like the flowers, finite. We are forever scarred by our own impending death.

Crane's own education about real war was still in the future. (In fact, it was the very success of *The Red Badge of Courage* that made that education possible, indeed almost unavoidable, for editors thought that a man who could make up war out of whole cloth could do something even finer with the real thing.) Meanwhile a shortened version of the novel was serialized in newspapers by the editor Irving Bacheller's syndicate, and Bacheller soon hired Crane to make a trip to the West and Mexico, writing newspaper sketches as he went. Crane received a contract for the book publication of the novel during a stay in Lincoln, Nebraska, in February 1895, where he'd gone to research a piece on the suffering of farmers during a terrible drought.

Accounts of what Crane was like before the publication of *The Red Badge* are scarce and unreliable; many were written decades after his death. So we are doubly lucky that Crane's brief sojourn in Nebraska should have brought him face to face with a witness as sharp-eyed and sensitive as Willa Cather, who was a junior in college at the time.

Only five years had gone by when Willa Cather tried to

remember her chance meeting with Crane in that winter of
1895. The circumstances of the encounter were dramatic,
and rendered more so by Cather's readiness for precisely
such a meeting; Crane was the first man of letters she had
ever met. He wandered into her life like one of the threadbare but self-reliant young men of her later novels—Tom
Outland, say, in *The Professor's House.*

> It was, I think, in the spring of '94 [February of
> 1895, in fact] that a slender, narrow chested fellow
> in a shabby grey suit, with a soft felt hat pulled over
> his eyes, sauntered into the office of the managing
> editor of the *Nebraska State Journal* and introduced
> himself as Stephen Crane. . . . I had seen many a
> tramp printer come up the *Journal* stairs to hunt a
> job, but never one who presented such a disrepu-
> table appearance as this story-making man.

She paid particularly close attention to his body: "He was
thin to emaciation, his face was gaunt and unshaven." His
hands, however, were "singularly fine; long, white, and del-
icately shaped, with thin, nervous fingers."

Cather worked part-time at the paper, and had read
proofs for the syndicated version of *The Red Badge of Courage* the previous December: "In this way I had read it very
carefully." She skipped classes to learn what she could
about this slovenly and strangely jaded man who was only
two years older than she was. He carried a copy of Poe in his
pocket—or so she remembered, though perhaps he only reminded her of Poe. But what struck her most was his sense
of urgency. While drafting a letter he asked her for the
spelling of a word. "I haven't time to learn to spell," he explained. "I haven't time to dress either; it takes an awful
slice out of a fellow's life." He was waiting for money from
Bacheller, so that he could travel on to New Orleans and
Mexico, and Cather made the mistake of suggesting that in
ten years he'd laugh at his present distress. "I can't wait ten
years," he remarked. "I haven't time."

Cather's piece cannot be read as simple reportage. She is remembering Crane through at least two distorting lenses: his death in 1900, which provided the occasion for her memoir; and her own fascination with Edgar Allan Poe, of whom she was determined to see Crane as a late avatar. An air of portent and premonition hangs over Cather's account. She allows herself to play the fortune teller after the fact, for she knows the portents will be fulfilled by an untimely death.

> Crane was moody most of the time, his health was bad and he seemed profoundly discouraged. Even his jokes were exceedingly drastic. He went about with the tense, preoccupied air of a man who is brooding over some impending disaster. . . . His eyes I remember as the finest I have ever seen, large and dark and full of lustre and changing lights, but with a profound melancholy always lurking deep in them. They were eyes that seemed to be burning themselves out.

"I am convinced," Cather concluded, "that when I met him he had a vague premonition of the shortness of his working day. . . . He drank life to the lees, but at the banquet table where other men took their ease and jested over their wine, he stood a dark and silent figure, sombre as Poe himself."

But no mystical divination of impending disaster, no fin-de-siècle vision of doomed youth, is needed to explain Crane's sense of urgency. He was sick, more desperately perhaps than his friends could gauge. He told Cather he was going to Mexico "to do some work for the Bacheller Syndicate and get rid of his cough," and those twin imperatives, work and health, loomed large in the five years that remained of his life.

On the way to Mexico, Crane stopped to observe—and perhaps participate in—the rites of invalidism at a resort in Hot Springs, Arkansas. He portrayed the scene with the martial rhythms and images of *The Red Badge*, and his eye, as usual, cut to the fact of physical pain and infirmity:

> Crowds swarm to these baths. A man becomes a creature of three conditions. He is about to take a bath—he is taking a bath—he has taken a bath. Invalids hobble slowly from their hotels, assisted perhaps by a pair of attendants. Soldiers from the U.S. Army and Navy Hospital trudge along assisting their rheumatic limbs with canes. All day there is a general and widespread march upon the baths.

The gloomy march must have seemed like a view into the future for Crane. The pace of his life thereafter was fraught with urgency, as he tried, ever more desperately, to shape what time he had left according to the contours of his imagination. The bizarre events that ensued, back in New York and then off the coast of Florida, would amply justify a belief in Crane's ominous fate. The challenge is to discern the working of Crane's own hand in these extraordinary episodes.

SIX

Lines

I F *The Red Badge of Courage* brought Crane fame and some welcome cash, it never seems to have given him much pleasure. His recorded comments about it, even before its publication, were impatient. To his editor, who'd suggested some revisions, he sardonically offered to cut the word *Red* from the title: "That would shorten it." And during the summer of 1895, sending along yet one more forwarding address to the same editor, Crane added, "As a matter of fact I dont [*sic*] care much to see the page proof." Such remarks are wholly characteristic of Crane's methods as a writer. He worked quickly and intensely on a new project, but once the performance was done he wanted nothing more to do with it.

An exception, though, was the book he claimed was his favorite among his works, the collection of gnomic poems titled *The Black Riders*. "Personally, I like . . . 'The Black Riders,' better than I do 'The Red Badge of Courage,' " he wrote.

The reason is, I suppose, that the former is the more ambitious effort. In it I aim to give my ideas of life as a whole, so far as I know it, and the latter is a mere episode, or rather an amplification.

The Black Riders came out during the spring of 1895, soon after the twenty-three-year-old Crane's return from Mexico. It was, therefore, his first commercially published book, and he and his publishers were eager to make a splash. To gauge the shock of the book's *appearance*—in two senses of that word—we need to know something about the state of American poetry at the end of the century.

If American poetry during the 1890s were confined to a club of Harvard boys sitting at the feet of George Santayana, literary historians might be pardoned for dismissing the decade as a "poetic twilight," or "the big blank of American poetic history." E. A. Robinson lamented the diminished energies of poets like George Cabot Lodge and Trumbull Stickney: "these little sonnet-men . . . Who fashion, in a shrewd, mechanic way, / Songs without souls, that flicker for a day," while T. S. Eliot, who entered Harvard in 1906, complained that in his youth there was not "a single living poet, in either England or America, then at the height of his powers, whose work was capable of pointing the way to a young poet conscious of the desire for a new idiom."

But beyond the walls of Harvard there was a great deal of interesting poetry written in the United States during the 1890s, now routinely passed over—in anthologies and literary histories—in the leap from the deaths of Whitman and Dickinson to the Imagist stirrings of 1912. Some of the most vital poetry of the period—always excepting Robinson and the early Frost—was produced by writers better known for their prose: Hamlin Garland, Ellen Glasgow, and Stephen Crane. Crane's experimental poems continue to be read (when they are read at all) in relation to the nineteenth-century Methodism of Crane's father and his maternal great-uncles. Such an approach only partly explains Crane's obsessive themes and images, however. I want to suggest an alternative perspective on these poems, by relating them to two currents of thought in the 1890s: the permutations of the Arts and Crafts movement in the United States and, to a lesser degree, the intense interest in psychical research.

Even by the flamboyant standards of book design in the 1890s, Crane's *The Black Riders and Other Lines*, published by the Boston firm of Copeland and Day in the spring of 1895, was remarkable. A book of sixty-eight short poems, it was designed first to seduce, then to alarm its readers. The cover promised elegance and a certain decadent luxury. A black orchid swooped over a surface of light gray, with the same design mirrored on the back. The orchid was meant to suggest the audacity of the book, in both structure and theme. As the designer of the book, Frederic Gordon, explained, "The orchid with its strange habits, extraordinary forms and curious properties seemed to me the most appropriate floral motive, an idea in which Mr. Crane concurred."

But the lush packaging belied the contents of the book—the surplice hid a hair shirt. It was as though the cover of the book was a product of the Aesthetic Movement of the 1880s, while the printed pages themselves announced another aesthetic altogether. A page design of almost puritanical austerity confronted the reader. The "lines"—"I never call them poems," Crane insisted—were untitled, identified only by Roman numerals. They were printed uniformly high on the page, so that the shortest ones, of three or four lines, seemed suspended over a gulf of white, with wide margins on the sides. The severe design was unrelieved by ornament, and there was no table of contents. Most arresting of all, the "lines" were printed entirely in capital letters. Critics complained of the layout, but

Crane was delighted. "I see they have been pounding the wide margins, the capitals and all that but I think it great," he wrote his publishers. The book was certainly not ignored. As Carlin Kindilien has remarked, "Reviewers who might have quickly scanned the work of a new poet were stalled into close reading by the bizarre format."

Crane's intense interest in the *look* of his poems may well have had something to do with his companions during the fall of 1893, when he wrote most of *The Black Riders*. He was working in Manhattan as a poorly paid freelance journalist and completing the manuscript of *The Red Badge of Courage*. His friends and roommates were young artists and illustrators, including Frederic Gordon. They lived in various rooming houses and lofts on the East Side. Crane said later that they all "slept on the floor, dined off buns and sardines, and painted on towels or wrapping paper for lack of canvas."

Crane seems early on to have conceived of his "lines" as texts to be looked at and read, rather than recited or sung. When an editor and friend, John D. Barry of *Forum* magazine, arranged a public reading of some of Crane's poetry in April of 1894, Crane refused to attend, saying that he "would rather die than do it." This refusal has been taken for modesty or stage fright; but it also seems likely that Crane instinctively resisted a presentation of his poems that would remove them, so to speak, from the page. It was Barry who probably suggested that Copeland and Day—a firm closely related to the Arts and Crafts movement inspired by William Morris—might be interested in Crane's poems.

Crane insisted on calling his poems "lines" for at least two reasons. As a newspaper reporter and avid sportsman, he wanted first to distance himself from a stock image of "poets" as long-haired, indoor, pretentious types. But the specific word he chose to use instead, "lines," suggests that Crane also wanted to emphasize the concrete fact of these poems, that they are lines of print on the page. He welcomed Copeland and Day's suggestion to print the lines entirely in uppercase letters—this would further emphasize the materiality of the poems. With uppercase letters, not only the bases of the letters but the tops as well are on the same level, thus giving the lines a more uniform lateral extension—they are even more "linear."

Crane was working as a professional journalist when *The Black Riders* was published, and it cannot be by accident that the capitalized columns of words evoke newspaper headlines. It was during the 1890s that tabloid journalism, under the innovative direction of Crane's bosses Pulitzer and Hearst, became the alarmingly successful force that it remained until the arrival of television. The opening lines of Crane's title poem, added after the decision to set the book entirely in caps, suggest scare headlines,

> BLACK RIDERS CAME FROM THE SEA.
> THERE WAS CLANG AND CLANG OF SPEAR
>   AND SHIELD,
> AND CLASH AND CLASH OF HOOF AND
>   HEEL,
> WILD SHOUTS AND THE WAVE OF HAIR. . . .

while a wire-service laconicism reigns in the fourteenth poem in the book,

> THERE WAS CRIMSON CLASH OF WAR.
> LANDS TURNED BLACK AND BARE;
> WOMEN WEPT;
> BABES RAN, WONDERING.

The idea of looking at a newspaper as though for the first time is in fact the theme of one of the few poems in *The Black Riders* that address contemporary reality: "WHAT IS THIS?" an otherworldly sage asks, regarding a newspaper. "OLD, OLD MAN, IT IS THE WISDOM OF THE AGE," the poet answers. Unfortunately, recent editors do not reprint the poems in their original capitalized form, thus losing the meaning of the unorthodox typography.

The critical reaction to Crane's poems was mainly one of bafflement, and to a great extent this is still the case. William Dean Howells, who had encouraged Crane after the vanity-press publication of Crane's slum novel, *Maggie: A Girl of the Streets,* lamented that Crane had not "given [the poems] more form." Six months later he was more explicit:

> These things are too orphic for me. It is a pity for you to do them, for you can do things solid and real, so superbly. . . .
>
> I do not think a merciful Providence meant the "prose-poem" to last.

One critic complained that Crane was making "alleged poetry that is without rhyme or meter," while another said of the lines, "In their futility and affectation they strike the impartial reader as so much trash."

Since the 1890s, interest in Crane's poems has been sporadic and, for the most part, lukewarm. The Imagists in the 1920s recognized a neglected precursor, and Carl Sandburg's familiar poem "Letters to Dead Imagists" acknowledges a shared use of free verse and concrete imagery. For the New Critics, Crane's poetry fared badly when it was noted at all; it lacked the complexity and ambiguity that critics like R. P. Blackmur and Cleanth Brooks admired. In his biography of Crane, published in 1951, John Berryman dealt with the poems only in passing, and with almost palpable embarrassment. Daniel Hoffman's full-length study of 1956 was the first serious reading of Crane's poetry, and raised many of the questions of genre, tradition, and influence that remain unanswered. Hoffman found unexpected resemblances between Crane's lines and certain prose poems of the South African novelist and feminist Olive Schreiner, but his most convincing pages relate Crane's themes to possible sources in Methodist tracts by Crane's father and uncles. In his standard history of American poetry, Roy Harvey Pearce dismisses Crane as "not counting for much as a poet." One is left with the impression that Crane's experimental lines have not yet found their audience and remain, in crucial ways, illegible. What follows is an attempt to reopen the book.

Two stories have come down to us about the genesis of Stephen Crane's poems. One suggests that a sympathetic ghost from the spirit world inhabited Crane's mind and spoke through the poems; the other specifies that the ghost was Emily Dickinson. The first story comes from Hamlin Garland, and the second from the editor John D. Barry. Garland, I will argue, misinterpreted what happened, while Barry fabricated it.

"I have got the poetic spout so that I can turn it on or off," Crane wrote his friend Garland in May 1894. Garland, himself a poet, was profoundly impressed. Like Crane, Garland is best known for his contributions to American realism. In the stories of *Main-Travelled Roads* (1891, 1896), as well as in the fine (and unjustly forgotten) poems collected in *Prairie Songs* (1893), Garland gave a disillusioned view of life and labor in his native Midwest—a vision at the furthest extreme from the heartland idylls of the most popular American poet of the 1890s, James Whitcomb Riley.

Garland published several versions of his first encounter with Crane's poetry, but in all of them the idea of a "poetic spout" is central. In the winter of 1894, as Garland tells it, Crane handed him a sheaf of poems and pointed to his own temple: "I have four or five more standing in a row up here—all they need is to be drawn off." In another version, Crane, at Garland's urging, sat and wrote one of these down. "Thereupon with my pen he wrote steadily, composedly, without a moment's hesitation, one of his most powerful poems. It flowed from his pen like oil."

No performance could have been more exciting to Garland at the time. He was profoundly interested in psychical research, and had himself just spent six weeks testing a psychic "for voices and the movement of objects without contact." The previous year he had presided at a meeting in Boston of the American Psychical Society. His account of Crane's writing resembles a case study for the *Psychical Review,* to which he was a contributor. "The composition of these lines," he concluded with regard to Crane, "was an entirely automatic, subconscious process. . . . *It was precisely as if some alien spirit were delivering these lines through his hand as a medium*" (Garland's emphasis).

Who might this alien spirit have been? The second story handed down to us about Crane's lines offers an answer. One evening in the spring of 1893, Crane paid a call on William Dean Howells, whom he had met through their mutual friend Hamlin Garland, at his house on what is now Central Park South. At this time (so the story goes), Howells took down a volume of Emily Dickinson's recently published poetry from the shelf and read a few poems aloud. "Mr. Crane was deeply impressed," reports John Barry, "and a short time afterward he showed me thirty poems in manuscript, written, as he explained, in three days. These furnished the bulk of the volume entitled *The Black Riders.*"

American poets tend to work in such isolation that an account like this of direct cross-pollination seems irresistible. And indeed, no one has seriously challenged Barry's account, which appeared in the *Bookman* in 1901, a year after Crane's death. Why, after all, would Barry invent the Dickinson recital and its explosive aftermath? The answer is that he thought he had made a scoop, as he soon made clear:

> It was plain enough to me that they [Crane's lines] had been directly inspired by Miss Dickinson. . . . And yet, among all the critics who have discussed the [*Black Riders*], no one, to my knowledge, at any

rate, has called attention to the resemblance between the two American writers.

Barry was so proud of his discovery that he may well
have invented an episode to establish the "direct inspiration" that he thought was "plain enough." One can even
piece together a possible line of thought on Barry's part.
Howells had, after all, written a very favorable review of
Dickinson in *Harper's* in 1891. Wouldn't he have been likely
to have spoken of Dickinson to Crane—a daring poet of the
past and a daring writer of the present—and maybe even to
have read some of her poems aloud? That at any rate, Barry
might have reasoned, would explain the astonishing similarity of the two poets' work.

Barry might have saved himself the trouble, however, for
he was by no means the first to note the resemblance. Several critics in the 1890s had already compared Crane and
Dickinson, including the aging but still influential Thomas
Wentworth Higginson, Dickinson's mentor and posthumous editor. Crane's poems reminded Higginson of "a con-
densed Whitman or an amplified Emily Dickinson. . . . He
grasps his thought as nakedly and simply as Emily Dickinson; gives you a glance at it, or, perhaps, two glances from
different points of view, and leaves it there." And Mark Antony De Wolfe Howe, in the *Atlantic* of February 1896, saw
a link between Crane's and Dickinson's use of a similar
form:

> The parable form into which many of the fragments
> are cast gives them half their effectiveness. The au-
> dacity of their conception, suggesting a mind not
> without kinship to Emily Dickinson's, supplies the
> rest.

In fact, many critics, including some of the most prominent,
noted the similarity—with the conspicuous exception of

Howells himself, who mentions Dickinson neither in his own review of *The Black Riders* nor in his letters to Crane.

But what these critics noted as resemblance does not run very deep, and hardly constitutes the direct inspiration that Barry thought was so evident. They point to a shared audacity, but in this regard Crane is compared to Whitman almost as often as to Dickinson. No one has yet advanced a convincing claim of influence between Dickinson and Crane, and in fact their approaches to poetry are quite different.

We have to look elsewhere to understand the genesis of Crane's poems, beginning with a closer look at Garland's reports. Garland, I believe, misconstrued the evidence Crane gave him. He was struck by Crane's claim that he had more poems waiting.

> "I have four or five up here," [Crane] replied, pointing toward his temple, "all in a little row," he quaintly added. "That's the way they come—in little rows, all ready to be put down on paper."

What amazed Garland, and aroused his interest in unusual psychic phenomena, was that "the verses were composed in the mind all ready to be drawn off." But Garland missed Crane's emphasis. Crane's point was not that the poems were up in his head, but that, as he put it (twice), they were "in a little row." It was the way they were arranged that interested Crane, an arrangement readily transferred to paper; as Garland reported, "He wrote steadily in beautifully clear script with perfect alignment and spacing, precisely as if he were copying something already written and before his eyes."

We have already seen how Crane's publishers found ways to emphasize this "alignment" when they set Crane's "lines" in capital letters. But it has escaped critical notice that the major imagery in *The Black Riders* is also based on "little rows." Patterns of rows, lines, and ranges are everywhere in the book. The title poem, "BLACK RIDERS CAME FROM THE SEA," itself suggests black characters moving from the inkwell across a page. Had Crane not added this poem, the book would have opened with the following:

THREE LITTLE BIRDS IN A ROW
SAT MUSING.
A MAN PASSED NEAR THAT PLACE.
THEN DID THE LITTLE BIRDS
   NUDGE EACH OTHER.

THEY SAID, "HE THINKS HE CAN
   SING."
THEY THREW BACK THEIR HEADS
   TO LAUGH.
WITH QUAINT COUNTENANCES
THEY REGARDED HIM.
THEY WERE VERY CURIOUS,
THOSE THREE LITTLE BIRDS IN A
   ROW.

A similar plot will repeat itself in several other, more vigorous poems: a man enters a barren place; he confronts someone sitting there reading, regarding, or holding something; words are exchanged. But what is striking here is the emphasis on the birds sitting "in a row." The tired theme of competing with the expressiveness of nature—"HE THINKS HE CAN SING"—is subordinated to the image of lineation.

Similarly, in his well-known poems about mountains, Crane emphasizes less the size or the threat of the mountains (as most critics have claimed) than their arrangement, specifically in ranges. It is as though he has unpacked the phrase "mountain ranges," literalized it.

ONCE I SAW MOUNTAINS ANGRY,
AND RANGED IN BATTLE-FRONT.

AGAINST THEM STOOD A LITTLE MAN;
AYE, HE WAS NO BIGGER THAN MY FINGER.

This is a frequent inflection of Crane's obsession with rows—as lines of battle—and suggests a link between the "lines" and *The Red Badge*.

The image of ranges is central in another poem, the fifth one in the collection.

ONCE THERE CAME A MAN
WHO SAID,
"RANGE ME ALL MEN OF THE WORLD IN ROWS."
AND INSTANTLY
THERE WAS TERRIFIC CLAMOR AMONG THE
    PEOPLE
AGAINST BEING RANGED IN ROWS.

Garland called this poem "an ironic comment on the reformer," and perhaps it is; but Crane's treatment of social control, with its militaristic deployment of people, is here subsumed by his obsession with the pattern of ranges and rows.

THERE WAS A LOUD QUARREL, WORLD-WIDE.
IT ENDURED FOR AGES;
AND BLOOD WAS SHED
BY THOSE WHO WOULD NOT STAND IN ROWS,
AND BY THOSE WHO PINED TO STAND IN ROWS.

What Crane is visualizing in such poems, I believe, is the lines of poetry themselves, deployed on the page. And he adds a new element to this pattern, in the poem just quoted, with the spilling of blood: "BLOOD WAS SHED / BY THOSE WHO WOULD NOT STAND IN ROWS. . . ." Blood, in Crane's lines, is almost always associated with ink. It is a metaphor that works in two directions for Crane: blood is expressive, like ink (this leads to imagery of embarrassment, blushing, etc.); ink is expressive, like blood (revealing what is hidden deep in the heart, etc.). "I COULD

NOT SEE MY WORDS," Crane writes in one poem, "NOR THE WISHES OF MY HEART."

The most explicit poem in this regard is the following:

> MANY RED DEVILS RAN FROM MY HEART
> AND OUT UPON THE PAGE.
> THEY WERE SO TINY
> THE PEN COULD MASH THEM.
> AND MANY STRUGGLED IN THE INK.
> IT WAS STRANGE
> TO WRITE IN THIS RED MUCK
> OF THINGS FROM MY HEART.

In poems like this it is hard to say which way the metaphor works: whether the poem is about the evil in the heart or about the difficulties of writing. This uncertainty holds even when the theological background to the metaphor is most evident, the idea that Holy Writ is washed in the blood of Christ. Crane has a biting poem on the theme in his second, and inferior book of poems, *War Is Kind:* "A little ink more or less! / It surely can't matter? . . . What? / You define me God with these trinkets? . . . Show me some bastard mushroom / Sprung from a pollution of blood. / It is better."

"The poetic corner in the human head becomes too soon like some old dusty niche in a forgotten church," Crane wrote. He wanted to clean and air the church, and one way he did it, as I have been suggesting, was to recall poetry to its basis in lines of type. We are now in a position to speculate about the tradition to which Crane's verse belongs. The place to look is the printed page itself, and specifically the ideology behind the printing of those pages. Crane's lines were printed first in book form by Copeland and Day, then, during the following five years, in the little magazines of Elbert Hubbard. Fred Holland Day and Hubbard were leaders in the Arts and Crafts movement in the United States, and specifically in the attempt to recall the art of printing to something higher than "the debasement that had come to it as a result of a century of mechanical 'improvements,' " as William Orcutt, one of Copeland and Day's printers, wrote.

From 1893 to 1899, Herbert Copeland and Fred Day produced some of the finest book designs ever printed by an American publisher. While in important ways they were followers of William Morris's Kelmscott Press, with its interest in the medieval ornament of illuminated manuscripts, they also looked to more severe book designs from which Morris himself had taken inspiration. They hired some of the most talented young artists to illustrate their books—including Will Bradley (who designed the cover of *War Is Kind*), Frederic Gordon, the young John Sloan, and Maxfield Parrish—and concentrated in their list on poetry, particularly by younger and little-known writers like Crane. The firm produced ninety-six books in all, fifty-four of which were poetry.

But it was Day's emphasis on typography that interests us here, and in particular his conviction that the choice of a typeface should correspond in a meaningful way to the contents of the book. Type, as Orcutt wrote, was "always intended as a vehicle for the thought it conveyed." Nor was the return to certain pre-industrial methods merely an issue of aiming for an archaic look. As Orcutt observed,

> To set a volume in a particular face of type just because that font happened to be out of use somehow offended me. To use any old decoration to fill in a hole on a page seemed sloppy business—but at the time I had no notion why I didn't like it. Printers did not talk about the 'language of type' in those days. They had forgotten (if they had ever known) that Aldus and Jenson, and now William Morris recognized that type was always intended as a vehicle for the thought it conveyed, and that to select a type haphazard, with no reference to the text, was nothing less than sacrilegious.

Given such practices, it is not surprising that Crane was worried when Copeland and Day promised him that "the form in which we intend to print *The Black Riders* is more severely classic than any book ever yet issued in America." Crane was afraid that by "classic" they meant "old English type . . . some of my recent encounters with it," he complained, "have made me think I was working out a puzzle." But they meant just the opposite: a typeface so simple and austere that Crane's "lines" would have the stark power of a telegram or a newspaper headline.

Fred Day was a man of elegance, born into a sufficiently wealthy Boston family that his publishing ventures had the flair of an expensive and refined hobby. An eclectic genius, Day was also a pioneering figure in photography, and was the patron and mentor of one of his models, Kahlil Gibran. At the other extreme of the Arts and Crafts movement was Elbert Hubbard, the indefatigable marketer of "hand-made" products from his Roycrofters Community in East Aurora, New York. ("Imagine a town named *East* Aurora!" Theodore Dreiser scoffed.) For the anti-establishment Hubbard, Crane's poetry represented as much an extension of his own rough-hewn aesthetic as a way to thumb his nose at the aesthetic standards of Boston, and especially at Howells, who Hubbard felt regarded him as a *Philistine*—hence the title of Hubbard's very popular literary magazine in the 1890s.

We may wonder, then, why Crane's poetry had such peculiar appeal to some of the leading proponents of a return to earlier, artisanal modes of production. What, we might ask, would a thoroughgoing Arts and Crafts poetry look like? What uses of language would correspond to the pre-industrial forms and artisanal finish of Arts and Crafts furniture and architecture? In his little 1900 book on William Morris, Hubbard describes a brass doorplate "so polished and repolished, like a machine-made sonnet too much gone over, that one can scarcely make out its intent."

One idea for an Arts and Crafts poetry is that it be, like

Roycrofters furniture, *rough-hewn*, with the mark of the hand still on it. Crane's abandonment of rhyme and regular stanza probably carried this meaning for Hubbard and Day. One might argue that the relation between Crane's austere lines and the more opulent prosody of Howells or Tennyson, say, is analogous to that between Arts and Crafts designers and the heavy forms of Victorian design. Also the medievalizing subjects and props in some of Crane's poems would have appealed to the man who called himself, only half-jokingly, "Fra Elbertus," as well as to Day, who was profoundly interested in the Middle Ages. One thinks of the spears and shields of the title poem, as well as the much-anthologized "A YOUTH IN APPAREL THAT GLITTERED" (which in fact is more a critique of medievalizing tendencies than an invocation of them).

But apart from these attractions, Crane's poetry had one overriding appeal to proponents of the Arts and Crafts aesthetic: namely, that the demand for an intimate relation of theme and typeface could find few better solutions than Crane's use of a nexus of imagery that drew on figural permutations of lines of type. The printing of Crane's lines in capital letters on unadorned pages reinforced this primacy of typography.

Crane's achievement in his experimental "lines" is part of a larger literary history that I can only touch on here. *The Black Riders* is one indication of a sort of international crisis of the poetic line (*"Crise de vers"* was the title of Mallarmé's meditation of 1896) that occurred during the 1890s. Yeats was drawn to the work of William Morris and to the illuminated manuscripts of Blake, while Mallarmé turned to experiments with typography in his *Un Coup de Dés* (1897), exploring, as the philosopher Stanley Cavell notes in another context, "the interest there may be in the fact that all writing is visible, is made with, say, ink on paper, or successive letters." There is in Crane's work, as in that of Mallarmé and Yeats, a renewed interest in the materiality of writing poems, as though poetry, after a century of trying to align itself with ordinary speech or song (Wordsworth's speech or Whitman's song), had forgotten its material existence on the page. The general neglect of American poetry in the 1890s has obscured the importance of *The Black Riders* in this larger story.

SEVEN

Crane In Love

STEPHEN CRANE RETURNED to New York from his western trip in the late spring of 1895 and proceeded to westernize, or at least rusticate, himself. "Damn the east!" he proclaimed that fall. "I fell in love with the straight out-and-out, sometimes-hideous, often-braggart westerners because I thought them to be the truer men. . . . They are serious, those fellows. When they are born they take one big gulp of wind and then they live." There was now a cluster of Cranes outside Port Jervis—Edmund had moved his family there, and served as the town's postmaster. By summer Crane had moved in with Ed and was working steadily and quickly at his fourth novel, *The Third Violet*. Temporarily forgotten was his previous existence as hustling urban newspaperman. "I live in Hartwood, Sullivan Co., N.Y., on an estate of 3500 acres belonging to my brother," he told an inquisitive editor, "and am distinguished for corduroy trousers and briar-wood pipes. My idea of happiness is the saddle of a good-riding horse." Hartwood was both hearth and health spa for Crane; he could hunt, fish, ride, and sail among the paying customers at his brother William's lodge. "I am cruising around the woods in corduroys and feeling great," he reported in July. "I have lots of fun getting healthy."

From his rustic remove, one hundred miles from Manhattan, Crane could take a fresh look at the city, "the land," as he put it, "where all bad newspaper articles come from." He was weighing his next move while waiting for the book publication of *The Red Badge of Courage* in October. In *The Third Violet* he let himself muse on his earlier life in the city, while at the same time setting the agenda for the extraordinary year to come. In this most personal and autobiographical of his novels, he allowed his deepest thinking about love and work to surface. In remarkable ways, *The Third Violet*, like his earlier novels, predicts Crane's life, and in particular his erotic life, during 1896; it lays out his choices and sketches what his future would fulfill.

Crane's view of the city had always been that of an outsider, a stranger, a temporary sojourner. His rootless life there, drifting from one boardinghouse to another, and from one newspaper stint to another, stood for a larger rootlessness in his life during the early years of the 1890s. He wrote with complete assurance, complete authority, about urban subjects, but his favorite perspective was that of innocent eyes—those of *Maggie,* never mistress of the city's ways, or of the wandering waif of Crane's baby sketches— or newcomers from the sticks like George and his mother. Crane had less in common with an urban temperament like Dreiser, or even Howells, than with such westerners as Hamlin Garland and Willa Cather, both of whom felt an instinctive kinship with him.

After his return from the West, Crane increasingly tried to assemble a world elsewhere, outside the disguises and dirt of the city, a sort of pastoral green realm where he could feel more at home. "You don't know," he told his friend Willis Hawkins, "how that damned city tore my heart out by the roots and flung it under the heels of it's [*sic*] noise." "I shall stick to my hills," he assured his editor. And with *The Third Violet,* he managed to name that place of escape. It is a double world, as pastorals generally are, combining nature and art. Specifically, Crane fused the natural landscape around Sullivan County with the island of imaginative and erotic release he had discovered among the young painters, designers, and illustrators who were his closest companions during his early years in New York City. What these young artists meant to his writing has never received adequate attention, but from the sparse documentation of Crane's daily life during the early 1890s—idealizing memoirs, posed photographs, Crane's own reticent or self-promoting letters, and the pages of *The Third Violet*—one can piece together a sense of their importance to him.

None of the artists Crane knew in those days achieved anything like the fame he did, but they shared with him a seriousness and ambition about their art. By 1893 or so several of them were regularly employed, while he was still engaged in the uncertainties of freelancing, a fate he described later as, "of all human lots for a person of sensibility . . . the most discouraging." The artist C. K. Linson, seven years Crane's senior and one of his closest friends, must have seemed particularly advanced in his career. Trained in Paris at the École des Beaux-Arts and the Académie Julian (where he was a classmate of Gauguin's), Linson worked with steady success as a painter and illustrator. In 1893 a major gallery wished to show his work. He made enough money to share the rent for a studio with a couple of other artists; it was a quiet place where Crane wrote many of his early city sketches.

Why then did Crane spend so much time in the company of artists rather than with his fellow journalists, poets, and novelists? Part of the reason was surely chance, for Lin-

11. *Crane and C.K. Linson on the roof of Linson's studio,*
42 West 30th Street, in 1894.

son was a cousin of Crane's Port Jervis and Syracuse friend Louis Senger. But the company of artists also reinforced several of Crane's deepest notions of how to approach the city. Crane had, for example, the outsider's sense of the visual shock of the city—its unnatural colors in incongruous combination. He made George Kelcey, in *George's Mother*, a newcomer in order to heighten this sensual charge.

> He had a vast curiosity concerning this city in whose complexities he was buried. It was an impenetrable mystery, this city. It was a blend of many enticing colors. He longed to comprehend it completely, that he might walk understandingly in its greatest marvels, its mightiest march of life, its sin.

The idea of the city as a mystery, pervasive in nineteenth-century European writing, took on for George, as well as for Crane, the specific coloring of sin—the metropolis as Babylon.

The bohemian life of Crane's artist friends promised the best access to these enticing colors—literal and metaphorical. Crane was often hungry and usually broke during the early 1890s, but he relished a sense of living under cover. In a tribute to the former Art Students League on East Twenty-third Street, in which several artists he knew had studios, and where he often spent the night, Crane observed that "this staid puritanical old building once contained about all that was real in the Bohemian quality of New York." What happened inside, Crane implied, was anything but puritanical: "The exterior belies the interior in a tremendous degree. It is plastered with signs, and wears sedately the air of being what it is not. The interior however is a place of slumberous corridors rambling in puzzling turns and curves."

Crane's rather hooded meaning in such passages needs deciphering. The proximity of nude models and the art students' informal intimacy with them—which he'd read about in the wildly popular *Trilby* and soon wrote about in the less popular *The Third Violet*—helped to provide the "blend of many enticing colors" he was seeking. "Everyone was gay, joyous, and youthful in those blithe days," he wrote of the building, "and the very atmosphere of the old place cut the austere and decorous elements out of a man's heart and made him rejoice when he could divide his lunch of sandwiches with the model." Even so, while Crane's letters hint at unspecified transgressions, the truth was probably closer to a bit of doggerel he wrote at the time: "We are too thin to do sin." (Sex required sandwiches.) In any case, what attracted Crane was the bohemian mood as much as its practices, so far from the prohibitions of his parents' narrow creed, though still preserving its language of sin and damnation. Women, for Crane, were still somewhat unreal during the early 1890s, as is evident in the sketchy treatment of Maggie herself, with her rather shadowy physical existence. (Crane may well have been a virgin when he wrote *Maggie*, though in the absence of evidence this must remain more hunch than hypothesis.) He knew the painters much better than he knew their models.

Literary bohemia never had deep roots in the United States until the Greenwich Village scene of the 1920s, and Crane's brief sojourn in it has concealed deeper and less easily understood aspects of his relations with visual artists. Before the technical advances that, in the mid-1890s, made photography an alternative way of presenting images in the popular press, there was a close and symbiotic relation between journalists like Crane and illustrators like Linson. (The friendship of the painter Hawker and the journalist Hollanden, in *The Third Violet*, is emblematic of this partnership.) As Linson remembered, one of his first thoughts on meeting Crane was the possibility of a business arrangement.

145

12. *Crane at ease on a couch in Linson's studio, c. 1893.*

Did this young author want an illustrator? I was "on the job," though they did not say it that way then. There were many illustrators, too. I did not ask, but as the work of writers must come to the illustrators by way of editors, it was our feeling that to editors most illustrators were like tramps scrabbling for handouts. But to the tramps, most editors were pirates. . . . "And most writers are punk," was Crane's notion.

Linson and Crane collaborated on several projects, including a feature on Pennsylvania coal mines in 1894. Crane's approach, from the first sentence, invited illustration: "The breakers squatted upon the hillsides and in the valley like enormous preying monsters eating of the sunshine, the grass, the green leaves."

Linson and Fred Gordon, who rented one of the biggest studios in the Art Students League (he later designed the cover of Crane's *The Black Riders*), profited from their friendship with Crane, but he got more in return than a quiet place to work and sleep. For during the 1880s and 1890s, a period in American art when open-eyed "realists" like Thomas Eakins and Winslow Homer were the exception rather than the rule, it was illustrators like Linson who were investigating the urban mysteries and offering their findings in newspapers and magazines like *Harper's Monthly*, the illustrator's best market for topical drawings. As Robert Bremner points out in his study of American attitudes towards poverty, newspapers did not make regular use of illustrators until the late 1880s, and by the mid-1890s photographers began to supplant them. Crane's years among illustrators were precisely these, when illustrators were *the* investigators of city life. Illustrators explored the slums and their inhabitants and followed health inspectors and policemen on their rounds. Linson himself, for example, had drawn the *Harper's* illustrations for sections of Walter Wyckoff's important book *Workers*. Wyckoff, who

147

dressed as a tramp and wandered from job to unskilled job to assemble material, may well have provided the idea for Crane's own slum masquerade, "Experiment in Misery."

But these illustrators were also aspiring painters, and they provided Crane with a powerful metaphor for his own verbal art. Crane's use of painterly metaphors is so pervasive that one comes to take it for granted, without pausing to ask about its significance. The primary colors of his titles—*The Red Badge of Courage*, "The Bride Comes to Yellow Sky," "The Blue Hotel" (and subtler shades like "The Third Violet," "A Dark-Brown Dog," and "A Grey Sleeve," not to mention "The Black Riders")—are notorious and often parodied. Crane liked to begin his stories with arresting brushstrokes of color, as in the opening sentence of *George's Mother*: "In the swirling rain that came at dusk the broad avenue glistened with that deep bluish tint which is so widely condemned when it is put into pictures." In such passages, Crane invited his readers to see a close tie between his writing and the visual arts. He wanted his words to capture the visual and emotional shock of the city, and he wanted his verbal art to arise from the unconventional ways of living and working that he found among painters. The fullest record of those ambitions is *The Third Violet*.

The Third Violet is among Crane's unfairly forgotten works. A novel long out of print until quite recently and almost never discussed, it is nonetheless one of Crane's most engaging and revealing creations. Its portrait of bohemian life is nuanced and precise, its social satire incisive; Crane was as aware of his predecessors in these modes as he was in the writing of *Maggie*. The novel's love interest is deliberately vague, for Crane was experimenting with what he called his "quick style," a highly idiosyncratic use of "sketch-like" narrative. The book also sheds light on Crane himself at a crucial moment in his literary and emotional career.

148

13. *Linson's oil portrait of Crane, 1894.*

Crane rarely risked a love story, and most critics have regarded *The Third Violet* as a regrettable mistake. "What made Crane think he could write effectively at length about a courtship resists inquiry," John Berryman remarked. Crane wrote it quickly, in less than three months, and sent the manuscript to the editor Ripley Hitchcock in late December 1895. His recorded remarks about the novel are apologetic—"It's pretty rotten work," he wrote a friend on New Year's Eve—though the modesty was probably in large part bait for praise. And some praise came, though mostly from English reviewers who thought the book very informative about American manners. "We have never come across a book that brought certain sections of American society so perfectly before the reader as does *The Third Violet*," one reviewer noted.

The action of *The Third Violet* is so thin that the novel struck some readers as being almost experimental in its plotlessness. A painter from New York named William Hawker takes refuge for a few summer weeks with his family on their shabby farm in Sullivan County. He's poor, and his family is poorer—"the commonest kind of people," says a visitor in the region. Despite the gap in their incomes, Hawker falls in love with a society heiress, Grace Fanhall, who is sojourning with fashionable friends at the local Hemlock Inn. Hawker's close friend, the writer Hollanden, tries to advance the match, but Hawker's pride and Fanhall's prejudice complicate matters. A rival, the wealthy Yale man Oglethorpe, enters the scene and seems to reach an understanding with Miss Fanhall.

The dejected Hawker returns to New York and resumes his bohemian life with a group of artist roommates. The model Florinda O'Connor—a Trilby clone—is in love with Hawker. She represents the free sexual life of the bohemian artists—the world chronicled in *La Bohème* and so many other turn-of-the-century romances—as opposed to the rigid rituals of high-society courtship. Florinda, who poses in the nude for pay, is made to seem almost a prostitute; in a scene in a music hall, the successful painter Pontiac talks freely of her physical charms. "Stunning figure," he keeps repeating, to Hawker's annoyance, "stunning."

But Hawker only has eyes for Grace, who has dropped one violet on the tennis court at the Hemlock Inn, given another to him in parting, and, at the end of the novel, presents him with an ambiguous third. The ending is open to the point of opacity. Grace bursts into tears as she tells Hawker to leave.

> "Oh, do go. Go. Please. I want you to go."
>
> Under this swift change, Hawker appeared as a man struck from the sky. He sprang to his feet, took two steps forward and spoke a word which was an explosion of delight and amazement. He said: "What?"
>
> With heroic effort, she slowly raised her eyes until, a-light with anger, defiance, unhappiness, they met his eyes.
>
> Later, she told him that he was perfectly ridiculous.

Do the lovers realize how silly they've been and live together happily thereafter or, after the same realization, call the whole thing off? We are left hanging.

Crane is so reticent about his characters' feelings that much of the emotional curve of the novel must be derived from the halting and elliptical conversations of the lovers. As John Berryman has finely observed, the book "produces in many of its human passages an odd, slight sense of *instead*, as if we were not hearing whatever it is that matters." One reviewer called it "an étude in conversation . . . the jerky, fragmentary talk of real life," and surely it has a place in the mainly later and mainly British development of the novel of pure dialogue, from Henry James's *The Awkward Age* to the early novels of Anthony Powell, Aldous Huxley, and Ivy Compton-Burnett. Here, for a characteristic example, are the lovers in a rowboat on a lake at night, as

Hawker cuts through the sentimental view of how artists live:

> "But, still, the life of the studios—" began the girl.
>
> Hawker scoffed. "There were six of us. Mainly we smoked. Sometimes we played hearts and at other times poker—on credit, you know—credit. And when we had the materials and got something to do, we worked. Did you ever see these beautiful red and green designs that surround the common tomato can?"
>
> "Yes."
>
> "Well," he said proudly, "I have made them. Whenever you come upon tomatoes remember that they might once have been encompassed in my design. When first I came back from Paris I began to paint, but nobody wanted me to paint. Later, I got into green corn and asparagus—"
>
> "Truly?"
>
> "Yes, indeed. It is true."
>
> "But, still, the life of the studios—"
>
> "There were six of us. Fate ordained that only one in the crowd could have money at one time. The other five lived off him and despised themselves. We despised ourselves five times as long as we had admiration."
>
> "And was this just because you had no money?"
>
> "It was because we had no money in New York," said Hawker.
>
> "Well, after a while, something happened—"
>
> "Oh, no, it didn't. Something impended always, but it never happened."

The wealthy Miss Fanhall is determined to place Hawker in the idealized life, outside all commerce, of the studio, while Hawker is just as determined to place himself, with the Warhol-like detail of the tomato can, among the workers.

The ambiguous position of the striving and starving artist is caught in his own name, which combines the solitary ruthlessness of the bird of prey with the shop vendor who hawks his wares.

Hawker is evidently an impressionist painter—"Does that shadow look pure purple?"—and one could make a case that the sketchy finish of the book owes something to Crane's efforts to reproduce, in prose, effects like those his friends were producing in paint. ("You are a pure impressionist," Conrad told Crane a few years later.) Crane may well, especially in the later chapters of the book, have been experimenting with verbal equivalents of painterly "sketchiness." Many of the artists he knew were trained in Paris during the 1870s and 1880s—Hawker is said to have "worked pretty hard in Paris"—when artists, as a recent commentator has remarked, increasingly were "not fully committed to the high finish that had been a hallmark of the preceding generation . . . [and] the sketch had achieved a new level of acceptance."

Hawker, like the French Impressionists, is an open-air painter; one reason he has left New York is to work outside. *The Third Violet* neatly splits in half, country then city, and Crane's sketches of the Sullivan County countryside are particularly vivid. In these passages Crane seems to be revisiting regions of past imaginative power that he is reluctant to leave behind, for example, the odd wit of the Sullivan County sketches he'd written just after leaving Syracuse. The first sentence of the novel recalls their exuberant animism and mystical sense of the woods around Port Jervis:

> The engine bellowed its way up the slanting, winding valley. Grey crags, and trees with roots fastened cleverly to the steeps, looked down at the struggles of the black monster.

Crane lets himself linger over the description of a brook in the valley: "A little brook, a brawling, ruffianly little brook, swaggered from side to side down the glade, swirling in white leaps over the great dark rocks and shouting challenge to the hillsides." The country as Crane dreams it is a place of almost animal contentment, where Hawker's father is oxlike and he himself is closely linked to his charming setter Stanley. This is a green world ripe for love, as Hawker and Fanhall wander the countryside together.

The city of the second half of the book is the negation of these attunements. Far from being complete and harmonious, it is, as Crane presents it, already in ruins, in constant disrepair. Crane imagines the cobblestones of the city as having been banished from the countryside.

> When the snow fell upon the clashing life of the city, the exiled stones, beaten by myriad strange feet, were told of the dark silent forests where the flakes swept through the hemlocks and swished softly against the boulders.

This is partly Hawker's projection, his longing for the trees near the Hemlock Inn where he achieved a measure of intimacy with Miss Fanhall. But it also evokes Crane's own sense of alienation in the modern metropolis, the feeling that made him want to "stick to his hills."

This urban alienation is most acute in an extraordinary paragraph about Florinda's life amid the continual disrepair of the city. In this scene, Hawker is accompanying Florinda on her walk home through the dark and sinister streets of the city at night.

> Florinda lived in a flat with fire escapes written all over the face of it. The street in front was being repaired. It had been said by imbecile residents of the vicinity that the paving was never allowed to remain down for a sufficient time to be invalided by the tramping millions, but that it was kept perpetually stacked in little mountains through the unceasing vigilance of a virtuous and heroic city government which insisted that everything should

be repaired. The alderman for the district had sometimes asked indignantly of his fellow-members why
this street had not been repaired, and they, aroused,
had at once ordered it to be repaired. Moreover,
shopkeepers whose stables were adjacent placed
trucks and other vehicles strategically in the darkness. Into this tangled midnight Hawker conducted
Florinda. . . . Grim loneliness hung over the uncouth shapes in the street which was being repaired.

Part of the charge of this passage is the ambiguous social position of these two walkers. Given his appearance and
her address, they could easily be mistaken for a prostitute
and her john. The "grim loneliness" hanging over "uncouth
shapes," the "tangled midnight" the couple wanders into—
these hark back to Maggie's last night on the streets. Florinda herself strikes Hawker as an innocent victim suffering
some kind of exile, as though she would be more at home in
the country:

As they stood on the steps of the flat of innumerable
fire escapes, she slowly turned and looked up at him.
Her face was of a strange pallor in this darkness and
her eyes were as when the moon shines in a lake of
the hills.

As she enters her apartment building, Crane notes one
more detail indicating her ambiguous social position:
"There was a little red lamp hanging on a pile of stones to
warn people that the street was being repaired." Red lights
in the city have, of course, their own notorious associations.

Crane is suggesting that the loneliness of urban life, its
condition of exile, is partly the result of the constant growth,
and therefore constant incompleteness, of the city. Baude-
laire's anguished elegy, "Le Cygne," in the face of Baron
Haussmann's demolition and reorganization of Paris, Howells's dismay at the changes in lower Broadway in *A Hazard
of New Fortunes*—these are the analogues for Crane's evo-

155

cation of a city in disrepair. The pile of gravel in the opening scene of *Maggie* is part of the same response. For Crane, the city is a place where people are displaced, never entirely at home. In *The Third Violet*, Crane suggests that the disrepair of the city threatens all human intimacy; urban dwellers no longer know where they belong or with whom. The "fire escapes written all over the face" of Florinda's building are as intelligible as the city gets. In a city full of the unemployed—the "tramping millions" that filled New York during the depression years of the 1890s—it's increasingly difficult to tell who's who: "A peaceful citizen emerged from behind a pile of debris, but he might not be a peaceful citizen, so the girl clung to Hawker." Maggie's difficulty in reading the faces of strangers on her final night has become, in *The Third Violet*, the ordinary experience of walking down a dark city street.

Crane conceived of *The Third Violet* as a self-portrait, partially disguised. In one exchange in the novel he invited his readers to do the same: "I don't believe a word of it is true," a guest at the Hemlock Inn tells Hollanden, after hearing his life story. "What do you expect of autobiography?" Hollanden replies. But while *The Third Violet* obviously drew on Crane's happy months at Hartwood, and on his earlier life among painters in New York, it did something else, and something odder as well. For the book was as much about Crane's future as about his past. Specifically, it was Hawker's erotic dilemma—torn between the remote and upper-class Grace Fanhall and the physically immediate and working-class Florinda O'Connor—that established and predicted the terms of Crane's own sexual proclivities and activities during the rest of his life. As usual with Crane, the steps were curiously schematic. He pursued women as deliberately as he did his literary career. Indeed, the two were often hard to distinguish, for he courted women in his letters after working out the terms of courtship in his novels. In this regard the "sketchiness" of *The Third Violet* assumes a new meaning, as Crane tried to "flesh out" in real life what he had outlined in his imagination. *The Third Violet,* with its rustic swain and socialite, was the blueprint for his pursuit of a real woman, one Nellie Crouse of Akron, Ohio.

There was, of course, nothing particularly original about the way Crane divided Hawker's affections between Fanhall and Florinda. Indeed, some such split between idealized and sexual love was so common at the turn of the century that Freud, analyzing men "in whom the tender and the sensual currents of feeling are not properly merged," called it in 1912 "the most prevalent form of degradation in erotic life." Crane's originality, here as elsewhere, was in his approach. As soon as *The Third Violet* was completed, almost to the day, he set out with great deliberation to live those erotic alternatives during the next twelve months of his life. To put it bluntly, he found Grace Fanhall in Nellie Crouse. Failing in his courtship of "Miss Fanhall," Crane turned to a series of Florindas: Amy Leslie, Dora Clark, and finally Cora Taylor. (One lingers for a moment over the similar names: Florinda, Flora, Dora, Cora of Florida. . . .)

The seven extraordinary letters that Crane wrote to Nellie Crouse during the first three months of 1896 are the most impressive and revealing in his correspondence. They are also the most carefully written and most often quoted— almost always out of context—of all Crane's letters. They were written at a critical point in his life, as he made the shift from unknown freelancer in the newspaper business to world-famous author of *The Red Badge of Courage.*

Who, then, was Nellie Crouse? It seems hardly to have mattered to Crane, since he knew almost nothing about her, and since if he hadn't written these letters to her, one feels he would have found someone else to send them to. She was a pretext, a prop, an occasion. She was a society belle of good family, eminently eligible, and soon to marry a man

157

14. *Nellie Crouse with a dog, Akron, Ohio, winter 1896.*
If she hadn't existed, he would have invented her.

she had met at a Harvard ball. Her letters to Crane have disappeared.

They met at a social tea, to which Crane was invited by his friend and former roommate Lucius Button, in January of 1895, just before Crane's departure for the West and Mexico, and when *The Red Badge of Courage* was beginning to appear in serial form in newspapers. This was their only meeting, but Nellie stuck in Crane's memory during the following year, until he worked up the courage to write to her, on New Year's Eve of 1895, as though in immediate fulfillment of a New Year's resolution. He told her in his first letter that she was the reason he left Mexico the previous spring. Someone he'd seen reminded him of her. He assured Nellie that he hurried home because he intended to see her, but although he cut short his journey in May, he didn't write to her until the end of December. Thus, a whole year went by between their meeting and his first letter.

The delay is easily explained. Crane, always anxious about his worthiness as a suitor, tended to key his pursuit of women to his publishing success. A year earlier, right after the publication of *Maggie,* he had written three pretentious letters to an older, married woman called Lily Brandon Munroe. He waited to write Nellie Crouse until after the appearance of *The Red Badge of Courage* in October 1895 and directly after a dinner in his honor held in Buffalo.

In fact, Crane's first letter to Nellie Crouse was a cover letter, enclosing the invitation to the Buffalo occasion, along with a souvenir menu and a newspaper account. The dinner had been arranged by Elbert Hubbard, champion of Crane's poetry and editor of the *Philistine* magazine, the most popular "little magazine" during the 1890s. Hubbard promoted work he considered daring and unconventional, and he assembled a group of literary men—conspicuous for its mediocrity, since Howells, Bierce, and others begged off—to celebrate the extraordinary promise of young Stephen Crane.

Crane's first letter to Nellie documents his importance,

but it also issues an invitation—or perhaps a challenge. He invites her to live her life the way he lives his: "The lives of some people are one long apology. Mine was, once, but not now. I go through the world unexplained." It's an extraordinary credo, this refusal of self-definition. Crane wants his life to be open to the future, improvisatory, even if it gets him into trouble.

Having established his credentials as a rising star and credible suitor, he tells her about the episode in Mexico that reminded him of her existence:

> I was in southern Mexico last winter for a sufficient time to have my face turn the color of a brick sidewalk. There was nothing American about me save a large Smith and Wesson revolver and I saw only Indians whom I suspected of loading their tomales with dog. In this state of mind and this physical condition, I arrived one day in the city of Puebla and there, I saw an American girl. There was a party of tourists in town and she was of their contingent. I only saw her four times—one in the hotel corridor and three in the street. I had been so long in the mountains and was such an outcast, that the sight of this American girl in a new spring gown nearly caused me to drop dead. She of course never looked in my direction. I never met her. Nevertheless I gained one of those peculiar thrills which a man only acknowledges upon occasion. I ran to the railroad office. I cried: "What is the shortest route to New York." I left Mexico.

"I suppose you fail to see how this concerns you in anyway!" Crane concludes. "And no wonder! but this girl who startled me out of my mountaineer senses, resembled you."

This little anecdote, apparently so harmless and off the cuff, serves to establish the terms of Crane's courtship of Nellie Crouse. She is the distant, unapproachable American girl, glimpsed among a party of upper-class tourists—precisely the situation in which Crane had met her in New York. (And the situation in which Hawker first glimpsed Miss Fanhall.) He, on the other hand, is the quintessence of unsuitability. With his revolver and his sunburned face, he resembles the Indians he lives among: "I had been so long in the mountains and was such an outcast. . . ." In the other letters to Nellie, Crane continues to portray himself as a rustic, out-of-doors kind of guy. He closes his second letter with a reminder that "a young [*page torn*] corduroy-trousered, briar-wood-[smoking]-young man—in Hartwood, N.Y. . . . is eagerly awaiting a letter." That is to say, he's again in the mountains—in New York rather than Mexico. "I am by inclination a wild shaggy barbarian," he boasts in another letter.

What's extraordinary about the Puebla episode is the nationalist twist Crane gives it. He portrays himself as someone changed by his Mexican experience into a foreigner: "There was *nothing American about me* save a large Smith and Wesson revolver. . . ." He arrives in Puebla "and there I saw an *American* girl." He continues to stress the girl's Americanness, and claims he left Mexico because of this crisis in his national identity. It soon becomes clear that this anxiety about nationality is really anxiety about his own social status. (The American girl is wearing "a spring gown.") Crane wonders whether he really is of the same society as these society girls—the one in Puebla and the other in Akron—whether they come from the same America he does.

If the first letter documents Crane's distinctiveness, the ones that follow try to establish hers as well—though not with regard to social class. Of course Crane doesn't have much to go on: the brief encounter a year earlier and a handful of letters. But he is up to the challenge. He invites her to believe herself more distinctive than she ordinarily does (or is). He tells her that when he first met her, "I believed I saw in your eye . . . that the usual was rather tiresome to you." It is her "knowingness" that he harps on, above all.

> Your admission that many people find you charming, leads me to be honest. So prepare. I called once in 34th St, when you were there didn't I? Well, I was rather bored. I thought you were very attractive but then I was bored, because I had always believed that when I made calls, I was bored. However to some sentence of mine you said: "Yes, I know," before I had quite finished. I dont remember what I had said but I have always remembered your saying: "Yes, I know." I knew then that you had lived a long time. And so in some semi-conscious manner, you stood forth very distinctly in my memory.

Her perceptiveness, which cuts through his boredom, makes him want to know her, as a kindred spirit: "I have said sometimes to myself that you are a person of remarkably strong personality and that I detected it in New York in that vague unformulating way in which I sometimes come to know things." When she sends him a photograph, he assures her that "there is something in your face which tells me that there are many things which you perfectly understand which perhaps I don't understand at all. This sounds very vague but it is nevertheless very vague in my mind." He tells her that "the light of social experience in your eyes" terrifies him. He is reinventing her, with Grace Fanhall as his model, and for the most part she doesn't seem to mind.

But the implication that he and Nellie have been through it all gets him into trouble. He has bragged of being "an intensely practical and experienced person," and she has bridled at the second adjective, assuming, understandably, that he means sexual experience. He quickly tells her, in his next letter, that he did not call himself "experienced" to warn her, but "in a sort of wonder that anyone so prodigiously practical and experienced should be so attracted by a vague, faint shadow—in fact a woman who crossed his vision just once and that a considerable time ago." All this talk of experience has also made her worry about his drinking. "Why, in heaven's name, do you think that beer is any more to me than a mere incident?" he asks in exasperation. Her concern must have served as an unwelcome reminder of the straitlaced world of his parents.

Throughout his seven letters to Nellie Crouse, Crane flirts with the idea of going to visit her in Akron—to bridge, so to speak, the social divide. In his second letter, dated January 6, 1896, he tells her he plans to go back to Arizona "to study the Apaches more"—again stressing his wild streak—and reminds her that his route will pass through Akron. A week later he promises her, with an obvious though perhaps unintentional sexual innuendo, that "when Akron becomes possible to me, I shall invade Akron." On January 26 he assures her that, despite the delay, he is "quite serious over the stop-off at Akron" in February. Then he retreats into vagueness. On February 5 he mentions a possible trip to England, and wonders whether she might "come east in the summer?" In his sixth letter (February 11) he is considering a trip to Chicago later in the month, or perhaps in March, but suggests alternatively that he accompany her on a trip to Europe she is planning.

What's clear from this constantly postponed trip (and in the postponement of writing Nellie in the first place) is that Crane doesn't really want to see her. What interests him is that this is a courtship that must take place *in writing*. This keeps the courtship at a distance, in the realm of possibility. "You have been for me a curiously *potential* attraction" he tells her. When Hawker first meets Miss Fanhall—herself a socialite tourist among tourists—in *The Third Violet* he is drawn to "the—the—the distance in her eyes." To preserve that distance is Crane's strategy in his letters to Nellie.

Letters also allow Crane to present himself in the best possible light—which for him means in writing. (One thinks of Kafka's fantasy: "Could it be that one can take a girl captive by writing?") Crane is acutely aware that he did not make much of an impression on Nellie when they first met. Much of his correspondence is taken up with self-deprecating remarks about his social awkwardness. In society "I am often marvelously a blockhead and incomparably an idiot," he assures her. "I reach depths of stupidity of which most people cannot dream." In particular, what he calls a "social crisis" can leave him "witless and gibbering."

This social unease corresponds to his fantasy of his own smallness. (Crane was about five-foot-seven, short but not particularly diminutive.) The pretext for his first letter to Nellie was that he was looking for their mutual friend Lucius Button: "I suppose it is his size. He could be so easily overlooked in a crowd." The implication is that Crane would be more conspicuous than the lost Button. But now, in his fourth letter, he confesses that "in all social situations I am ordinarily conscious of being minute."

But if he stutters in public, he struts in the privacy of writing, where he can both keep his distance and bridge it. Still there are misunderstandings. It turns out that Nellie takes "social crises" as a major failing. The kind of man she likes best is the "man of fashion," the smooth performer in public. And to make matters worse, she suggests that maybe Crane could learn something from his reviewers! She's challenging him on both sides: his fluent writing (which she implies could be better) and his social confusion (which she deplores).

His pathetic attempts to respond are painful to read. He assures her that she's got him all wrong, that her preference for the man of fashion "came nearer to my own view than perhaps you expected."

> I have indeed a considerable liking for the man of fashion if he does it well. The trouble to my own mind lies in the fact that the heavy social life demands one's entire devotion. Time after time, I have seen the social lion turn to a lamb and fail—fail at

Lucius Button   S.C.

15. *Crane and the "lost button"—his friend Lucius Button—on Linson's roof, 1894.*

precisely the moment when men should not fail. . . . I like the man who dresses correctly and does the right thing invariably but, oh, he must be more than that, a great deal more. But so seldom is he anymore than correctly-dressed, and correctly-speeched, that when I see a man of that kind I usually put him down as a kind of an idiot. Still, as I have said, there are exceptions. There are men of very social habits who nevertheless know how to stand steady when they see cocked revolvers and death comes down and sits on the back of a chair and waits.

None of this convinces Nellie. To make matters worse, she has inadvertently opened an old wound by invoking a distinction that Crane had examined closely in *The Third Violet.* There he had sketched the differences between the true aristocrat (Hawker) and the man of wealth and fashion (Oglethorpe). Now, in the face of Nellie's challenge, he argues that the true aristocrat is a man of breeding, not necessarily of wealth.

> I swear by the real aristocrat. The man whose forefathers were men of courage, sympathy and wisdom, is usually one who will stand the strain whatever it may be. He is like a thorough-bred horse. His nerves may be high and he will do a lot of jumping often but in the crises he settles down and becomes the most reliable and enduring of created things.

This is precisely how Crane had described Hawker, as "a thoroughbred" despite his poverty. To Nellie, Crane denounces those who "chant 143 masses per day to the social gods and think because they have money they are well-bred." For the etiquette manuals that proliferated in the 1890s (of which he himself owned a few) he has only scorn: "These people think that polite life is something which is to be studied, a very peculiar science, of which knowledge is only gained by long practice." But true "form," he argues, "is merely a collection of the most rational and just of laws which any properly-born person understands from his cradle."

During the early months of 1896, when Crane himself was beginning to enter proper society on the strength of *The Red Badge*, he was particularly insistent on his own claims to being "properly-born." Two days after his first letter to Nellie, he responded to the editor John Northern Hilliard's request for biographical information for a feature on him. The letter, as noted earlier, is almost entirely taken up with Crane's pedigree. On the strength of that genealogy, Crane successfully applied in April of 1896—the spring of his courtship of Nellie—for membership in the Sons of the American Revolution.

One's discomfort with Crane's obsession about being among the "well-born," particularly during the immigration-anxious 1890s, is mitigated somewhat by the more democratic code of conduct he expects from the man of good breeding. His best thoughts about how he lives his own life are derived from his characterization of the "real aristocrat."

> The final wall of the wise man's thought . . . is Human Kindness of course. If the road of disappointment, grief, pessimism, is followed far enough, it will arrive there. Pessimism itself is only a little, little way, and moreover it is ridiculously cheap. The cynical mind is an uneducated thing. Therefore do I strive to be as kind and as just as may be to those about me and in my meagre success at it, I find the solitary pleasure of life.

In his next letter to Nellie he says he "will be glad if I can feel on my death-bed that my life has been just and kind according to my ability. . . ."

But all his high-minded talk fell on deaf ears. He pre-

167

tended to agree with her assessment of "the man with the high aims and things," which she had told him she liked in her soul, but not in her heart. But this was obviously her view of Crane himself; she was letting him down easy. This is the last letter but one, and Crane must already have felt the distance widening. He no longer addressed her as "Miss Crouse"—things had become too intimate for that—but he didn't dare another salutation, and settled for none at all.

Crane's last letter to Nellie is an amazing document. It is in fact a compilation of three letters, jotted down between March 1 and March 18. Throughout the correspondence he and Nellie had competed to see who could be the more blasé. "How dreadfully weary of everything you are," he had written in the fourth letter. "There were deeps of gloom in your letter which might have made me wonder but they did not, for by the same token, I knew of them long ago." The next letter repeats a more laconic version of the same thing: "But then you are very tired. I am, too, very tired." "For my own part," he assures her, "I am minded to die in my thirty-fifth year. I think that is all I care to stand." The final letter, though, moves into a new key, part genuine depression (one feels), and part histrionics:

> Dear me, how much am I getting to admire graveyards—the calm unfretting unhopeing [*sic*] end of things—serene absence of passion—oblivious to sin—ignorant of the accursed golden hopes that flame at night and make a man run his legs off and then in the daylight of experience turn out to be ingenious traps for the imagination. If there is a joy of living I cant find it. The future? The future is blue with obligations—new trials—conflicts. It was a rare old wine the gods brewed for mortals. Flagons of despair—.

There is a draft of a poem among Crane's papers with the refrain "Flagons of despair," and Crane may have simply enclosed in this last missive to Nellie an earlier prose

16. *Formal portrait of Crane, taken in Washington, D.C.,*
    at the time of his last letter to Nellie Crouse— "My pen is dead." March 1896.

draft. But by this time he knew that his courtship had failed (she had presumably shown him the door), and that in a quite literal sense it was a failure of writing. His last note to her reads in full:

> Really, by this time I should have recovered enough to be able to write you a sane letter, but I cannot—my pen is dead. I am simply a man struggling with a life that is no more than a mouthful of dust to him.
>
>

Yours sincerely
STEPHEN CRANE

With that deliberately formal valediction, the correspondence ends.

Having failed with Fanhall he turned to Florinda. By an odd coincidence, that February he was revising *Maggie* for republication, which Appleton's was planning to issue as a sort of follow-up to *The Red Badge*. It was as though he was preparing his imagination for another immersion in the demimonde. By late spring he was back in New York City, and up to his neck in the vice-ridden district of the Tenderloin, sketching its low-life inhabitants: "The people of the Tenderloin, they who are at once supersensitive and hopeless, the people who think more upon death and the mysteries of life, the chances of the hereafter, than any other class, educated or uneducated." And it was with one of their company, as he walked the city streets as innocently as Hawker with Florinda, that Crane ran afoul of the New York police. But that is another episode.

EIGHT

Dora

THE ELEVATED TRAIN tracks that cast their crablike, ambiguous shadows over so many of Stephen Crane's New York sketches are gone from lower Sixth Avenue, taking with them the dives and dance halls that a hundred years ago gave that once kinetic thoroughfare the nickname Satan's Circus, and leaving nothing much. In the long, gray succession of supermarkets and furniture stores, interrupted for a green moment by the florists of the West Twenties, no landmark stands out, with the single, startling exception of the Jefferson Market Courthouse. That great, red-brick fantasy in Ruskinian Gothic, at the corner of Tenth Street, once concealed in its nether regions the Women's House of Detention and now, saved from developers by a deal with the city, houses a branch of the New York Public Library.

Well before its most recent transformation, the ironies of the courthouse's physiognomy were apparent to shrewd observers. Crane, who delighted throughout the 1890s in unmasking the façades of Gilded Age architecture, saw that something could be made of a courthouse and prison masquerading as a place of worship. "The windows were high and saintly," he wrote in a sketch in 1896, "of the shape that is found in churches. From time to time a policeman at the door spoke sharply to some incoming person. 'Take your hat off!' He displayed in his voice the horror of a priest when the sanctity of a chapel is defied or forgotten."

The story of the Dora Clark case has been told many times, always as a tale of gallantry and coincidence, with Stephen Crane coming to the rescue of a woman wrongly accused of prostitution. I want to suggest that most of the apparent coincidences were nothing of the kind, while other real coincidences have been overlooked. Crane's reputation may suffer a bit under scrutiny, but it should be clear by the end of this story that scrutiny was precisely what he invited.

It wasn't by accident that the Jefferson Market Courthouse served as the setting for one of the stagiest episodes in the novelist's amazingly theatrical life. The twenty-four-year-old Crane, a star reporter since the publication of *The Red Badge of Courage* a year earlier, had decided in the fall of 1896 that the building would be the focus for a series of sketches on police activities in the tony entertainment district of the Tenderloin. The wedge of Manhattan bordered by Forty-second Street to the north and Twenty-third Street to the south, and lying between Fourth and Seventh avenues, had received its appetizing name, according to legend, from police captain Alexander "Clubber" Williams, who was transferred to the district in 1876 after long toil in less rewarding areas. "I've had nothing but chuck steak for a long time," Williams reportedly said, "and now I'm to get a little of the tenderloin."

Crane's series, to be published in Hearst's young and showy New York *Journal*, was announced in the *Bookman* in September 1896, and Crane began collecting material immediately. On Monday, September 14, he attended sessions of the magistrate's court (also housed in the Jefferson Market building), sitting on the bench next to the shrewd and evenhanded magistrate Robert C. Cornell. Among the cases Cornell dismissed that week (records of convictions have not survived) were an attempted suicide and the theft of "good and lawful money of the United States to the amount and of the value of forty five cents." Like other city magistrates, Cornell had a steady caseload of assaults and petty thefts; but increasingly during the mid-1890s, he also heard cases related to police efforts, under a new reform administration headed by commissioner Theodore Roosevelt, to clean up gambling, prostitution, and illegal liquor sales in the Tenderloin.

Crane began to explore the literary possibilities of the courthouse in a superb sketch of 1896 called "An Eloquence of Grief." It allowed him to pursue one of his major preoccupations: the physiognomy of crime and modern punishment. Characteristically, he turned his attention to the spectators, who struck him as worshipers at a strange shrine. They wore "an air of being in wait for a cry of anguish, some loud painful protestation that would bring the proper thrill to their jaded, world-weary nerves—wires that refused to vibrate for ordinary affairs." Crane sets the reader up for something nerve-shattering; the policeman's cutting voice and the pointed stained-glass windows contribute to an atmosphere where everything is menacingly *sharp,* as though only incisive violence will make an impression on this blasé crowd.

The spectators get what they are after when a female defendant—accused of stealing clothing from her mistress, and questioned by a lawyer "with the air of a man throwing flower pots at a stone house"—is remanded to jail. Her wealthy accusers turn one way and the woman another, "toward a door with an austere arch leading into a stone-paved passage."

173

> Then it was that a great cry rang through the court-
> room, the cry of this girl who believed that she
> was lost.
>
> The loungers, many of them, underwent a spas-
> modic movement as if they had been knived. . . .
>
> People pity those who need none, and the guilty
> sob alone; but innocent or guilty, this girl's scream
> described such a profound depth of woe—it was so
> graphic of grief, that it slit with a dagger's sweep the
> curtain of common-place . . . [and] a man heard ex-
> pressed some far-off midnight terror of his own
> thought.

This aesthetic frisson was as far as Crane could go (and for
most writers of the 1890s it would be far enough) in deciphering the tensions of the magistrate's court from his observer's perch.

But what Crane was after, and what the *Journal* encouraged in its reporters, was to go beyond passive "reporting"
of the news to *making* it. "The *Journal,* as usual, ACTS,"
Hearst once boasted, "while the representatives of ancient
journalism sit idly by and wait for something to turn up."
This ambition neatly fit Crane's write-it-then-live-it temperament. He had already shown in his Asbury Park "Parade Sketch" both a talent for turning an ordinary
assignment into a newsmaking event and a knack for pre-
cipitating incidents.

The events of the night of September 15 are still obscure, but Crane's hand in them was probably far more active than has been thought. According to the *Journal* (in its
headnote to Crane's own account of the night's events, published the following Sunday), Crane, after sitting in on the
proceedings at the magistrate's court, "had seen but a ka-
leidoscopic view of the characters who passed," and now
"he must know more of that throng of unfortunates; he
must study the police court victims in their haunts." So he
arranged to meet two chorus girls at a Turkish smoking par-

lor on West Twenty-ninth Street. (Two, one assumes, to re-
duce the impression of an assignation—the kind of "bird
and bottle supper" that was chic at the time.)

The women accompanied Crane a few blocks uptown to
the Broadway Garden, a popular resort where he interviewed them for his *Journal* series. Before they left, at 2
a.m., they were joined by Dora Clark, an acquaintance of
one of the women. Crane escorted one of the chorus girls to
a cable car, and returned to find the other two women being
placed under arrest by a policeman. The policeman had
spotted them from the vestibule of the Grand Hotel, and
accused them of soliciting two men who had just passed by.
Convinced of their innocence, Crane claimed that one of
the women, the chorus girl, was his wife, but it was a defense he couldn't use twice. Against the advice of fellow reporters and of Commissioner Roosevelt (an acquaintance of
Crane's and an admirer of *The Red Badge*), Crane testified
that morning in Dora's behalf, before Magistrate Cornell at
the Jefferson Market Courthouse.

The weird and dreamlike circularity of these events
gives one pause. One feels, obscurely, that Crane orches-
trated the whole departure from and return to Magistrate
Cornell's benign bench. And of course the good magistrate,
after noting that Crane was no stranger to the court, sent
the parties home: Dora justified, the arresting officer
Charles Becker humiliated, Crane looking like a gentleman
and glad to portray himself as such in the Sunday spread
allotted to his "Adventures of a Novelist." In that rather arch
report Crane refers to himself throughout as "the reluctant
witness," when of course he wasn't anything of the kind.

Crane's version of the story is suspiciously suited to his
own uses. Consider the way Dora innocently enters the
scene:

> They [Crane and the two chorus girls] were on the
> verge of departing [from the Broadway Garden]
> when a young woman approached one of the chorus

175

girls, with outstretched hand.

"Why, how do you do?" she said. "I haven't seen you for a long time."

The chorus girl recognized some acquaintance of the past, and the young woman then took a seat and joined the party.

The implication is that it was entirely by chance that Dora joined the party, an implication accepted by Crane's biographers. (Stallman: "Unknown to Crane, Dora Clark—also known as Ruby Young—was a streetwalker who had several times been arraigned for soliciting.") The assumption is questionable, to say the least; on the contrary, it seems highly likely that Crane knew precisely who Dora was. It should be remembered that he set out to "study the police court victims in their haunts," and Dora was such a victim, having been arrested by Becker and his associates at least four times during the previous three weeks and arraigned at the Jefferson Market Court.

The coincidences are less glaring if we assume that Crane was cruising for a crisis, one in which he would be a participant, and that the chorus girls flagged down Dora Clark as someone who might help spark one. It has been suggested that Crane may have been the target for police entrapment. But he was not arrested—johns in the 1890s generally weren't—nor was he required to testify in Dora's behalf. He did so voluntarily because, as he put it, "a wrong done to a prostitute must be as purely a wrong as a wrong done to a queen." It's probably closer to the truth to say that the target for entrapment was Officer Charles Becker himself, and that Dora Clark was the bait.

"Picturesque as a wolf," was how Crane described the imposing officer, who "suddenly and silently . . . appeared from nowhere and grabbed" the two girls. But Charles Becker, who was destined for greater scandals than this, had come from somewhere not so different from Crane himself. Indeed, Becker's early career runs strangely parallel to Crane's, like a dark shadow. He was born a year earlier than Crane, in July 1870, and like Crane passed his childhood in Sullivan County in New York, not far from Crane's family haunts around Port Jervis. He came to New York City in his late teens, gravitating first to the Bowery (where he served as a bouncer in German beer gardens), before following his brother into a profession in 1893. The similarities to Crane's career are striking; the major difference, of course, is that the Becker brothers joined the police force instead of the press.

Becker was sworn in on November 1, 1893, Crane's twenty-second birthday, after saving up the $250 fee— nearly a third of a new recruit's annual salary—exacted of police candidates by the corrupt chieftains of Tammany Hall. Three months later the Lexow hearings into New York City police corruption began, and the New York *Press* (for which Crane worked in 1893) pursued investigations of its own into police graft. Becker had modeled himself after the most famous policeman on the force, the same Clubber Williams who had given the Tenderloin its name. Notorious for his graft and brutality—his nickname came from his innovative use of a nightstick—Williams was "retired" in January 1895, as Roosevelt continued his efforts to clean up the police.

Crane's friendship with Roosevelt was already progressing by July 20, 1896, when the commissioner invited him to stop by police headquarters: "I have much to discuss with you about 'Madge' "—*Maggie,* that is. By August, Roosevelt, who considered himself an expert on western life, felt comfortable enough with Crane to offer criticism of his story "A Man and Some Others": "Some day I want you to write another story of the frontiersman and the Mexican Greaser in which the frontiersman shall come out on top; it is more normal that way!" Already concerned about what

177

Crane might write about the New York police, Roosevelt defended their methods for controlling crowds at Madison Square Garden. "I will say one thing for them at the Bryan meeting [it was an election year]; we have not had a single complaint of clubbing or brutality from any man claiming to have suffered."

In mid-October Dora Clark pressed charges of wrongful arrest and harassment against Officer Charles Becker. Crane's role in instituting the proceedings remains obscure. Did he send a telegram to Roosevelt in late September 1896 saying that he was planning to press charges against Becker, "with the result that an aroused and resentful police department bent all its unscrupulous energies to discrediting Crane and making New York too hot for him to live in"? The telegram that Crane's friend Fred Lawrence remembered helping to send has never come to light, nor is there any evidence that Crane was in Philadelphia at the time, as Lawrence claimed (in a letter to Thomas Beer in 1923).

The story does imply that Crane may have had more of a hand in the events than he wanted to be known. Still the perfect gentleman, he was again willing to risk his reputation and testify at the trial, this time at police headquarters, with a police commissioner presiding. Roosevelt, probably sensing the likelihood of embarrassment in the press, excused himself, ostensibly in order to stump for McKinley. Instead, Frederick Grant, son of Ulysses, stepped in, and his most conspicuous act was to keep Crane waiting from mid-afternoon until 3 a.m. before calling for his testimony.

It seems likely that Crane encouraged Dora to press charges, to prolong an affair that promised further journalistic rewards. The press was solidly in Crane's favor—one of their own against the corrupt police. What Crane apparently didn't count on was the speed with which the police department's wrath would shift from the feisty prostitute to the self-righteous newspaperman. If Crane did not start as a target for the police (for having the audacity to announce a series on the metropolitan cops), he certainly ended up as one. Adding to the hostility, someone may well have noticed that Crane had written for the *Press* in 1893 during its investigations of police corruption.

The vigorous cross-examination was aimed at portraying Crane as a man of dubious morals. He was questioned about the apparatus for opium use that he kept in his apartment (a memento from the piece he'd written on opium dens a few months earlier, in which he'd described in detail what it felt like to smoke the stuff). Then Becker's lawyer turned to the real dirt that the gumshoes had found on Crane. Hadn't he shared an apartment the previous summer with a woman called Amy Huntington—also known as Amy Leslie—living there "as husband and wife for six months"? Crane refused to confirm or deny it, but a janitor was brought to the stand to support the charge, and the police had made their point about Crane's morals.

Becker was acquitted: an honest mistake in the course of duty, perhaps he was overzealous, etc. It's hard to substantiate the rumors that Crane was so harassed by the police after the Becker trial that he was forced to leave New York. Thomas Beer makes this claim—"My name in New York is synonymous with mud," he has Crane saying—and Crane did seize the first opportunity to leave New York, signing on with the Bacheller Syndicate in October to cover the Cuban uprising.

And there the Dora Clark affair ends, at least as far as we can trace Crane's part in it. But one more odd coincidence intrudes, a case of "foreshadowing" that, given Becker's eventual downfall, would be considered too obvious were it to appear in a work of fiction. Before leaving for Cuba, Crane wrote a piece about the federal prison at Ossining, New York, for Pulitzer's *World*. "The Devil's Acre" is a fitting pendant for Crane's sketch of the Jefferson Market Courthouse: twin explorations of the kind of housing that modern society provides for crime. Like the courthouse-as-church, the inner rooms of Sing Sing are treated by Crane as though they're interesting examples of interior decoration:

> The keeper unlocked a door in a low gray building within the prison inclosure at Sing Sing. The room which he and his two visitors then entered was furnished sparsely. It contained only one chair. Evidently this apartment was not the library of a millionaire.
>
> The walls and ceiling were of polished wood and the atmosphere was weighted heavily with an odor of fresh varnish. . . . The chair, too, was formed of polished wood. It might have been donated from the office of some generous banker.

It was the electric chair, of course, patiently waiting, Crane wrote, for "its next stained and sallow prince."

We pick up the trail of Officer, now Lieutenant, Becker sixteen years later. He was indicted in 1912 for conspiring to murder his gambling partner Herman Rosenthal in front of the Metropole Hotel. Lieutenant Becker was the centerpiece of the famous case that made the considerable reputations of, among others, the then district attorney (and within two years governor) Charles Whitman and the police reporter Herbert Swope. Those reputations required a conviction, despite what still seems a shaky case. So Charles Becker was convicted, and was the first New York City policeman to die in the electric chair, on July 30, 1915, at Sing Sing.

Becker is allowed a curtain call in Fitzgerald's *The Great Gatsby*, published in 1925 when the memory of the Rosenthal murder was still vivid. The mobster Meyer Wolfsheim tells Nick Carraway he'd rather be drinking across the street, at the old Metropole: "I can't forget so long as I live the night they shot Rosy Rosenthal there." "Four of them were electrocuted," Nick remembers. "Five," says Wolfsheim, "with Becker." Among the wonderful list of guests who attend Gatsby's party are "the Chester Beckers and the Leeches, and a man named Bunsen, whom I knew at Yale"—names which, decoded, suggest the public (Bunsen) burning of Charles Becker.

NINE

Shipwrecks

THROUGHOUT THE Dora Clark affair, Stephen Crane had portrayed himself as a man to whom things happen. The "reluctant witness" was willing to testify, but his testimony revealed little of his effort to be where things were likely to happen, and nothing at all of his complicity in prolonging events once they had been set in motion. Crane's journalism allowed him to educate himself in the phenomenology of disaster—fires, murders, mining accidents, shipwrecks. When he found himself in the midst of such events, he was prepared to make the most of them. Three months after the Dora Clark affair had run it course, Crane plunged into another highly visible and ambiguous episode, and again he found it professionally useful to conceal his own hand in its unfolding.

"Shipwrecks," he wrote in "The Open Boat," "are *apropos* of nothing. If men could only train for them and have them occur when the men had reached pink condition, there would be less drowning at sea." The strange fact is, however, that in certain specific ways Crane *did* train himself for the sinking of the *Commodore* in January 1897, not to avoid drowning but to prevent the literary equivalent: the fate of having nothing to say. The shipwreck in this case was apropos of plenty; as so often occurred in his life, Crane had written the story before he lived it. For Crane, the *Commodore* disaster was merely the culminating episode in a lifelong involvement with shipwrecks, actual and metaphorical. In some of his earliest journalism Crane had written about shipwrecks on the Jersey shore, developing techniques of style and emphasis that he would use to advantage in drafting "The Open Boat." Metaphors of shipwreck recurred in his father's sermons, and gave an evangelical cast to Crane's own writings about disasters at sea. Something in the fact of shipwreck ran so deep in Crane's imagination that it seemed only a matter of time before he found himself lost at sea.

The New Jersey coast, Crane wrote in an unpublished sketch of 1891, was "the land of shipwrecks and summer resorts, of horror at sea and hilarity on land." In the late fall of 1896, Crane found himself in another coastal resort littered with wreckage and lined with hilarious hotels. Apparently eager to avoid the New York City police, whose wrath he had incurred with his testimony against Officer Charles Becker, Crane accepted an offer to cover the nationalist uprising in Cuba. The Bacheller Syndicate outfitted him with a money belt and seven hundred dollars in Spanish gold, and he traveled by train to Jacksonville, Florida, the port for vessels running the naval blockade to provide arms and men to the insurgents in Cuba.

Crane was accompanied as far as Washington by a newspaperwoman named Amy Leslie. She was a former trouper with light-opera companies, performing under her given name Lillie West; now in her mid-thirties, she made her living as the theater critic for the Chicago *Daily News.* We don't know when Crane first met her. Their names were

183

first linked when she refused an invitation to the Buffalo dinner in Crane's honor, in December 1895, with the words "My most gentle thoughts are tinged with envy of you who are so lucky as to meet Stephen Crane." This sounds a bit like a proposition, and Crane may have treated it as such. Six months later Stephen Crane and Amy Leslie were lovers. Of this fact we would remain more or less in the dark had not Crane been forced to concede, during his cross-examination at the Becker trial, that he shared an apartment with one "Amy Huntington." (She was apparently as drawn to disguise as Crane was.)

But apart from such bare facts, we know virtually nothing about this love affair. The letters Crane wrote to Amy Leslie—those that have survived—all date from the end of the affair. What commentary these letters have attracted has centered on Crane's caddishness in professing his undying love to one woman while courting another, namely Cora Taylor, whom Crane met shortly after his arrival in Jacksonville, and got to know as he waited impatiently for a boat to take him to Cuba. But there is no serious reason to doubt Crane's capacity to love two women at the same time. Scholarly objections seem based on moral grounds rather than psychological ones.

What is clear from the letters, however, is that Crane's associations with each woman ran deeper than love. The choice between them took on an almost allegorical significance. In choosing his wife he was also choosing his life. Amy represented literary New York, the Dora Clark episode, the city—in short, everything that Crane was in flight from. Cora stood for adventure, the sea, the great world— everything Crane was in quest of. In his letters to Amy from Jacksonville he links her insistently to the land. As long as he's grounded, unable to leave, he thinks of her: "Today we are spending in misery at the hotel with a strict rule about drinking [it's Sunday] and no one to play with. I can do nothing but think of you." And in another letter:

> My Beloved: It has been altogether a remarkable se-
> ries of circumstances which has delayed us here so
> long and it breaks my heart to think that I might
> have had you with me a few days longer. . . . The
> boat we are going over on is a yacht chartered by the
> world.

"The world" is of course Pulitzer's *World,* but for Crane it is
the wide world itself that he's setting off for, Amy and the
constraints of New York that he's leaving behind.

Crane's first days in Jacksonville were laced with in-
trigue. Sometime during the last week of November, he reg-
istered at the classy Saint James Hotel under the name
Samuel Carleton, joining other correspondents there in
search of passage to Cuba. The filibustering business—the
illegal transport of guns to the nationalist rebels—was at its
height in the fall of 1896. Despite official U.S. neutrality,
American sentiments were strongly in favor of the Cuban
insurgents against Spanish rule. The U.S. Navy winked at
the not-so-secret resupply operations, while the tabloids of
Pulitzer and Hearst drummed up support for the Cuban
cause.

Crane was aware of the risks involved. A filibustering
vessel had sunk the year before, and another had recently
been fired upon by the Spanish. While several American
correspondents were already working in Cuba, they were
assumed by the Spanish to be spies, and treated accordingly
when captured. Crane hastily composed a will, assuring his
brother William in a cover letter that he had "acted like a
man of honor and a gentleman" in the Dora Clark case.
Then in a sort of private will he arranged payments to Amy
Leslie, through an intermediary, for money she had lent
him. By late December he'd found a ship willing to take
him, the *Commodore,* which had made several successful
trips to Cuba; Crane signed on as a seaman at twenty dollars a month. He dined with its captain, Edward Murphy, at

17. *Crane on horseback, probably taken in Florida, 1896.*

the Hotel de Dream, a house of assignation named for its former owner, one Ethel Dreme, and run on the New Orleans model by Cora Taylor, an attractive and sophisticated woman who was pleased to entertain the author of *Maggie* and *George's Mother.*

Despite frequent rumors of its existence, Crane's correspondence with Cora has never come to light, leaving the precise emotional tenor of their relations open to speculation. Much has been made of Crane's psychological need to "rescue" fallen women, from the fictional Maggie to the real Dora and Cora; John Berryman developed such a theory at length. It doesn't fit Cora very well, however, for when Crane met her she had already escaped from a stifling marriage to an English officer called Captain Donald Stewart, son of a former commander in chief of British forces in India. Six years older than Crane, Cora was born into a respectable Boston family, and was related on her mother's Quaker side to the poet John Greenleaf Whittier; she had chosen a bohemian existence as deliberately as Crane. She had traveled farther and faster than he had, acquiring experience abroad amid the upper crust, and trailing a mysterious and romantic "past." Photographs of her suggest a woman at home in her skin, as the French say; she was unashamed of her appetites and unabashed in seeking their fulfillment. She considered herself a "new woman," and what she had to offer Crane was, among other things, an unhypocritical view of sex. "I wonder," she wrote in her journal, "if husbands are so often unfaithful because their wives are good? I think so. They cannot stand the dreary monotonies and certainties." By the time Crane met her, Cora knew a good deal about the secret lives of husbands.

After some delays, the *Commodore* was loaded with a cargo of guns, and readied for departure on New Year's Eve. Twenty-seven men were aboard, including sixteen Cuban

18. *Cora at the time of her marriage to Donald Stewart,
in England, 1892.*

passengers and Stephen Crane. Motoring downriver from Jacksonville in a thick fog, it ran aground twice, and once had to be tugged off a sandbar by a U.S. customs ship, the *Boutwell.* (That the illegal vessel was aided rather than intercepted suggests complicity between the Navy and the management of the *Commodore.*) Early the following morning, as the ship continued, with the *Boutwell*'s blessing, out to sea, something went wrong in the engine room. The cause is still a mystery: whether the hull was damaged in the groundings, or whether an explosion had occurred, owing perhaps to sabotage, the boat was drawing water fast and the seas were high. Three lifeboats were released and filled; two of them, with the Cuban passengers aboard, made land safely the following morning. The third foundered, and seven men drowned. Crane joined the captain, the oiler, and the cook in the last boat to leave the *Commodore*, an open ten-foot dinghy. The nearest land, the area near Daytona Beach, was fifteen miles away.

Crane wrote two accounts of the *Commodore* disaster; both are highly selective, as interesting for what they exclude as for their contents. The major source for details of the shipwreck is Crane's newspaper version, written during the days immediately following the disaster and published in the New York *Press* on January 7, 1897, with the title (perhaps supplied by an editor) "Stephen Crane's Own Story." It is usually regarded as a "factual" account, as opposed to the "after the fact" narrative of the subsequent and far more famous "The Open Boat." But "Stephen Crane's Own Story" is no less "literary" than the later story; in some ways it is more openly mythical and allusive. It describes an episode more harrowing and morally ambiguous than any recorded in "The Open Boat."

"Stephen Crane's Own Story" is full of omen and augury, New Year's resolve and disappointment. The narrative begins with a scene of feeding, as though the ship is taking its holiday dinner:

189

It was the afternoon of New Year's [actually New Year's Eve]. The *Commodore* lay at her dock in Jacksonville and negro stevedores processioned steadily toward her with box after box of ammunition and bundle after bundle of rifles. Her hatch, like the mouth of a monster, engulfed them. It might have been the feeding time of some legendary creature of the sea.

But the monster is quiet: "She loaded up as placidly as if she were going to carry oranges to New York, instead of Remingtons to Cuba."

Crane surrounds the launching of the *Commodore* with portents. As the boat leaves the dock, she gives "three long blasts of her whistle, which even to this time impressed me with their sadness. Somehow they sounded as wails." The cook tells Crane that he doesn't "feel right about the ship somehow," while an old seaman in the pilothouse murmurs that he is "about through with [filibustering]." And of course the *Commodore*, after ominously running aground twice, finally goes down for good, all omens fulfilled.

Crane's "Own Story" is a newspaper account, and it's worth asking what purpose all this impending doom is meant to serve. Is it just for literary effect—"foreshadowing" artfully added after the fact? Surely it serves that function, and was intended to do so. But might it not have another purpose too, as a story Crane is telling about himself, hence its apt title, "Stephen Crane's Own Story"? The omens would then be Crane's way of confessing his own readiness—even appetite—for disaster. And the shipwreck would merely be the fulfillment of that preparation.

The straightforward narration of the shipwreck itself is complicated by a moral dilemma. As the captain and the other three men in the dinghy look back at the abandoned *Commodore*, they watch her "floating with such an air of buoyancy" that they joke about whether she might not sink at all. Suddenly they are shocked to see that there are men

190

aboard her. "There were five white men and two negroes. This scene in the gray light of morning impressed one as would a view into some place where ghosts move slowly." Their reappearance makes them seem like revenants, come to accuse the men in the dinghy.

> The men on board were a mystery to us, of course, as we had seen all the boats leave the ship. We rowed back to the ship, but did not approach too near, because we were four men in a ten-foot boat, and we knew that the touch of a hand on our gunwale would assuredly swamp us.

That's the reasoning of the crew in *Lord Jim*; it is not the way a captain is supposed to reason. For can it truly be said that Captain Murphy really was, as the code of the sea demands, the last man to leave the *Commodore?* Of course the situation is anomalous: the men have apparently *returned* to the ship. But the reason the captain leaves last is so that all others aboard are accounted for and provided for before he is. In the case of the *Commodore* the men on deck were manifestly not provided for. (Do the captain's responsibilities to his passengers and crew end the moment all have left the ship, he last?)

Crane explains the situation as follows. The seven men had returned to the ship when their lifeboat foundered alongside. They had made makeshift rafts in the meantime and wanted the dinghy to tow them. The captain acquiesces to this crazed request. Two men jump to a raft, but the first mate, apparently understanding the situation as one in which the sacrifice of the chief officers is called for, "threw his hands over his head and plunged into the sea."

> He had no life belt [Crane writes], and for my part, even when he did this horrible thing, I somehow felt that I could see in the expression of his hands, and in the very toss of his head, as he leaped thus to

191

death, that it was rage, rage, rage unspeakable that was in his heart at the time.

Meanwhile, at the captain's urging, the other men jump onto rafts, and Crane is struck by their entreating faces. He watches one man jump down "and turn his face toward us. On board the *Commodore* three men strode, still in silence and with their faces turned toward us. . . . There they stood gazing at us."

The men on the foremost raft throw a line to the dinghy, although the impossibility of the task is clear to everyone:

> But we tried it, and would have continued to try it indefinitely, but that something critical came to pass. I was at an oar and so faced the rafts. The cook controlled the line. Suddenly the boat began to go backward, and then we saw this negro on the first raft pulling on the line hand over hand and drawing us to him.
>
> He had turned into a demon. He was wild, wild as a tiger. He was crouched on this raft and ready to spring. Every muscle of him seemed to be turned into an elastic spring. His eyes were almost white. His face was the face of a lost man reaching upward, and we knew that the weight of his hand on our gun-wale doomed us. The cook let go of the line . . . and the rafts were suddenly swallowed by this frightful maw of the ocean.

It is a nightmare passage, its horror enhanced by the Last Judgment coloring Crane casts it in, with its demons and its doomed men consigned to the pit ("the frightful maw of the ocean"). The lost ones look longingly at the saved, while the guilt of the saved is assuaged only by the overstepping gesture of "the demon." (There's no moral imperative to rescue demons.)

"Stephen Crane's Own Story" comes to a close with the remark "The history of life in an open boat for thirty hours would no doubt be very instructive for the young, but none is to be told here now." Already Crane is saving the best, or the least problematic, for "The Open Boat," which would take him not days but months to write.

Stories of disaster and survival at sea were a popular genre in the nineteenth century, particularly up to the Civil War, before sails gave way to steam and the whaling fleets of New England were destroyed. After the war such stories took on an elegiac air, lamenting the lost days of wooden ships. Anthologies of accounts of shipwrecks, of which R. Thomas's *Narratives of Remarkable Shipwrecks* (1835) was probably the most popular in America, served as sources for Poe and Melville, and probably for Crane as well. These anthologies generally repeated the same well-known stories, adding recent disasters to the familiar names: the *Phoenix* (1780); the *Earl of Abergavenny* (1805), in which the captain, Wordsworth's brother John, lost his life; the *Medusa* (1816), which provided the subject for Géricault's famous painting. Long before the *Commodore* disaster, Crane had explored the possibilities of this genre, in some of his Jersey shore journalism, as though in preparation for the work he would put into "The Open Boat."

We know little about Crane's activities while he worked on "The Open Boat" during the month or two after the shipwreck, and some of the reports are conflicting. Stallman confidently states that Crane wrote the story "in waterfront cafés, at the St. James Hotel, and at the Hotel de Dream," but this is conjecture, probably fueled by images of Hemingway. There are reports of a visit to Port Jervis a week after the shipwreck: "In Hartwood he frenziedly wrote 'The Open Boat,'" the editors of Crane's letters claim.

Ralph Paine, a reporter for the *Journal*, remembered Crane reading the story aloud to Captain Edward Murphy at the Hotel de Dream, and claimed to have heard this exchange:

> "Listen, Ed. I want to have this *right,* from your point of view. How does it sound so far?"
>
> "You've got it, Steve"—said the other man, "That is just how it happened, and how we felt. Read me some more of it."

Some such conversation may well have occurred, but Crane had reasons other than literary accuracy for talking to Captain Murphy. He was still trying to get to Cuba, and Murphy had access to boats.

There were other complications. We can safely conjecture that during the writing of "The Open Boat" Crane was courting (or being courted by) Cora Taylor, and his thoughts about shipwreck began to intermingle with his thoughts about love. Sometime in late January or February Crane wrote on a strip of paper saved by Cora:

> Love comes like the tall swift shadow of a ship at night. There is for a moment the music of water's turmoil, a bell, perhaps, a man's shout, a row of gleaming yellow lights. Then the slow sinking of this mystic shape. Then silence and a bitter silence—the silence of the sea at night.

This passage—with its ambiguous reference to the "sinking" of the ship (does it sink into darkness or into the water?)—may well have more to do with Amy Leslie than with Cora. While certainty about such things is impossible, it seems likely that Crane's sense of guilt at abandoning Amy Leslie joined with his guilt at abandoning the men on the rafts. In any case, romantic entanglements provide the backdrop for Crane's great story of disaster at sea.

If "Stephen Crane's Own Story" is a portrait of the lost, "The Open Boat" is a portrait of the saved. In the way it excludes moral ambiguity from its narrative it resembles the most famous representation of shipwreck in the nineteenth century. Before Géricault painted his *Raft of the Medusa* (1818–19), he had considered, and made sketches of, other moments of the shipwreck narrative, including the notorious episode in which the treacherous captain and officers of the ship, safe in their lifeboats as they headed for the North African coast, let drop one by one the ropes with which they had agreed to tow the raft to shore. Géricault chose instead to depict the survivors at the moment when they spot a ship on the horizon. He minimized the historical specificity of the wreck; the original title of the painting was simply *Scene of a Shipwreck.* By letting the raft take up almost the whole painting, Géricault focused all his attention on making the viewer feel that he or she was on the raft, participating in the ordeal. "His composition," as the leading Géricault scholar has noted, "does not invite contemplation but participation."

Crane, like Géricault, worked by a process of negation in order to increase the immediacy of his account. He eliminated the whole horrifying episode of the raft and the tow rope—so similar to the *Medusa* narrative—from "The Open Boat"; the only trace is the "scene in the grays of dawn of seven turned faces" that haunts the captain. Crane said nothing about the *Commodore*'s mission. As in *The Red Badge of Courage,* he called the men in the boat by their profession—the captain, the oiler, the cook, the correspondent—not by their proper names. As *The Red Badge* could be a description of any soldier's fate, so "The Open Boat" could be the story of anyone lost at sea.

Crane's main challenge (like Géricault's) was to find techniques to put the reader into the open boat. His solution was to manipulate point of view so that any perspective from outside the boat was rejected. The story's famous opening is meant to accomplish this:

> None of them knew the color of the sky. Their eyes glanced level, and were fastened upon the waves that swept toward them. These waves were of

the hue of slate, save for the tops, which were of foaming white, and all of them knew the colors of the sea.

A few paragraphs later Crane entertains an outside perspective only to reject it:

In the wan light, the faces of the men must have been gray. Their eyes must have glinted in strange ways as they gazed steadily astern. Viewed from a balcony, the whole thing would doubtlessly have been weirdly picturesque. But the men in the boat had no time to see it, and if they had had leisure there were other things to occupy their minds. The sun swung steadily up the sky, and they knew it was broad day because the color of the sea changed from slate to emerald-green, streaked with amber lights, and the foam was like tumbling snow. The process of the breaking day was unknown to them. They were aware only of this effect upon the color of the waves that rolled toward them.

Complete absorption is what Crane is after, hence the emphasis on color and the men's knowledge of it.

While "The Open Boat" is often considered Crane's best story, there is something a bit evasive and overdone about much of the performance. Its man-against-nature grandiloquence, so dear to English teachers, is often compared to Greek tragedy as some sort of ultimate statement of the human condition. (As Lord Jim says, "Weren't we all in the same boat?") The story is probably overrated, though its splendid beginning and ending make this easy to do.

The complex interweaving of irony and sublimity in its opening paragraphs is justly admired:

The horizon narrowed and widened, and dipped and rose, and at all times its edge was jagged with waves that seemed thrust up in points like rocks.

Many a man ought to have a bath-tub larger

than the boat which here rode upon the sea. These waves were most wrongfully and barbarously abrupt and tall, and each froth-top was a problem in small boat navigation.

The opening paragraphs establish the oscillating moods of the story, from sublime description to ironic, almost amused detachment. The brilliant detail of the bathtub—with its homely image of domestic safety opposing, and yet prefiguring, the perils of a swamped boat—is characteristic of Crane's later prose.

But it is the story's ending that will occupy us here, not only for its summing up of the pattern of guilt and expiation in "The Open Boat," but also for the way it echoes and builds on Crane's earlier, pre-Jacksonville accounts of disasters at sea. After holding the boat offshore during the night, with the oiler and the correspondent taking turns at the oars, the men in the dinghy prepare to run the boat through the surf towards shore, jumping free when the boat swamps. "An overturned boat in the surf is not a plaything to a swimming man." Three men make it safely to land, with the help of a man onshore.

> But suddenly the man cried: "What's that?" He pointed a swift finger. The correspondent said: "Go."
> In the shallows, face downward, lay the oiler. His forehead touched sand that was periodically, between each wave, clear of the sea.

And a few lines later, as the survivors are warmed with blankets, coffee, "and all the remedies sacred to their minds,"

> The welcome of the land to the men from the sea was warm and generous, but a still and dripping shape was carried slowly up the beach, and the land's welcome for it could only be the different and sinister hospitality of the grave.

197

> When it came night, the white waves paced to
> and fro in the moonlight, and the wind brought the
> sound of the great sea's voice to the men on shore,
> and they felt that they could then be interpreters.

Interpreters, that is, of the rightness of this particular ending, with the sacrifice of one, and him the strongest, of the
four men. The appropriateness of the sacrifice depends,
however, on an episode of which there remains barely a
trace in the story: the abandonment of the men on the raft.

The closing image of a drowned man washed up in the
surf had a long foreground in Crane's career. The juxtaposition of sea and shore had early come to seem, in Crane's
view, an emblem for the lost and the saved, with the pounding surf as the dividing line. His language, as he wrote of
shipwrecks, had taken on some of the cadences of his father's sermons, in which shipwreck figured as the fate of the
lost sinner. In his *Arts of Intoxication,* for example, J. T.
Crane used shipwreck as an image of those lost to drink and
calling for help, "while all through the night, one after another, men, women, and little innocent children are dropping, dropping from the icy wreck, and the busy waves are
piling the dead along the shore. . . ."

Crane's education in the lore of shipwrecks had begun
early. "On many parts of the [Jersey] shore the rotting timbers of wrecked vessels lie thick," Crane had written in
1891, after accepting a commission to memorialize one of
these wrecks, that of the *New Era* of 1854. The ship had
come from Bremen with 380 passengers in steerage, many
of them German emigrants. It hit a sandbar north of Asbury
Park and foundered within view of spectators onshore.
"Men fought with each other like wild beasts for the possession of stray spars or casks," while men onshore got a line
out to passengers on a lifeboat. The boat capsized three

times in the heavy surf and "but five of the fourteen who started reached the shore alive." "When dawn came," Crane wrote, "the storm cleared and the bright sun-rays fell upon the grey up-turned faces of many corpses."

The image of bodies washed up in the surf recurs in Crane's interesting sketch "The Ghostly Sphinx of Metedeconk," published two years before "Stephen Crane's Own Story," and in the same paper, the New York *Press.* "The Ghostly Sphinx" is a love story in the guise of a shipwreck narrative. Its plot, briefly, concerns a love affair between a sea captain and a maiden. He must leave for a voyage to South America; she pouts. When the ship returns it founders off the coast in a storm, while the woman watches from the beach.

> From time to time seamen tried to swim to the shore, and for an instant a head would shine like a black bead on this wild fabric of white foam. . . . Once she espied something floating on the surf. . . . A monstrous wave hurled the thing to her feet and she saw that her lover had come back from Buenos Ayres.

A corpse washed up on the shore is the ending of both Crane's versions of the wreck of the *Commodore,* with the love interest replaced by a vision of "brotherhood": "There was this comradeship that the correspondent, for instance, who had been taught to be cynical of men, knew even at the time was the best experience of his life."

But the *Commodore* episode had a happy ending for Crane. It's the oiler who dies, a substitute sacrifice to the monstrous sea, and Crane is reunited onshore with his lover, Cora Taylor of Jacksonville. Just as Crane's literary accounts of shipwrecks are fulfilled, as it were, in a real one, another pattern in his life goes from literary to literal. His long fascination with prostitutes and fallen women—from the fantasies of *Maggie* to the Dora affair—reaches its ful-fillment in the worldly Cora, madam of the Hotel de Dream.

It is as though a pun hidden in three names had been worked out: Cora is like Dora. Cora *como* Dora. Commodore.

TEN

Real War

CRANE HAD grandly succeeded once in depicting war, and editors were understandably determined to have him succeed many more times in the same vein. But Crane knew that there were limits to his powers of imagining human conflict, and he had a horror of repetition. His letters soon turned bitter like a well run almost dry. "People may just as well discover now that the high dramatic key of The Red Badge cannot be sustained," he complained in the late fall of 1896, as he was completing his placid novel, *The Third Violet.* He announced several times that he'd written his last war story—as he churned out "A Grey Sleeve," "The Little Regiment," and the rest—and denounced the corner that he'd painted himself into with "the cursed Red Badge." That fall he told his friend Willis Hawkins that "I have invented the sum of my invention in regard to war." Thus it was partly to restock his imagination that Crane relentlessly pursued real war during the spring and summer of 1897. But something else was driving him as well, a nagging sense that, like Henry Fleming on the eve of battle, he hadn't yet been tested. *The Red Badge of Courage* remained a hypothesis without experiments.

Cuba had given Crane one of his finest stories. It hadn't given him a war. On March 11, 1897, he wrote to his brother William of his frustrated attempts to evade the naval blockade and reach the fighting in Cuba:

> I have been for over a month among the swamps farther south [than Jacksonville], wandering miserably to and fro in an attempt to avoid our derned U.S. Navy. And it can't be done. I am through trying. I have changed all my plans and am going to Crete.

As long as the United States remained neutral over Spanish claims to Cuba, Greece—where hostilities with Turkey were simmering—seemed a more promising site for international conflict than the Caribbean, and war correspondents quickly shifted continents. The abruptness of Crane's own change of direction—both in the rhythm of his letter and in the rhythm of his life—is striking. He had already adopted the peculiar point of view of the war correspondent, to whom the various sites of battle have a certain abstract equality. If not Cuba, then Crete; any storm in a port.

Crane signed on with Hearst's New York *Journal* to cover the impending Greco-Turkish conflict. Determined not to be left behind, Cora sold the Hotel de Dream and, all bridges burned, followed Crane to New York, where she managed to secure a job with the *Journal* as well. It was someone's idea, probably Cora's own, that she could be marketed as "the first woman war correspondent," and she was. He took one boat to England, she took another—apparently to preserve appearances. Some commentators have suspected that Crane was less than enthusiastic to have her along, though this theory rests (rather shakily) on the unappealing portrayal of the actress-turned-reporter Nora Black in Crane's potboiler *Active Service*. In any case, she stayed out of sight while Crane's English admirers made much of him.

Throughout Crane's English visit and the Greek campaign, it is difficult to trace Cora's presence; one must, for the most part, imagine her at Crane's side. At a luncheon at the Savoy, though, thrown by the star reporter and popular novelist Richard Harding Davis, Crane turned up with Cora, "A bi-roxide blonde who seemed," Davis wrote, "to be attending to his luggage for him." Later in Greece, Davis described her as a "commonplace dull woman old enough to have been his mother and with dyed yellow hair." Some of Davis's bile can be safely attributed to his injured sense of a male domain—the clubby clutch of war reporters—invaded by an ambitious woman. Davis was also highly competitive with Crane and was already sensing a rival on the rise. But it's also quite possible that Cora, feeling sheepish and out of place, did come across as somehow *de trop.*

Crane traveled with Davis to Paris, took a train to Marseilles, and arrived in Athens by ship on April 8. (Cora took a slower land route.) Two days later he wrote to William, boasting that he might be named a member, on the strength of his writings, of Prince Constantine's personal staff. "Wont that be great? I am so happy over it I can hardly breathe. I shall try—I shall try like blazes to get a decoration out of the thing." Otherwise, he found Athens unimpressive: "not much ruins, you know. It is mostly adobe creations like Mexico although the Acropolis sticks up in the air precisely like it does in pictures." Crane's biographers have explained away the letter's bravura as mere posturing for William's sake, the bohemian brother seeking to impress the respectable small-town magistrate who was seventeen years his senior. But surely it is no more posturing than Crane's letters to Nellie Crouse, say. What it shows more clearly is Crane's sense of the theatricality of war when seen from a distance. War viewed as a spectator sport, a matter of decoration and disguise, continued to be one side—the seductive side—of Crane's response to war.

And what a neat little month-long war it turned out to be, for Crane and his fellow reporters. It was eminently viewable, a choreographed drama in what William James called "the supreme theatre of human strenuousness." It also provided Crane a perfect vehicle for testing the techniques of scale and point of view that he'd worked up in *The Red Badge of Courage.* "From a distance it was like a game," he wrote. "There was no blood, no expression, no horror to be seen."

As Crane slowly makes his way towards his first encounter with real war, it is remarkable how closely he recapitulates the sequence of impressions and events in *The Red Badge of Courage,* as though to confirm the rightness of each detail. His novel is the lens through which he views real war. Chance seems, as it did with the sinking of the *Commodore,* to play into Crane's hand. The French steamer *Guadiana,* en route from Marseilles to Athens, makes an unscheduled stop—"a mild digression," Crane calls it, as though he's already within a written narrative—at Crete, to deliver mail to the fleet of European powers (the "Concert") harbored there as a sort of joint peace-keeping force. It is early morning, as in the opening visionary scene of *The Red Badge.* Just as Henry Fleming's first impression of the Union Army was of a great body at rest, Crane's first impression of this naval fleet in battle array is distinctly corporeal:

> It was the fleet of the Powers . . . this most terrible creature which the world has known. . . . This fleet was the living arm and the mailed hand of the Concert. It was a limb of Europe displayed, actual, animate.

At the same moment he notes the sound of a crying baby on his ship, "who disliked the motion of the steamer [and] continued to cry in the cabin." Such seemingly random juxtaposition—the great armed body of Europe, the crying baby—is the dominant stylistic trait of Crane's Greek reporting.

The same association of crying babies and preparations for war reappears at the end of Crane's dispatch, as night descends and the *Guadiana* steams out of the harbor:

> The hand of Europe was hidden by the hills lying in evening peace. The mother of the sick baby had come on deck and to the inquiries of some good-natured passengers she replied gratefully that it was rather better.

The obvious interpretation, if interpretation is called for, is that Europe is the mother, and Greece the sick baby. But Crane himself was sick on the trip to Athens, and sicker still when he arrived. As in his earlier baby sketches, a self-portrait may be implied, for Crane's illness and his consequent sense of increased vulnerability continue to color his vision of war.

As soon as he arrives in Athens, Crane, like his fictional character Fleming, is besieged by rumors of impending fights and incompetent officers: "Constantly the news comes from the frontier that the Greek soldiers are kept from fighting—pitching into the Turks—only by the superb control which the officers have over them." Battle is still, as it was for Fleming early on, merely speculative: "This talk sounds like four glasses of cognac on the shady side-walk before a café." Crane heads for the frontier (without Cora, who as a woman was refused a pass by the Greek authorities in Athens) to join the Greek troops there, but hears that the real fighting is elsewhere. On April 29, Crane announces that he has "heard the first rumors of the hard fighting in Thessaly," and he heads that way as quickly as possible, in the company of Richard Harding Davis and John Bass, the head of the *Journal* staff.

The party of correspondents takes the faster route to Thessaly on ship by way of Athens. But Crane is too sick to travel any further. Again (like Fleming) he's forced to wait.

Instead of battle, he writes about war correspondents. "The advantage of international complication is the fact that it develops war correspondents," he writes on May 1. Not until May 4 does he see real war at last, at the second battle at Velestino. Crane is honest about what he saw and didn't see, and about his illness:

> Some other correspondents saw more of the battle than I did. I was rather laid up and had hurried on from Pharsala when I learned of the strong attack on Velestino. I . . . did not spare myself. But I only arrived at noon of the second day. I had seen skirmishes and small fights, but this was my first big battle.

The battle itself, as Crane recounts it, closely resembles the imagined battle of *The Red Badge*. It begins with a defeat and ends with victory, followed by incomprehensible orders from above. Like Fleming, Crane complains bitterly about the cowardly behavior of the Greek officers. "To be sure, the army retreated from Velestino," he observes, "but it was no fault of the army."

It is war as spectacle and symphony that first impresses Henry Fleming, and the same is true of Crane, as he tries to convey his first impressions of battle. He takes us closer and closer to the fray, then abruptly switches our point of view:

> The roll of musketry was tremendous. From a distance it was like tearing a cloth; nearer, it sounded like rain on a tin roof and close up it was just a long crash after crash. It was a beautiful sound—beautiful as I had never dreamed. It was more impressive than the roar of Niagara and finer than thunder or avalanche—because it had the wonder of human tragedy with it. It was the most beautiful sound of my experience, barring no symphony. The crash of it was ideal.

This is one point of view. Another might be taken from the men who died there.

That extraordinary transition, as the perspective suddenly shifts, registers the other side of war for Crane, what the World War I poet Wilfred Owen called the pity of war. As night falls Crane watches sporadic shells light up the darkness: "By the red flashes I saw the wounded taken to Volo," the port city nearby.

Crane is intensely aware, during his second day of battle at Velestino, of how written accounts tend to falsify the experience of battle, especially the passage of time. "War takes a long time," he observes. "The swiftness of chronological order of battle is not correct. A man has time to get shaved, or to lunch or to take a bath often in battles the descriptions of which read like a whirlwind." But the corrective is not to make the descriptions read, as Crane says elsewhere, "with the celerity of a stone chariot." Instead, Crane experiments with a disjunctive, collage-like approach for depicting battle, with brief, paragraph-long vignettes juxtaposed as though at random:

> I noticed one lieutenant standing up in the rear of a trench rolling a cigarette, his legs wide apart. In this careless attitude a shot went through his neck. His servant came from the trench and knelt weeping over the body, regardless of the battle. The men had to drag him in by the legs.
>
> The reserves coming up passed a wayside shrine. The men paused to cross themselves and pray. A shell struck the shrine and demolished it. The men in the rear of the column were obliged to pray to the spot where the shrine had been.
>
> An officer of a battery sent a man to the rear after another pair of field glasses, the first pair having been smashed by a musket ball. The man brought a bottle of wine, having misunderstood. Meanwhile the Turks were forming on a little green

hill 1,200 yards off. The officer was furious over the man's mistake, but he never let go of that bottle of wine.

Of course, upon closer inspection the three events are anything but random. They all involve a sort of miscue, an abortive act that casts the proceedings in a different light. Each vignette focuses on the effect of gunfire on an automatic gesture—rolling a cigarette, crossing oneself, waving a bottle. Freud called such miscues parapraxes, and thought they were symptomatic, like dreams, of the repressed workings of the unconscious in everyday life. But what Crane's miscues reveal is not, as in Freud, the activity of the unconscious; the interruptions come from outside, not from within. They reveal, instead, the sheer fact—or facticity—of the human body, the way it gets in the way, asserting its awkward presence under the worst possible circumstances. Again Crane is registering, with his extraordinary eye for such things, the fate of the human body in conflict: the lieutenant with his legs apart; the servant dragged to cover by *his* legs; the hand holding tenaciously, but unconsciously, the wine bottle. Of course, there is something grimly comical about these scenes as well, arising from the physical automaticity that the French philosopher Henri Bergson found at the core of comedy.

A fourth vignette in the same sequence also documents an interruption by a bursting shell:

> A member of the Foreign Legion came from the left, wounded in the head. He was bandaged with magnificent clumsiness with about nine yards of linen. I noticed a little silk English flag embroidered on his sleeve. He was very sad and said the battle was over. Most wounded men conclude that the battle is over.

That last sentence sets the tone and the perspective for Crane's best writing on the Greek war.

From the battle of Velestino on, Crane is intent upon reporting not the usual narrative of battle—victories and reverses, courage and cowardice—but its true face. He is forever issuing correctives. "People imagine war to be one long muscular contortion with a mental condition corresponding to it." Not at all, Crane reports. Soldiers wait idly for weeks, and suddenly there is unbelievable carnage. "People would like to stand in front of the mercury of war and see it rise or fall, and they think they ought to demand it, more or less, in descriptions of battle." But Crane points out that in a battle on the scale of Velestino (as in *The Red Badge*), it's often impossible to say who's winning.

When Velestino turns out to be the critical stand of the Greeks, Crane devotes the rest of his dispatches—across two more weeks—to what he sees as the true, as opposed to the "journalistic," results of war. For Crane had decided that the real product of war was not the realignment of nations and governments. The real product of war was the mutilation of human bodies. Some of the most vivid passages in his Greek reporting are almost unbearable in their patient probing of war's atrocities.

> On the lonely road from Velestino there appeared the figure of a man. He came slowly, and with a certain patient steadiness. A great piece of white linen was wound around under his jaw, and finally tied at the top of his head in a great knot, like the one grandma ties when she remedies her boy's toothache. . . .
>
> Under other circumstances one could have sworn that the man had great smears of red paint on his face. It was blood: it had to be blood, but then it was weirdly not like blood. It was dry, but it had dried crimson and brilliant. In fact, the hue upon his face was so unexpected in its luridness that one first had to gaze at this poor fellow in astonishment. He had been shot in the head and bandaged, evidently,

according to the ability of the nearest comrade. Now as he went slowly along two things smote the sense of the observer—first, the terrible red of the man's face, which was of the quality of flame as it appears in old pictures, and second, this same ridiculous knot in the linen at the top of the head which simply emphasized one's recollection of New England and the mumps. . . . He was hurt and he was going to Volo. Even as he plodded across the ridge a train loaded with other wounded rolled down the valley. It had started a long time after he had started, and it would be at Volo much sooner, but one can, perhaps, understand why he did not wait for it at Velestino. A rabbit, when it is hurt, does not wait for a train; it crawls away immediately into the bushes. And so this man had started for Volo.

Most accounts of war, as Elaine Scarry has noted, tend to shift the wounding and killing of men to the margins, as mere incidental aspects of war. "But if injury is designated 'the by-product,' what is the product?" she asks. Crane answers this question eloquently with his portrait of the wounded soldier on the road to Volo.

Behind him was the noise of the battle: the roar and rumble of an enormous factory. This was the product. This was the product, not so well finished as some, but sufficient to express the plan of the machine. This wounded soldier explained the distinct roar. He defined it.

One pauses at the brilliant pun on "finished," and on the confident use of repetition—"This was the product. This was the product . . ."—expressing both the repeated functions of machinery and the pathos of the spectator's shocked response. It is the confirmation and culmination of an idea Crane had already sketched in *The Red Badge of Courage*:

> The battle was like the grinding of an immense and terrible machine to him. Its complexities and powers, its grim processes, fascinated him. He must go close and see it produce corpses.

Early and late, Crane had no doubts about the real products of war.

Just how remarkable, then, was Crane's reportage from Greece? "The written and spoken record of war over many centuries certifies the ease with which human powers of description break down in the presence of battle," writes Scarry, "the speed with which they back away from injuring and begin to take as their subject the most incidental or remote activities occurring there, rather than holding onto what is everywhere occurring at its center and periphery." Crane's war reporting is a sustained and startling exception to the kinds of materials Scarry attacks. Crane's characteristic strategy in his war reportage is to move from evasion and distraction—the usual patriotic claims about the reasons for a given war—to precisely the realization, the violent unmasking of war, that Scarry finds so rare. This revelation dawns on him again and again, as though it's constantly in danger of being lost sight of:

> You can repeat to yourself, if you like, the various stated causes of war, and mouth them over and try to apply them to the situation, but they will fail to answer your vague interrogation. The mind returns to the wonder of why so many people will put themselves to the most incredible labor and inconvenience and danger for the sake of this—this ending of a few lives like yours.

Crane anticipates, here and elsewhere, the disillusionment and anger of writers like Wilfred Owen and Robert Graves twenty years later, as they tried to make sense of the carnage of World War I. Crane's writings about war were particularly poignant for that later generation. As Ford Madox

Ford said of Crane's influence: "The idea of falling like heroes on ceremonial battle-fields was gone forever; we knew that we should fall like street-sweepers subsiding ignobly into rivers of mud."

After the retreat from Velestino, Crane returned to Athens to rest for a few days; he was still sick, apparently. Then he returned to the front to cover the evacuation of the wounded. Just before the armistice was signed on May 20, he found himself aboard a hospital ship that resembled in its horror the raft of the *Medusa*.

> The ship is not large enough for its dreadful freight. But the men must be moved, and so 800 bleeding soldiers are jammed together in an insufferably hot hole, the light in which is so faint that we cannot distinguish the living from the dead.

Characteristically, Crane developed the details of this Last Judgment scenario:

> Near the hatch where I can see them is a man shot through the mouth. The bullet passed through both cheeks. He is asleep with his head pillowed on the bosom of a dead comrade. . . .

"There is more of this sort of thing in war," Crane concluded, "than glory and heroic death, flags, banners, shouting and victory."

Crane was too sick to travel when the war sputtered to a close during the days following the armistice. Like one of the wounded himself, he took to his bed in Athens. When he was well enough to walk, he joined the well-known correspondent Julian Ralph to see the sights, which did not impress him. (Nor did Crane's blasé response impress Ralph, who was shocked at Crane's ignorance of Greek history and architecture.) Before Crane's and Cora's departure, they commissioned photographs of themselves in war correspondent attire, perched on rocks that are obviously props. War as theater had reasserted itself.

That fall of 1897 Crane turned his attention once more to the subject of war. He drew both on the structure of *The Red Badge of Courage* and on his experiences in Greece, as though to correct his imagined battles with the real thing. The result was one of his finest stories, "Death and the Child," which predictably recapitulates Crane's obsession with wounds, corpses, and cowardice, but less predictably returns to his earlier interest—particularly apparent in the baby sketches of 1893—in the play of children.

Joseph Conrad, whom Crane had met for the first time in October, remembered Crane playing with the Conrads' infant son Borys that winter. Conrad observed Crane gazing at the six-week-old baby:

> this was his usual attitude of communion with the small child . . . whose destiny it was to see more war before he came of age than the author of "The Red Badge" had time to see in all the allotted days of his life. In the gravity of its disposition the baby came quite up to Crane; yet those two would sometimes find something to laugh at in each other. Then there would be silence, and glancing out of the low window of my room I would see them, very still, staring at each other with a solemn understanding that needed no words or perhaps was beyond words altogether.

It was this capacity for intense absorption that Crane admired in babies and in soldiers. In "Death and the Child" he found a way to bring infants and infantry together. In contrast to them, Crane conceived of his anti-hero, Peza, an Italian correspondent of Greek origin who, in a burst of naive patriotism, decides to join the Greek troops he is covering. Peza is clearly a version of Henry Fleming. He arrives at the front eager to live his fictive view of war. Where the

213

19. *War as a stage: Crane in war correspondent's attire, on fake rocks, in a photography studio in Athens, 1897.*

20. *Cora as correspondent, same rocks, same studio.*
Inscribed to "me old pal Stevie," from "Imogene Carter," Cora's pen name.

soldiers are all absorption, Peza is all distraction, pestering the officers to let him fulfill his fantasies of heroism. The casual behavior of the soldiers as they await orders doesn't fit his notions of war. They look at Peza curiously and speculate about his identity: "Then, on the verge of his great encounter toward death, he found himself extremely embarrassed, composing his face with difficulty, wondering what to do with his hands, like a gawk at a levee."

Peza finally persuades an officer to let him join in the fray. When the officer tells him to equip himself with the bandolier of a dead soldier, Peza balks. His encounter with the corpse is much like Henry's in the wooded chapel scene in *The Red Badge*. Once armed, he can't rid himself of the notion that he has somehow put himself in the arms— Crane puns on the word—of death; he has put on mortality. Like Fleming again, he panics when the shells come too close. Soldiers in the trenches watching his neck-clutching flight weigh two explanations—cowardice, or a wound— the same ambiguous poles of *The Red Badge*.

The similarities to Henry Fleming are obvious. But Crane's genius, here, is to introduce another, radically contrasting point of view, that of a child deserted by his parents.

> A child was playing on a mountain, disregarding a battle that was waging on the plain. Behind him was the little cobbled hut of his fled parents. . . . The child ran to and fro, fumbling with sticks and making great machinations with pebbles. By a striking exercise of artistic license the sticks were ponies, cows, and dogs, and the pebbles were sheep. . . . His tranquility in regard to the death on the plain was as invincible as that of the mountain on which he stood. . . . Once he looked at the plain and saw some men running wildly across a field. He had seen people chasing obdurate beasts in such fashion, and it struck him immediately that it was a manly thing which he would incorporate in his game.

216

The contrast between Peza's distraction and the absorption of the child could hardly be sharper, but Crane further develops it by introducing an odd little theory of psychic functioning, a sort of economy of attentiveness that resembles eighteenth-century theories of the sublime and the beautiful. Peza is struck by the relative cool of "a straggle of wounded men":

> Peza tried to define them. Perhaps during the fight they had reached the limit of their mental storage, their capacity for excitement, for tragedy, and had simply come away. Peza remembered his visit to a certain place of pictures, where he had found himself amid heavenly skies and diabolic midnights— the sunshine beating red upon desert sands, nude bodies flung to the shore in the green moon-glow, ghastly and starving men clawing at a wall in darkness, a girl at her bath with screened rays falling upon her pearly shoulders, a dance, a funeral, a review, an execution, all the strength of argus-eyed art; and he had whirled and whirled amid this universe with cries of woe and joy, sin and beauty, piercing his ears until he had been obliged to simply come away.

In these passages Crane is mapping out two possible responses to overwhelming experience. One is Peza's psychic overload, the passive observer who, having had his fill, simply turns away. The extreme of this behavior is Peza's panic-stricken retreat, all fuses blown. But the alternative is the game of the child, whose active play incorporates and reproduces aspects of the fighting, thus mastering it. Crane defines both approaches in artistic terms: the child's "artistic license" contrasts with Peza's passive overload in the art museum.

A remarkably similar theory of psychic economy, advanced by Freud late in his life, accounts for Peza's panic-stricken passivity in contrast to the steady absorption of children and soldiers. Freud found himself obliged to explain certain phenomena that posed a challenge to his conviction that dreams are always the fulfillment of a wish. He described two phenomena in which people repeat, in dreams and in waking fantasy, the unpleasant events to which they have been exposed: soldiers after the trauma of war and children in their play. It happens that these are precisely the subjects of Crane's "Death and the Child." And here one is tempted to recall Freud's repeated acknowledgment that he was anticipated in his insights by artists and writers.

The specific game Freud analyzed, in which a child threw a toy out of sight and then reclaimed it, was in Freud's view a response to the disappearance or expected disappearance of parents. Freud's hypothesis was that "the child turned his experience [of the mother's disappearance] into a game. . . . At the outset he was in a passive situation—he was overpowered by experience; but, by repeating it, unpleasurable though it was, as a game, he took an active part." Freud sums up the situation of the child: "He compensated for the [temporary disappearance], as it were, by himself staging the disappearance and return of the objects within his reach."

This is precisely the situation of the playing child in Crane's story: he has been abandoned by his fleeing parents. The theory of creativity implied in Freud—a theory based on the repetition of trauma rather than on the cathartic purging of it—is all but explicit in Crane. His child is the artist, repeating in different terms the horror of war, while Peza is the helpless victim, "overpowered by experience." In the final scene in the story, Peza, in full flight, climbs up to the mountainside where the child sits playing.

> The child heard a rattle of loose stones on the hillside, and facing the sound, saw a moment later a man drag himself up to the crest of the hill and fall panting. Forgetting his mother and his hunger, filled

with calm interest, the child walked forward and stood over the heaving form. His eyes, too, were now large and inscrutably wise and sad. . . .

"Are you a man?" the child asks.

Peza rolled over quickly and gazed up into the fearless cherubic countenance. He did not attempt to reply. He breathed as if life was about to leave his body. He was covered with dust; his face had been cut in some way, and his cheek was ribboned with blood. All the spick of his former appearance had vanished in a general dishevelment, in which he resembled a creature that had been flung to and fro, up and down, by cliffs and prairies during an earthquake. He rolled his eye glassily at the child.

The child repeats his question, and Peza, "palsied, windless, and abject . . . confronted the primitive courage, the sovereign child, the brother of the mountains, the sky and the sea, and he knew that the definition of his misery could be written on a wee grass-blade."

If we recapitulate for a moment Crane's involvement with war, a strange pattern emerges. First Crane imagines, with no previous experience of armed conflict, a soldier's response to a complex and barely comprehensible battle. Then he manages to experience such a battle himself, at Velestino. Then he *reimagines* that battle for a further story that in obvious ways repeats the plot of *The Red Badge of Courage.* A couple of months later, Crane would interrupt the relative peace of his sojourn in England to expose himself to fire again, in Cuba. It's clear that the playing child in "Death and the Child" is not the only person who repeats the trauma of war as though, by taking an active role, he might finally master it. For Crane, in the "artistic license" of his writing, is himself that playing child, fated to live and relive the traumatic structure of war.

ELEVEN

Ravensbrook

AFTER THE LITTLE WAR in Greece, Crane found himself, in the late spring of 1897, with no home to return to. New York was impossible, with the police turned against him because of the Dora Clark episode. What had made Jacksonville seem like home—namely, the presence of Cora Taylor—was now his wherever he went, while to return to Jacksonville would be to restore that part of Cora's reputation that she was most eager to shed. Hartwood was appealing, but it would be difficult to keep the Methodist Cranes in the dark about Cora, and she was not likely to be able to amuse herself in the wilds of Sullivan County, New York. England was more inviting for many reasons. The past—Dora's and Cora's—was unknown there; Crane's books, including the recently published *The Third Violet*, were bigger and more immediate hits with the British than with the American public; and friends with less restrictive moral codes were willing to help resettle Mr. and Mrs. Stephen Crane, as they now called themselves, in England.

One of those friends, Harold Frederic, the *New York*

Times man in London, found temporary rooms for the Cranes a few miles from his own house at Limpsfield, a village in Surrey, and a quick train ride from London. Crane had met Frederic during his brief stopover in London before traveling on to Greece, and had been impressed with Frederic's warm generosity. He remembered Frederic on that occasion as "a tall, heavy man, moustached and straight-glanced, seated in a leather chair in the smoking-room of a club, telling a story to a circle of intent people with all the skill of one trained in an American newspaper school." The two men had much in common. They had grown up in tight Methodist families in small towns. Their success in the city had progressed from newspaper work to the writing of novels. Both had published bestsellers in 1896; Frederic's *The Damnation of Theron Ware*, a Hawthornesque narrative of the erotic downfall of a young Methodist minister, had created something of a scandal as well. Frederic lived with a woman he wasn't married to, while keeping a second household for his wife and children. But something else drew Crane to Frederic. He was a man of the world—at home in England but still resolutely American—in ways that Crane sought to emulate. "Frederic was to be to me a cosmopolitan figure, representing many ways of many peoples; and, behold, he was still the familiar figure, with no gilding, no varnish, a great reminiscent panorama of the Mohawk Valley!"

If the Cranes were trying to "pass"—as husband and wife, as sophisticated world travelers, as people without pasts—Frederic soon found appropriate lodgings for them at Ravensbrook, a pretentious suburban villa sunk at the base of a steep slope. It took its name, according to legend, from Roman times, when some soldiers, looking for water, followed ravens to the stream that flowed by the house (and through its basement as well, according to Ford Madox Ford). Those ravens, perhaps, helped to inspire doleful speculations on the role of Ravensbrook in hastening Crane's death. In any case, several visitors remarked how damp the place was—a condition that cannot have been conducive to his health.

The Cranes' immediate neighbors were members of the Fabian Society, socialists who took many of their guiding ideas from William Morris, and numbered among their more prominent members George Bernard Shaw and Ford Madox Ford. Their rustic preferences in clothes and furnishings were familiar to Crane from his friendship with Elbert Hubbard and his similarly inspired Roycrofters Community. Asked to lecture to the Fabians, Crane spoke on the art of "wig-wagging," the language of flag signals that he had learned in Greece. It must have seemed a strange choice of topic for the politically inclined Fabians. Perhaps Crane intended to shock, or perhaps he simply chose a topic on which he had some expertise. In any case, if the Fabians were medieval in their tastes, they were modern in their morals; they were tolerant, in particular, of unorthodox marital arrangements. The Cranes would not be subjected to scrutiny on that score.

The ten months at Ravensbrook were unusually domestic for Stephen Crane. Cora, to be sure, was a "hostess" by profession, on intimate terms with the pleasures of respectable men, if not of respectable women. The rites of civilized elegance she and her "girls" had mimed for paying guests at the Hotel de Dream she could now perform, as it were, in reality. She set about furnishing the rooms in "old oak and that sort of thing." Looking beyond her immediate and disreputable past, she tracked down distant relatives on her father's side (the Howorths) among the minor English gentry.

As for Crane, he had so often been a guest in the rooms of others that he was eager to entertain on his own turf. While he complained occasionally about the abuses of the uninvited—more than once he had to book a room in a London hotel to finish a story—he was gladly willing to pay that price for the pleasures of company. H. G. Wells, Ford Madox Ford, Joseph Conrad—these and lesser names came to pay their respects that summer and fall of 1897.

With Conrad, whom he met through his British publisher in October, Crane forged a particularly close friendship. "I am a wanderer," Crane wrote his brother William in
October, and in Conrad he discovered a kindred soul. The
uprooted Yankee and the transplanted Pole found they had
much in common: an aristocratic code of conduct, an imaginative investment in the sea, an oblique and ironic approach to storytelling and to life. After their first meeting,
they wandered together through the London streets, while
Crane quizzed Conrad about the structure of Balzac's *Co-
médie humaine.* But while Conrad was older, more experienced, and far better read, in the eyes of the public he was
the lesser writer. Having spent his youth on shipboard, Conrad had come to writing relatively late, and was less advanced in his career than Crane. To his intense annoyance,
reviewers detected Crane's influence in his early works.
Conrad's admiration for Crane, and for "The Open Boat"
in particular, had a competitive edge. "I am envious of
you—horribly," he wrote. "Confound you—you fill the
blamed landscape—you—by all the devils—fill the sea-
scape. The boat thing is immensely interesting."

Crane, in return, admired Conrad's *The Nigger of the
'Narcissus,'* and singled out for praise the "simple treatment
of the death of Waite [*sic*]," which he found "too good, too
terrible," so that he "wanted to forget it at once." The plot of
that bizarre novel obviously struck close to home for Crane.
It recounts the tale of a black sailor who corrupts the mood
of a ship's crew by seeming to feign illness, when he is in
fact mortally ill; by the end of the novel, as he lies in bed
dying, he is fooling only himself. What James Wait died of
was tuberculosis; he was unable to acknowledge the fact of
his own disease. "I felt ill," Crane wrote Conrad, "over that
red thread lining from the corner of the man's mouth to his
chin. It was frightful with the weight of a real and present
death." Illness, the thread of blood at the dead man's mouth,
the weight of impending death—all converge in Crane's
fears about his own advancing tuberculosis. Indeed, it is al-

most as though Crane is confessing his fears to Conrad. After a visit in November, Conrad noted that Crane was "strangely hopeless about himself."

But the Cranes were nothing if not industrious, and Crane's writing during this period has a Scheherazade-like quality. To support their Ravensbrook establishment, which included two servants, Cora's companion from Jacksonville days Mrs. Ruedy, the dog Velestino, a butler, and frequent visitors, the Cranes prepared a weekly letter of society gossip and social observation that they sold to several American papers. These were the "articles" Crane referred to when he excused himself from writing letters home to Port Jervis: "I suppose it would be the proper thing for me to write long descriptions home of what I see over here but I write myself so completely out in articles that an attempt of the sort would be absurd."

In fact, Crane wrote very few letters during the summer of 1897; excluding an occasional request or business jotting, there are really only two, and both register deaths. On July 22, Crane wrote to console his brother Edmund over the death of his two-and-a-half-year-old son, whom Crane had played with a year earlier ("Good old Bill and the way he used to smoke my pipes!"). And a week later came another death in the family. Crane broke the news to Sylvester Scovel, a well-known war correspondent whom he and Cora had befriended in Jacksonville and seen again in Greece:

> *My dear Harry:* Old friends never write to each other. That is almost a law but tonight Cora and I want to speak to you because you are the only one will understand. Velestino has just died—not two hours ago. He died in Cora's bedroom with all the pillows under him which our poverty could supply. For eleven days we fought death for him, thinking nothing of anything but his life. He made a fine manly fight, with only little grateful laps of his tongue on Cora's hands, for he know [sic] that she

21. *Crane in his Ravensbrook study, with relics from his Western travels on the walls.*

was trying to help him. The V.S. told us that it was distemper. We are burying him tomorrow in the rhododendron bed in the garden. He will wear your collar in his grave.

Yours always
C.

P.S. If any of those pictures of him taken on the boat are at hand send them to us.

It's hard to gauge the precise tenor of these obituaries. Few lives engaged Crane's imagination more deeply than those of babies and animals. No irony is evident in Crane's evocation of the soldier's code: how they "fought death" for Velestino, while he carried on his own "fine manly fight."

But the summer had in store a further intimation of mortality, hitting, this time, even closer to home. On August 19, on the way to a party at the Frederics in a rented hack, the unfamiliar horse shied and the Cranes were violently thrown from the carriage. "We were almost killed ... ," Cora wrote Scovel; "you can picture our arriving covered with dust and blood." Crane told his brother Edmund that he was "badly shaken up," but that "the only result finally of the accident will be a small scar on the side of my nose."

Still, it took the Cranes several weeks to recover. Harold Frederic, baffled once in his hospitality, invited Stephen and Cora to recuperate in his summer place in the south of Ireland. Despite his poor health, Crane seized the occasion for another series of travel impressions—his "Irish Notes." Predictably jaunty as most of these are, with evocations of Irish rowdiness and roguery, another vision of impending calamity invades the finest sketch among them. Its title, "A Fishing Village," seems to promise one more picturesque pen portrait of the landscape in County Cork, and its first sentence keeps the promise: "The brook curved down over the rocks, innocent and white, until it faced a little strand of smooth gravel and flat stones." We expect an idyll still, until the brook takes a sinister turn, and so does Crane's mood:

It turned then to the left, and thereafter its guilty current was tinged with the pink of diluted blood. Boulders standing neck-deep in the water were rimmed with red; they wore bloody collars whose tops marked the supreme instant of some tragic movement of the stream. In the pale green shallows of the bay's edge, the outward flow from the criminal little brook was as eloquently marked as if a long crimson carpet had been laid upon the waters. The scene of the carnage was the strand of smooth gravel and flat stones, and the fruit of the carnage was cleaned mackerel.

Not until the end of this extraordinary paragraph, and the return to the smooth gravel and flat stones, do we know what the source of this bloodbath is. Meanwhile we have been invited to imagine all sorts of disasters to account for those nightmarish boulders "standing neck-deep in the water" and wearing "bloody collars."

The passage is witty, of course, with its crescendo of modifiers from *innocent* to *guilty* to *criminal*; the personification recalls the "ruffianly little brook" of *The Third Violet*. But the scene is also genuinely horrible. It is real blood, after all, even if it's only the blood of fish. (Is Crane thinking, perhaps, of Christ's invitation to the apostles, to make those fishermen "fishers of men"? This then would be the bloody harvest of the damned, with a clear demarcation of the guilty and the innocent.)

A bit later in the sketch, Crane contrasts a cheerful and optimistic fisherman—"the type America procures from Ireland"—with an older and wiser man: "bent, pallid, hungry, disheartened, with a vision that magnifies with microscopic glance any fly-wing of misfortune and heroically and conscientiously invents disasters for the future." Crane leaves no doubt about which vision he himself shares.

Crane returned to Ravensbrook in early September of 1897. The period that followed was astonishingly produc-

227

tive, as though the carriage accident had reminded Crane that time was short. In the course of roughly six months he completed his satirical novella of small-town life, *The Monster*; his remarkable westerns "The Bride Comes to Yellow Sky" and "The Blue Hotel"; and his Greek war story, "Death and the Child." In each of these great tales—which could easily be the peak achievements of six *years*—it could truthfully be said that Crane "magnifies with microscopic glance any fly-wing of misfortune and heroically and conscientiously invents disasters for the future." Again, one pauses to note the eerily predictive nature of Crane's imagination. For the disasters of the future turned out to be his own.

What, then, was the major source of Crane's foreboding? It is usually assumed that his main battle during the last three years of his life was with debts. "Dollars damned him," as A. J. Liebling succinctly argued. According to this theory—subscribed to by other chroniclers of Crane's life—Crane had to try to keep pace in his writing with Cora's extravagance; she spent what he earned, and the debts mounted. "In the working three months I have earned close to 2000 dollars," Crane wrote William at the end of October, "but the sum actually paid in to me has been only £20.17s.3d—about 120 dollars. In consequence I have had to borrow and feel very miserable indeed. I am not sure that I am not in trouble over it." This passage is often quoted as evidence of Crane's financial desperation, but later in the same letter Crane tells his brother that he won't ask him for money because "by the time this reaches you I will probably be all right again."

The case for Cora's villainy—her spendthrift ways bleeding her husband dry—is a shaky one at best. In this melodramatic account, she become a sort of vampire who feeds on Crane's vital (i.e., storytelling) powers. Some such fantasy seems to have guided Henry James's imagination as he wrote *The Sacred Fount* in 1898, in which a woman thrives while her husband withers away. Leon Edel confidently claims that this vampire fantasy was inspired by the Crane ménage. (If so, James added sexual expenditure to his critique, as though Cora's insatiable passion were diminishing Stephen's virile strength.)

There is no evidence, however, that Cora was any more extravagant than Stephen. The friends who came to visit were, after all, more his than hers. He was clearly as caught up in the fantasy of country-house elegance as she was. Why else would he try to track down his own noble ancestors in letters of the fall of 1897? As Cora's biographer, Lillian Gilkes, rightly says, Crane was "in process of exchanging his early bohemianism for the new look of an English squire"—a look that required a certain amount of money.

A more likely source of those "disasters for the future" that Crane invented was his own precarious health, of which the carriage accident, the deaths of children and dogs, and the reading of Conrad's eerie tale must have served as reminders. Biographers have shied away from the subject, understandably preferring to trace the more tangible—and better documented—fluctuations of the literary marketplace to the elusive conditions of Crane's frail body. It was part of Crane's code, as much martial as ministerial, to keep quiet about his own physical suffering—hence his praise of Velestino's "fine manly fight" against distemper. Financial ills could be safely broached in public, as occasions for jokes and histrionic self-pity; the young painters in *The Third Violet* complain of little else. But things of the body had to be kept hidden. If previous accounts of Crane's life merely preserve the concealment, they do so at the risk of failing to make sense of the achievement of his last years.

It is characteristic of the haze that still surrounds Crane's life that we have no idea of when the illness that killed him began. Perhaps this is true to some extent of all mortal illnesses: their etiology is so complex that it can probably be truly said that their genesis was in birth itself. All diseases are, in this special sense, congenital. What happened to Crane? someone asks in Hemingway's *Green Hills of Africa*. "He died," Hemingway answers. "He was dying from the start." But we are after something more specific and matter-of-fact, an indication of when Crane became aware that he had tuberculosis. Illness, ill-defined and undiagnosed in a characteristically nineteenth-century way, punctuates his whole life. He stayed out of school till he was eight because he was "sickly." He spent a few weeks recovering from the *Commodore* disaster and another few weeks recovering from the war in Greece. Had TB already set in? H. G. Wells said that the open boat killed Crane, but we cannot be sure. And later, in Cuba (to leap forward for a moment), he was seriously ill with "fever"—but which fever? "Cuban fever," Cora called it. Again, Crane himself had almost nothing to say about his illness. By the time he began to talk openly about it, he had already developed a flip distance from it, writing for example in 1899: "Cuba libre just about liberated me from this base blue world."

But the fall of 1897 was a critical juncture in Crane's declining health; it marked the beginning of his full awareness of his own impending death. The letter to Conrad about the death of James Wait was the closest he could come to an open confession of his fears, and so, in a slightly more disguised way, was the bloodbath in the Irish creek. The extraordinary productivity of those months, from September to March, was a brave attempt to stave off the inevitable. For Crane, to keep on writing meant to keep on breathing. In short, poverty didn't kill Crane; tuberculosis did. Money served, if anything, as a sort of dodge—or even metaphor—for illness. One might even say that two kinds of *consumption* fused in Crane's last years: he wasted money while his body wasted away.

Surely the social precariousness of the Cranes in England also had some bearing on the great tales of the fall of
1897. Despite obvious differences in plot and genre, all
these narratives turn on themes of social ostracism and pre-
tense. A mood of guilty secrets, of truth bursting from concealment, pervades them. And the American West, absent
from Crane's work during his two years of chasing real war,
reappears as the fitting landscape for these tales of disorientation. In the spring of 1895, he had traveled to Nebraska,
New Orleans, and Mexico, writing about drought conditions and the plight of the Mexican poor. Now he made a
second trip, one of the imagination, which resulted in his
two great westerns. Crane's study at Ravensbrook was apparently a sort of shrine to his idea of the West: a photograph reveals a pair of spurs resting on his desk, while a
Mexican blanket and a holster hang on the wall. The West
enters Crane's work as a place where people have the freedom and the latitude to live their fictions, where intimations
and prophecies are mysteriously fulfilled.

"The Bride Comes to Yellow Sky" loses none of its considerable charm and power if we note some obvious paral-
lels between its plot and the narrative that the Cranes were
living. Crane wrote the story in October, just after his convalescence in Ireland. He spun a tale of deceptive simplicity,
and borrowed his characters from dime-novel westerns.
Jack Potter, marshall of the west Texas town of Yellow Sky,
is bringing home his bride from San Antonio. For some unspecified reason he has concealed his marriage plans from
his hometown, and on the train—while the black porter and
the passengers joke about the awkward couple—he worries
about his welcome. Meanwhile, Scratchy Wilson, the town
outlaw and "the last one of the old gang that used to hang
out along the river," is drunk and shooting up the town, to
the immense discomfort of the men gathered in the Weary
Gentleman Saloon. The train pulls in, and Potter arrives at

his adobe house just as Scratchy is cussing it out and demanding that Potter come out and fight. Scratchy challenges Potter in the street; Potter tells him he doesn't have a gun because he has just married. "Well," says Wilson, dismayed and disarmed, "I s'pose it's all off now."

The first sentence of "The Bride Comes to Yellow Sky" is literally disorienting, as the West is converted into the East:

> The great pullman was whirling onward with such dignity of motion that a glance from the window seemed simply to prove that the plains of Texas were pouring eastward.

The rush of civilization is mirrored in smaller oppositions: the oxymoronic "whirling with dignity" and "pouring plains." The perspective of the sentence is also skewed, unlocalized. Whose glance are we following? Who would accept such evidence as proof that the plains are pouring eastward? The second sentence implies an even more radically naive point of view:

> Vast flats of green grass, dull-hued spaces of mesquite and cactus, little groups of frame houses, woods of light and tender trees, all were sweeping into the east, sweeping over the horizon, a precipice.

It is the perspective of one of Columbus's sailors, one almost feels, though their precipice was before them, not behind.

The story—one doesn't need to hammer the point home—mirrors the disorientation of Crane and Cora, passing for man and wife, in England. "Yellow Sky" is surely a plausible name for gas-lit, coal-clouded London. The bride is never named—she's nameless, as Cora must remain to Crane's family and to his New York friends. And she is described in much the way that people described Cora: "The bride was not pretty, nor was she very young." (Cora shrewdly wrote in her notebook that "a woman must be rather more than pretty—and may be rather less—to attract a fin de siècle man.") Potter's face is "reddened from many days in the wind and sun," and his hands are "brick-colored"—a possible echo of Crane's Mexican look, as he described it in his letters to Nellie Crouse: "I was in southern Mexico last winter for a sufficient time to have my face turn the color of a brick side-walk." And the autumnal mood of the story, its ironic elegizing of a disappearing West and the last of the bad guys, captures Crane's own sense of time running rapidly out.

One of the strangest aspects of the story is Potter's embarrassment about his marriage, to the point that he feels like a criminal:

> Of course, people in Yellow Sky married as it pleased them in accordance with a general custom; but such was Potter's thought of his duty to his friends, or of their idea of his duty, or of an unspoken form which does not control men in these matters, that he felt he was heinous. He had committed an extraordinary crime. Face to face with this girl in San Antonio, and spurred by a sharp impulse, he had gone headlong over all the social hedges.

The comedy of the passage lies in the exorbitance of Potter's feelings vis-à-vis his situation. He regards marriage as a crime, when it is usually considered the avoidance of one. The melodramatic description of his plight—"He was now bringing his bride before an innocent and unsuspecting community"—fits Crane in England better than it fits Potter in Yellow Sky.

Indeed, the story may be as much predictive as retrospective, for Crane was imagining that fall of 1897 what it would be like to return to Sullivan County, New York, and rejoin his "unsuspecting" family. "My idea," he told William, "is to come finally to live at Port Jervis or Hartwood. I am a wanderer now and I must see enough but—afterwards—I think of P.J. & Hartwood." If he brought Cora along, and there's no reason to think he didn't plan to, Port

233

Jervis would indeed be "an innocent and unsuspecting community." In the meantime Cora had to remain, like the bride, nameless and unnameable.

As the drinkers in the Weary Gentleman Saloon await Scratchy's arrival, one of them remarks that his rampage "means . . . that for the next two hours this town won't be a health resort." Crane was himself a weary gentleman at Ravensbrook, and health resorts were much on his mind. The fantasy of returning to Hartwood had partly to do with its restorative climate; Crane's brother William was convinced that the air there was particularly good for the lungs. In these last tales one is never far from Crane's sense of impending disaster.

Among the poems in *The Black Riders*, published just after Crane's return from the West, is a three-line, Zen-like riddle about the relation between expectation and experience:

> A MAN FEARED THAT HE MIGHT FIND AN
>   ASSASSIN;
> ANOTHER THAT HE MIGHT FIND A VICTIM.
> ONE WAS MORE WISE THAN THE OTHER.

Assassin was always a potent word for Crane. An aura of exoticism and sin surrounds the word in his early work, such as the description of the Virgil-like guide to the flophouse underworld in "An Experiment in Misery," who is "like an assassin steeped in crimes performed awkwardly."

I take it that of the two men in the poem, the second one is the wiser, though Crane implies that neither is a fool. Both know that fear, like hope, is self-fulfilling; the second man's greater wisdom lies in his understanding that our actions are more likely to destroy us than our sufferings. Of course, the two men are meant for each other, a fantasy that is played out in Crane's great story—perhaps his greatest— "The Blue Hotel."

234

The nine brief sections of "The Blue Hotel" also constitute a sort of riddle. Three strangers arrive at the Palace Hotel in Fort Romper, Nebraska, and by the end of the story one of them, "a shaky and quick-eyed Swede," lies dead in the local saloon, his eyes "fixed upon a dreadful legend that dwelt atop the cash-machine: 'This registers the amount of your purchase.' " The Swede is the man who "feared he might find an assassin"; he is convinced that he'll be killed in Fort Romper, and refuses to be reassured by another guest who says the Swede has been reading too many dime novels. The story shows how his fear is self-fulfilling. The intervening action, however, is so bizarre, and the narration so eccentric, that one has the feeling, reading and rereading this stunning story, of an accumulation of clues that doesn't quite admit a solution.

The opening paragraph has a jaunty, improvisatory feel, which is sustained throughout the story:

> The Palace Hotel at Fort Romper was painted a light blue, a shade that is on the legs of a kind of heron, causing the bird to declare its position against any background. The Palace Hotel, then, was always screaming and howling in a way that made the dazzling winter landscape of Nebraska seem only a gray swampish hush.

The painterly beginning is characteristic of Crane, but one pauses for a moment to note a curious resemblance between this passage and Wallace Stevens's "Anecdote of the Jar." While Stevens's civilizing jar, when placed upon a hill in Tennessee, "made the slovenly wilderness / Surround that hill," Crane's hotel has the opposite effect, making the landscape even wilder with its "screaming and howling." The conspicuousness of the hotel—"it was not to be thought that any traveler could pass the Palace Hotel without looking at it"—becomes a standard for the varieties of privacy and concealment displayed by the three guests at the hotel: the Swede; a "tall bronzed cowboy" headed for

235

Dakota Territory; and a "little silent man from the East, who didn't look it, and didn't announce it," and who has the curious name of Mr. Blanc.

While a blizzard rages outside, Pat Scully, the proprietor of the hotel, and his son, Johnnie, engage the guests in a game of cards, which is interrupted when the Swede accuses Johnnie of cheating. Johnnie challenges the Swede to fight; the Swede is victorious and walks through the storm to the Fort Romper saloon to celebrate. There he tries to persuade four men sitting at a table to drink with him. When they refuse, he tries to force one of them—a gambler, it turns out—to join him at the bar.

> There was a great tumult, and then was seen a long blade in the hand of the gambler. It shot forward, and a human body, this citadel of virtue, wisdom, power, was pierced as easily as if it had been a melon.

This denouement has often been interpreted as a demonstration of the deterministic fatality of human events, a reading supported by the story's ironic coda. The cowboy and the Easterner are sharing a claim "near the Dakota line" a few months later when they hear that the gambler has gotten off with three years in jail, "a light sentence," they agree. They replay the events at the blue hotel, and disagree over who was responsible. The cowboy blames the Swede for picking a fight with Johnnie. But Mr. Blanc responds,

> "You're a fool! . . . Johnnie was cheating. I saw him. I know it. I saw him. . . . We are all in it! This poor gambler isn't even a noun. He is a kind of adverb. Every sin is the result of a collaboration. We, five of us, have collaborated in the murder of this Swede. Usually there are from a dozen to forty women really involved in every murder, but in this case it seems to be only five men.

236

Let us leave aside Blanc's sexist joke, which reminds us how absent women are from Crane's later tales, and note instead how this gathering of responsibility for "sin" is the culmination of a good deal of lightly disguised religious material in the story. The Swede arrives at the hotel convinced that he won't survive the night: "I suppose I am going to be killed," he says, "before I can leave this house!" The case of paranoia that Crane is playing on is Christ's, in the narrative of the Last Supper. The card players' surprise is as great as the surprise of the disciples, who gape in disbelief that one of the faithful might betray Him. When Scully takes the Swede upstairs to convince him of his safety in the hotel, the Swede offers him "three silver pieces," a parody of Judas's earnings, and Crane repeatedly links the Swede's fate to Christ's: "The Swede made the gesture of a martyr"; "The Swede must have concluded that his hour was come." His hour does come when he insists that the gambler drink with him, an ironic echo (as was Scully's earlier offer of a drink) of Christ's Communion commandment at the Last Supper.

Such biblical allusions are hardly rare in Crane's work; the problem, here and elsewhere, is to say what function they serve. In "The Blue Hotel," Crane means the Last Supper to serve as an analogue for the story he is telling about the Swede, a story that hinges on the Swede's demand for certainty in his relations with other people and on his unwillingness to settle for any mystery or inscrutability in human appearances.

The story is poised on an axis of conspicuousness (the blue hotel) and concealment (the blizzard). The Swede finds concealment intolerable. He is—as Crane sometimes described himself—a compulsive studier of faces; he is also, again like Crane in Nebraska, a visitor from New York City. Newly arrived at the hotel, the Swede makes "furtive estimates of each man in the room"; his eyes "rove from man to man." Once the game has begun, the Swede "strode towards the men nervously, as if he expected to be assaulted.

237

Finally, seated, he gazed from face to face and laughed shrilly." When Scully tries to convince the Swede of the relative safety of Fort Romper, "the Swede scanned the old man as if he wished to see into his mind." Scully then shows the Swede a photograph of his daughter, as though this might clinch the argument. It is one of the more bizarre moments in the tale, but it adds to the pattern of obsessive attention to faces.

And the Swede's paranoia turns out—as cases of paranoia often do—to have some basis in fact: Johnnie *was* cheating. The Swede, we are made to feel, misses nothing that can be seen. His downfall occurs when he can't "see into" someone's mind. He is right about Johnnie but wrong about the gambler because, as the narrator assures us, no one could identify him by sight: "a scrutiny of the group would not have enabled an observer to pick the gambler from the men of more reputable pursuits."

It remains to say something about the peculiar aura hanging over "The Blue Hotel," an aura of disease and early death. The proprietor's name, Scully (for skull), suggests that this is, as the Swede fears, a place where people come to die, as though Crane were playing on the etymological kinship of *hotel* and *hospital*. The Swede himself seems tubercular, as Crane describes him. He is "shaky and quick-eyed" when he arrives, and, during the interview with Scully, "upon the Swede's deathly pale cheeks were two spots brightly crimson and sharply edged, as if they had been carefully painted." What Scully shows the Swede upstairs is "a ridiculous photograph of a little girl."

> The figure was as graceful as an upright sled-stake, and, withal, it was of the hue of lead. "There," said Scully, tenderly, "That's the picter of my little girl that died."

238

These are hardly words to reassure the hectic Swede.

In this allegory of illness, Crane seems to retrace, per-haps unconsciously, his visits to Saranac Lake to see Dr. Edward Trudeau, the famous lung specialist who ran a san-atorium there. Details of those trips are vague; we only know of them through Trudeau's brief reply, dated Septem-ber 16, 1898, to an inquiry from Cora. "Your husband," Trudeau wrote, "had a slight evidence of activity in the trouble in his lungs when he came back here this summer but it was not serious and he has improved steadily I under-stand since he came." Unless the phrase "came back here" refers to the remote location of the retreat, the wording seems to suggest a previous visit, possibly during the spring of 1897, immediately following the *Commodore* incident. But "The Blue Hotel" also prefigures Crane's later and final visit to a sanatorium—a hotel that is also a hospital—in the Black Forest.

"Beware of what you wish for in youth," Goethe wrote, "for you shall attain it in middle age." What Crane sketched in "The Blue Hotel" is a sort of theory of the self-fulfilling nature of desire. The story, like the other tales Crane wrote in the winter of 1897, has a confessional feel to it, as though he is plumbing his own deepest motivations. But he makes a wider point about how we are all in a sense entrapped by our fantasies. Crane was always drawn to the analysis of the double or duplicate life: the Swede who lives his life and death according to a dime-novel scenario; Christ who ex-periences life and death according to the prophecies of the Old Testament; and of course Crane himself, who obses-sively tried to live the plots he had already written. One pic-tures Crane with pen in hand in his Ravensbrook study, with the pair of spurs next to his inkwell, and the glass of flat beer he always kept in arm's reach when he was writing. One pictures him completing "The Blue Hotel," and preparing himself for his next dose of reality.

TWELVE

Wigwag and Spy

CRANE RETURNED TO Cuba in the spring of 1898 as though to unfinished business. Thirteen months earlier he had tried in vain to reach the island, baffled by the U.S. Navy and its official neutrality. But on April 11, 1898, Congress yielded to national war fever following the sinking of the battleship *Maine* in the harbor of Havana, and recognized Cuban independence from Spain. The Spanish-American War had begun. Crane sailed for New York three days later, the time it took him to assemble the fare. Conrad remembered his eagerness to leave—"at once that instant—lest peace should be declared. . . . Nothing could have held him back." Conrad added, "HE WAS READY TO SWIM THE OCEAN." Crane was as much in flight from England as to Cuba. His debts were mounting, his guests were legion, and he was sick. His tuberculosis had reached a stage at which it could no longer be ignored by the spring of 1898, and his actions and writings increasingly showed its effects.

Crane tried to hide his condition from Cora and their friends, but ominous signs multiplied as he prepared for Cuba. In late March Cora wrote to Sylvester Scovel, who was already involved in undercover operations off the Coast of Cuba. She noted that Crane was "rather seedy," and asked Scovel to "look after him a little . . . if he should be ill." Crane's complexion was undergoing a change as his condition worsened. Three successive passports—issued in January 1897, April 1898, and May 1900—describe his complexion as "clean," "medium," and "dark," respectively. Upon arrival in New York he tried to enlist in the Navy, according to Beer, but failed the physical—further evidence, if it is accurate, of his rapidly declining health. If he failed in signing up for the Navy, he succeeded with Pulitzer's (and Scovel's) *World,* and hurried on to Key West, where he arrived on April 25 to join the rest of the correspondents gathered there. As in Greece he was amazed by the sheer size of the press contingent, who monopolized all lines of communication. Crane's first dispatch takes an ironic view: "Propelled by the unmitigated efforts of some two hundred and fifty newspaper correspondents Key West furnishes a vast amount of news to the public. But if anything happens in another corner of the globe, Key West is the last place to hear of it." Actually there wasn't much news for another month, as the Spanish and the American naval fleets played hide-and-seek in the Caribbean, while the correspondents played poker and drank.

Crane's Cuba reporting and the later stories it inspired are in a different key from his Greek writings of the previous year. In Greece he was a cub war reporter, trailing behind such celebrities as Richard Harding Davis and Julian Ralph, and making the best of his consistent failure to scoop much of anything. The fighting was always elsewhere. Cora was with him then, too; she was the source of embarrassments, entanglements, and special arrangements. In Cuba he was unencumbered and a star. His reportage became increasingly jaded, sardonic. Also he was among American soldiers this time, whose language he spoke and whose moods he understood. But it was his own ambiguous position vis-à-vis the events he encountered that increasingly preoccupied him.

Two contrasting figures came to be, for Crane, the symbolic representatives for what he was up to in the Cuban campaign: the signalman (or wigwagger) and the spy. One was deliberately conspicuous in battle, often standing with his back turned, and horribly exposed, to enemy fire, as he signaled to ships offshore. The other was concealed, under cover, most effective when least seen. Both trafficked in signs and signals, codes and conundrums. And both were in considerable danger at all times. Crane's war can be understood as his progress from seeing himself as a wigwagger to seeing himself as a spy.

During the month of maneuvering at sea before American troops could be safely transported to Cuba, Crane spent much of his time aboard tugs chartered by the *World*, trying to make sense of the cat-and-mouse activities of the American and Spanish fleets. Meanwhile, he had become such a celebrity that he himself became the subject for journalists' reports. The novelist Frank Norris, for example—who had reviewed *Maggie* a few years earlier—noted Crane's incessant beer drinking and poker playing. Photos of Crane aboard the *Three Friends* capture a wild-eyed and disheveled figure. Crane wrote of his impatience for the fighting to begin and of his consequent need for distraction.

In the meantime, Crane described the naval maneuvers as an array of mysterious signs, requiring decoding by sharp-eyed experts. He was deeply impressed with those seamen who knew the language of warships. For the naval blockade of Cuban harbors to be successful, it was necessary to be able to identify ships immediately. In one dispatch he observed:

22. *Crane aboard the* Three Friends, *1898.*

To the eastward another steamer lifted a vague shadow over the horizon and an officer instantly remarked that it was the torpedo boat *Porter,* although how he could identify this vacillating uncertain form is known only to seamen.

Several of Crane's dispatches take comical pleasure in the press tug's misidentifications of passing ships. He himself began to learn the language: "See that yellow band on her forward funnel? Well, that is the easiest way to distinguish her from the *Dupont.*"

To Crane, such mysteries and enigmas of the sea were portents of the land war to come. "It was a peaceful scene," he wrote, as the battleship *New York* sailed past "a certain depression in the hills . . . indicating the position of Havana. . . . In fact it was more peaceful than peace, since one's sights were adjusted for war." Crane was intensely aware of how expectation clouds perception: "War's first step is to make expectation so high that all present things are fogged and darkened in a tense wonder of the future." In such passages, Crane is again brooding over the self-fulfilling nature of expectation, so marked in the shape of his own life.

Finally, late in the afternoon of June 10, 1898, a battalion of 650 marines began landing operations at Guantánamo Bay, and Crane was along. His first encounter with death was a particularly vivid one. A marine surgeon named John Blair Gibbs had noticed that Crane looked ill with malaria, and had invited him to come to his tent for a dose of quinine. Before the war Gibbs had a practice in New York City. He was a well-known yachtsman as well—precisely the sort of all-American man who figured in many later reports of the war. Gibbs was standing in his tent door, saying, according to one report, "Well, I don't want to die in this place . . ." when a bullet cut the sentence short. Gibbs, shot in the head, was pulled into the same trench where Crane had sought cover. "He took a long time to die," Crane wrote.

"He was long past groaning. There was only the bitter strife for air. . . . I held my breath in the common unconscious aspiration to help. I thought this man would never die. I wanted him to die." To Crane it must have seemed a cruelly ironic death. The doctor who had sought to heal him had himself died instead. "I was," Crane concluded, "a child who, in a fit of ignorance, had jumped into a vat of war."

Soon Crane apparently crossed the line from being a mere reporter to being a participant. Around midnight on June 11, Spanish soldiers stormed the American position. The American forces called for support from the gunboats in the bay below the camp. For this purpose, signalmen were needed, and Crane watched mesmerized as four marine wigwaggers sent messages. "Signaling in this way," as Crane explained in an article,

> is done by letting one lantern remain stationary—
> on top of the cracker-box, in this case—and moving
> the other over it to the left and right and so on in the
> regular gestures of the wig-wagging code. It is a very
> simple system of night communication, but one can
> see that it presents rare possibilities when used in
> front of an enemy who, a few hundred yards away, is
> overjoyed at sighting so definite a mark.

According to some reports (though not his own), Crane joined the wigwaggers, taking turns with them at their dangerous task.

After another three days, Crane was even more fully integrated into the war effort. The Spanish troops held a well about five miles from the American position, and it was, according to Crane, "the only water supply within about twelve miles of the Marine camp." Captain George Elliott had the assignment of taking the well and "destroying everything." He was short of officers, however, and, impressed with Crane's cool demeanor under fire, asked him to serve as his aide. (One notes the surprising intimacy, almost interchangeability, of the roles of soldiers and correspondents.) Crane accepted with alacrity, and found himself, in the four days of the fight at Cuzco—"really the tightest, best fight of the war"—carrying messages from Elliott to the other field commanders.

Strangely enough, the landscape of the battle—"a house, a well," and "the summit of a ridge," according to Crane—had been anticipated in one of his stories of 1895, "A Mystery of Heroism." In that Civil War story, a private bravely (and perhaps rashly) carries bottles of water under fire from a well to his fellow soldiers, only to have two officers squabble over the water and let it spill onto the ground. One English reporter actually remembered *Crane* performing this task: "Collecting about a dozen big bottles, he retired to the rear, filled them, and turned to climb the hill again—'his little person festooned with bottles,' as one who saw the incident described it afterwards. . . . This was only one of several occasions on which he showed his genuine pluck." But since this particular incident was only reported after Crane's death, it seems possible that the London *Daily Chronicle* reporter was remembering events through the lens of "A Mystery of Heroism."

At one point during the fight at Cuzco, the American gunships began firing mistakenly at an American position, and again a wigwagger was called for. Crane described the scene:

> And—mark you—a spruce young sergeant of marines, erect, his back to the showering bullets, solemnly and intently wig-wagging to the distant *Dolphin!*
>
> It was necessary that this man should stand at the very top of the ridge in order that his flag might appear in relief against the sky, and the Spaniards must have concentrated a fire of at least twenty rifles

upon him. His society was at that moment sought by none.

In the Cuzco affair and in later battles, Crane was startled by the extraordinary exposure of the American soldiers under fire. The men who captured his imagination most fully were those who were most exposed, whose business it was to be exposed, standing silhouetted against the sky and spelling out by means of flags or lanterns the positions of enemy troops.

Crane wrote of the wigwaggers again and again, and with each mention of them they became more central in his reporting, culminating in his great narrative—the finest piece of reporting, in the judgment of Richard Harding Davis, to emerge from the war—"Marines Signalling Under Fire at Guantanamo." With each description of these men, Crane's own self-identification with them becomes more emphatic. It was not mere coincidence that he had himself learned the language of wigwagging in Greece and apparently performed it in Cuba. Indeed, wigwagging provided one of his most vivid metaphors for his own sense of mission as a writer, giving a new specificity to the literary commonplace of the writer as beacon or torch bearer. (In this light, Crane's decision at Ravensbrook to lecture the Fabians on the subject of wigwagging becomes less incongruous.)

In "Marines Signaling Under Fire," Crane allowed himself to concentrate exclusively on the signalmen, and to see the battles at Camp McCalla and Cuzco from their point of view. What struck Crane most was the impassive expressions of these men, which stood in vivid contrast to the expressivity of their messages.

> I could lie near and watch the face of the signalman, illumed as it was by the yellow shine of lantern light, and the absence of excitement, fright, or any emo-

tion at all, on his countenance, was something to astonish all theories out of one's mind. The face was in every instance merely that of a man intent upon his business, the business of wig-wagging into the gulf of night where a light on the *Marblehead* was seen to move slowly.

Crane draws a contrast between the extraordinary *theatricality* of the scene and the *absorption* of the signalmen (to borrow two terms from the art historian Michael Fried). "These times on the hill resembled, in some days, those terrible scenes on the stage. . . . It was theatric beyond words. . . . Amid it all one could see from time to time the yellow light on the face of a preoccupied signalman."

Something like this relation of extreme experience and extreme absorption was Crane's ideal as a reporter. He noted again and again how the wigwaggers performed the "slow spelling of an important message" as they turned their backs to the battle. He was even more specific about the equation of wigwagging and writing:

> As I looked at Sergeant Quick wig-wagging there against the sky, I would not have given a tin tobacco-tag for his life. Escape for him seemed impossible. It seemed absurd to hope that he would not be hit; I only hoped that he would be hit just a little, little, in the arm, the shoulder, or the leg.
>
> I watched his face, and it was as grave and serene as that of a man writing in his own library.

Conspicuously calm, a cool messenger of feverish events, a trafficker in codes and signals—this description is as close as Crane ever came to specifying his own ideal of the writer. In the signalman sending messages to the ships offshore he found a perfect metaphor for how he had tried to live his life as a writer.

But another, contrasting figure had already begun to tug at Crane's imagination, and was to prove decisive for his conduct during his remaining six months in the Caribbean: the figure of the spy. At the very outset of the campaign, barely a week after his own arrival in Key West in late April, Crane had had the opportunity to interview Charles H. Thrall, whom he described in his "Pen Portrait of C. H. Thrall" as "a graduate of Yale . . . [who] has for years represented extensive American manufacturing interests in Cuba." Crane's portrait is laconic; the two men talk mainly about the mood of the inhabitants of Havana during the American blockade. It as though Crane means to preserve Thrall's cover, for Thrall—so appropriately named—was a spy. "We had been hearing a good deal about Thrall for a long time," Crane writes, with deliberate vagueness. "Everybody was aware of his immensely precarious situation. . . ." What caught Crane's sustained attention, however, were Thrall's eyes:

> Dressed in the universal linen or duck and with a straw hat on the back of his head, Thrall differs little from a certain good type of young American manhood. The striking thing about him now is his eyes. The expression of them will doubtless change as he breathes more of the peace of the American side, but at present they are peculiarly wide open, as if strained with watching. They stare at you and do not seem to think, and at the corners the lids are wrinkled as if from long pain. This is the impress of his hazardous situation still upon him.

Now Thrall, as it happens, had been recruited by Crane's friend and immediate boss at the *World*, Sylvester Scovel. Admiral William Sampson, the able commander of U.S. naval forces during the war, had asked Scovel if he knew of anyone who might be able to slip into Havana and ascertain the city's defenses. Scovel suggested Thrall, who had been in Cuba since 1891 as manager of the American-owned Havana Electric Company, and had recently fled to Key West. Then it was Scovel who used the rented tug of the *World* to drop Thrall off on Cuban soil and pick him up again.

Such complicity of reporters and soldiers may strike us as bizarre; in our time the roles often seem in opposition. But the U.S. apparatus for gathering intelligence during the 1890s was so primitive that the staff of the *World*, led by the knowledgeable Scovel, served, in effect, as a sort of proto-CIA. Scovel had been orchestrating undercover activities for the Cuban insurgents for several months before official U.S. involvement in the war. (When it became clear, in the last stages of the conflict, that the U.S. command had no intention of cooperating with the insurgents' plans for an autonomous Cuba, Scovel ran afoul of the authorities.) When Crane joined Scovel's staff, he joined a ring of spies. And when he interviewed Charles Thrall, that quiet man with the piercing eyes, he was speaking to a co-conspirator.

The skullduggery of Scovel and company did not cease with the landing of the Marines in early June. After the battles around Guantánamo Bay, where Crane had studied the conspicuous art of wigwagging, Scovel suddenly arrived with a new covert assignment, for which he recruited Crane. ("I fell into the hands of one of my closest friends," as Crane ruefully put it.) Scovel was working for Admiral Sampson again, who wanted to know the exact positions of the Spanish fleet in the harbor of Santiago. So Scovel and Crane with their Cuban guides landed the *World*'s tug thirteen miles west of Santiago and made the dangerous journey overland, past the Spanish sentries and over Mount St. Augustín, to a position above the harbor. "There upon the bosom of the green-fringed harbor," Scovel wrote, "lay Cervera's once-dreaded fleet." The information Scovel and Crane collected was decisive for the eventual U.S. victory at

Santiago, when the Spanish ships tried, with suicidal results, to run the blockade of the harbor.

Standing above Santiago, Crane and Scovel speculated
on what a good spot for a hospital the fine mountain air of
Mount St. Augustín would provide. "It was the kind of
country," Crane wrote in a dispatch, "in which commercial
physicians love to establish sanitariums." By the end of the
spying excursion, Crane was so ill that, as he put it, "I discovered that I was a dead man. The nervous force having
evaporated, I was a mere corpse." As usual, it's hard to say
precisely what fever Crane was suffering from—"my spinal
chord burned within me as if it were red hot wire." When he
had a relapse a few weeks later, it was first diagnosed as
yellow fever, then malaria.

In a grim rerun of the Greek campaign, Crane found
himself among the victims instead of the victors, too sick to
see the conflict to the end. He witnessed the confused battle
of San Juan Hill on July 1. Other reporters remembered
him roaming up and down the battle lines in a white rain-
coat, in full view of the Spanish snipers, as though he didn't
give a damn for his life. By July 4, Crane was so sick that
illness itself started to crowd out other subjects in his reportage, as he spent more and more time around doctors and
hospital tents. One of his most unnerving reports—compa-
rable in its apocalyptic power to some of Whitman's depic-
tions of the front in the Civil War—describes the interior of
a church that had been converted to a hospital. A man lay
on the altar table, which had been carried to the hallway so
the surgeons had enough light to operate.

> He was naked save for a breech-clout and so close,
> so clear was the ecclesiastic suggestion, that one's
> mind leaped to a phantasy that this thin, pale figure
> had just been torn down from a cross. The flash of
> the impression was like light, and for this instant it
> illumined all the dark recesses of one's remotest idea
> of sacrilege, ghastly and wanton. I bring this to you

251

merely as an effect, an effect of mental light and shade, if you like: something done in thought similar to that which the French impressionists do in colour: something meaningless and at the same time overwhelming, crushing, monstrous.

The power of the passage lies in the failed attempt to aestheticize the scene: the "mere effect" is overwhelmed by the "monstrous." On July 8, Crane boarded a hospital transport bound for Virginia flying the yellow flag of the "Cuban fever."

Crane's convalescence and his activities during the weeks that followed are vague, but it was apparently during this period that he made his way, perhaps for the second time, to the Adirondack retreat of Dr. Edward Trudeau, who treated TB patients at his well-known sanatorium near the Saranac lakes. Trudeau later assured Cora, who had somehow got wind of the visit, that Crane's case "was not serious." Presumably reassured, Crane boarded a tug towards the end of July in Pensacola, to follow the last—and, as it turned out, peaceful—phase of the war in Puerto Rico. A fellow reporter was shocked at Crane's condition, which he thought was much worse that it had been a month earlier: "Crane revealed the wreck of an athlete's frame—once square shoulders crowded forward by the concavity of a collapsed chest; great hollows where the once smooth pitching muscles had now wasted; legs like pipestems—he looked like a frayed white ribbon."

It is at this point—all battles over and peace taking hold—that the ambiguous figure of Charles H. Thrall intrudes again, as we enter one of the strangest and most mysterious phases of Stephen Crane's life. For Crane looked homeward only for a moment, cabling Cora from Key West on August 16; it was the last word she heard from him for three months. Crane was finished for the moment with white raincoats and wigwag flags. He'd been conspicuous, over-exposed almost, for three months of war. Now he felt like going underground—accomplishing the art of "vanishing," which he'd once described as his foremost trait. He made his way quietly to the Bahamas, and from there, disguised as a tobacco buyer, slipped illegally into Havana. The city was still under Spanish authority, pending the official transfer of power, which took place a month later. "I came into Havana without permission from anybody," Crane later wrote. "I was at a hotel [the Grand Hotel Pasaje] while the Government was firmly imprisoning nine correspondents on a steamer in the harbor. But no one molested me."

Havana was a grim place in the fall of 1898—unsure of its defeat or its "liberation," wary of its future in American rather than Spanish hands. Food was scarce, sanitation primitive. But for Crane it was all splendid—a return to that bohemian mood he'd known among his threadbare artist friends during the early 1890s, when he delighted in "experiments" with disguise and harmless deception. He wrote of his Havana companions the way he'd written of his friends in the Tenderloin:

> an unregenerate and abandoned collection of newspaper correspondents, cattle men, gamblers, speculators and drummers who have lived practically as they pleased, without care or restraint, going—most of them—wherever interest or whim led, with no regard for yellow fever or any other terror of the tropics.

So what was Crane up to? He was still under contract—to Hearst's *Journal* now, after a misunderstanding with the *World*—and filed desultory reports on conditions in Havana. He was in touch with his literary agent (though with no one else), requesting large sums of money. His apparent financial trouble has given rise to speculations about gambling debts or even blackmail. But the true motive for

Crane's Havana sojourn was probably both simpler and harder to define, and it was inseparable from Charles Thrall.

Around the first of September, Crane left the hotel and moved into the rooming house of Mary Horan, an Irish woman originally from New York City. Her house had served as Thrall's refuge during his spying missions the previous May. Crane was—it seems fair to say—retracing Thrall's footsteps: making his way illegally past the authorities, living undercover in Mary Horan's house, sitting in the chair where Thrall had sat, perhaps sleeping in the room where Thrall had slept. And in October, apparently, Thrall himself turned up, and the two men, like mirror images, sat down for a meal to celebrate the end of the war.

I say "apparently" because the evidence for this meeting is the story "This Majestic Lie"—a " 'personal anecdote' thing," Crane called it—which Crane wrote in Havana and sent to his agent in late October. The story does show conclusively just how closely Crane identified himself with Thrall, the American spy called "Johnnie" in "This Majestic Lie." In the story, Crane retraces Thrall's career as a spy, narrating the tale from the perspective of a bitter war correspondent. Crane contrasts the noise and chaos of Key West, before the invasion of Cuba, with the composed figure of Johnnie, the "little tan-faced refugee without much money":

> This happened and that happened and if the news arrived at Key West as a mouse, it was often enough cabled north as an elephant. The correspondents at Key West were perfectly capable of adjusting their perspective, but many of the editors in the United States were like deaf men at whom one has to roar. A few quiet words of information was not enough for them; one had to bawl into their ears a whirlwind tale of heroism, blood, death, victory or defeat—at any rate, a tragedy. . . . It is strange how men of

sense can go aslant at the bidding of other men of sense and combine to contribute to the general mess of exaggeration and bombast. But we did; and in the midst of the furor I remember the still figure of Johnnie.

In such passages Crane gives voice to his own self-disgust, his longing for a mode of writing less exaggerated and bombastic. "He was taciturn and competent," Crane concludes, "while we solved the war in a babble of tongues." And again, while Johnnie was "independent and sane . . . the rest of us were lulling the public with drugs." Just as Crane had compared the exposed wigwagger to a man writing calmly in his library, he thinks of the hooded, inconspicuous Johnnie as a new model for the kind of writer he'd like to be—competent, understated, disguised: "If Johnnie was to end his life and leave a little book about it no one cared—least of all Johnnie and the admiral. . . . On a dark night they heaved him into a small boat and rowed him to the beach."

In Crane's account, Johnnie the American spy is a character out of Conrad. He risks his life—"his fancy risk"—in order to inform the U.S. admiral about the defenses of Havana. But Havana, it turns out, is left out of the U.S. plans. It's the very futility of Johnnie's—and by extension Thrall's—endeavors that draws Crane's admiration, the willingness to risk all for nothing:

> One cannot think of the terms in which to describe a futility so vast, so colossal. He had builded a little boat, and the sea had receded and left him and his boat a thousand miles inland on the top of a mountain. The war-fate had left Havana out of its plan and thus isolated Johnnie and his several pounds of useful information. The war-fate left Havana to become the somewhat indignant victim of a peaceful occupation at the close of the conflict, and Johnnie's data was worth as much as a carpenter's

255

lien on the North Pole. He had suffered and labored for about as complete a bit of absolute nothing as one could invent.

But as Crane tells the story of Johnnie—the spy drifting among the cafés and bars of Havana, being cheated of his money by a restaurateur, being shot at, and catching "the fever"—one has the distinct impression that he's talking about himself, and that the futility is his own. The peculiar charge of living under cover seems as much Crane's as Johnnie's, the desire "to be splendidly imprudent . . . to make the situation gasp and thrill and tremble."

This identification culminates in the ending of "This Majestic Lie," when the doubles—the reporter and the spy—meet at a café in (Crane is precise) October 1898 to discuss "the subject of [Johnnie's] supreme failure." Johnnie orders extravagantly—the most expensive wine, the most exotic dishes. The story ends with the two of them, at Johnnie's urging, slipping out of the café—the same that had cheated Johnnie in May—without paying the enormous tab. And with that bit of private revenge, Johnnie remarks, "as far as I am concerned . . . the war is now over."

It was almost over for Crane as well. His little love affair with espionage, as he collected information useful only to himself, could hardly last much longer. It was his last fling as an infiltrator, a con man, a secret agent. No matter that he owed allegiance to no one, for hadn't Johnnie's (and Thrall's) information been as useless as his own? And then this strange dream was abruptly interrupted—for Cora had contacted, among others, such influential men as John Hay in order to find Crane and bring him home; and Conrad had sent an urgent, and rather indignant, letter. So Crane reluctantly boarded a ship to return to his other island home and—as it must have been clear to him by now—to his own death.

The Divided Ghost

CRANE'S LAST YEAR makes a gothic tale, scripted in part by Crane himself. After leaving Havana on December 24, 1898, he dawdled in New York for a few days, as though to postpone the inevitable end, then boarded a ship on New Year's Eve, bound for England. Cora greeted the *Manitou* at Gravesend, the mournful-sounding town where the Thames widens into the sea. The Cranes had been nine months apart, nine months almost incommunicado. But in the meantime Cora had acquired a new cage for her flown bird.

A week after his arrival in England, on January 17, Cora took Stephen to see Brede Manor, the ancient demesne in Sussex that friends had offered the Cranes at modest rent. The enormous house, with its high stone walls and Gothic windows, combined the features of a fortress and a church, as though to unite once more the divergent strains of Crane's ancestry. The oldest part of the house was medieval, with wings added during the Elizabethan period to give the house the form of an *E,* in honor of the queen's name. The massive oak doors of the house were for defense, and a chapel had been added to its southern end.

The house had less visible attributes as well. It was haunted, as Crane explained in his historical romance *The O'Ruddy*, part of which takes place at Brede. The ghost was that of Sir Goddard Oxenbridge, who could often be heard "tramping through the rooms in two sections." Crane explained the provenance of this divided ghost: "Bullets wouldn't harm him, nor steel cut him, so they sawed him in two with a wooden saw. . . . You hear him groaning at the bridge every night, and sometimes he walks through the house himself in two halves."

Despite its distinguished history, Brede Manor was, for Crane, less mansion than mausoleum. He took as his study a small room above the porch in the middle of the *E*; it had red walls and a single window overlooking the garden. It was here that Crane immured himself for long hours, a glass of diluted whiskey or flat beer at his side, writing incessantly. "We are living very quietly devoting all our attention to my work," he wrote his brother William in early March. What he worked on was mainly the series of stories set in an imaginary American town called Whilomville, loosely based on his memories of Port Jervis. Crane wrote these rather sentimental stories for money, counting the words as he went along. They concerned ordinary occurrences in the lives of children: a boy being teased for his new red mittens, another who goes out hunting for lynxes and scares a cow instead. Such idylls of small-town life sold easily to *Harper's* and to other family magazines.

Crane had first invented the locale of Whilomville (literally, "the town of once upon a time") for other purposes: to create a quiet backdrop for horrific events. In his novella *The Monster*, written before his departure for Cuba, he created a vivid account of social ostracism and hypocrisy. The story concerns a black servant who is literally defaced while saving his boss's child from a spectacular house fire. After the fire, the hideously disfigured Henry Johnson is nursed

258

23. *Brede Place, 1944 (photograph by Ames Williams).*

back to health by Dr. Trescott, his employer, who in turn loses his other patients because of his association with Johnson. The citizens of Whilomville regard Johnson's recovery as somehow contrary to nature, as though Trescott has brought a monster back, Frankenstein-like, from the dead. "He will be your creation," a neighbor warns the doctor.

In *The Monster*, Crane achieved an intensity missing from the later stories set in Whilomville. Part of the reason, surely, was the private theme of the tale, for *The Monster* (though critics, who have given a great deal of attention to the tale's racial themes, are strangely silent on this point) is about a doctor and a patient, and how illness alienates its victims, a theme increasingly close to Crane's obsessions.

Brede Place was a capacious house, if not a particularly comfortable one. It lacked plumbing, and had no sources of heat and light—no gas, no electricity—other than fireplaces and candles. But the supply of cold, dark rooms was seemingly endless, and through the spring and summer of 1899 guests came to fill them. From Port Jervis came William Crane's "difficult" daughter Helen, escorted by Crane's taciturn brother Wilbur, who, his duty done, quickly recrossed the Atlantic. Helen would benefit, William thought, from the civilizing influence of his younger brother's ménage—he assumed that Stephen and Cora were married—and from a year at a private boarding school in Lausanne. From Detroit came young Karl Harriman, a newspaperman who found Brede so welcoming that he stayed through the summer. And from the neighboring countryside came such old friends as the Conrads, H. G. Wells, and Ford Madox Ford. Henry James, the tenant of Lamb House at Rye, visited more than once.

The Cranes entertained lavishly, running up bills at the local butcher and grocer. Photographs of a garden party in late August show Crane looking lean and hungry in a boater and Henry James, appearing slightly embarrassed, nibbling on one of Cora's doughnuts. Much has been said

24. *Crane and a guest—she's usually identified as Cora, but this seems doubtful—at Brede Place.*

of James's "take" on the Cranes, and a dozen dubious anecdotes have bloomed in the blank of documentation. Clearly he liked them well enough to enjoy their company.

Crane's health, as must have been clear to James and other visitors, was bad again. He was hardly in a state to maintain the lavish lifestyle that Cora seemed to expect. He wrote William soon after his return to England, asking for a loan: "we are beastly short on ready money owing to my long illness." Health from now on meant productivity. In late August, when things again looked bad, Cora took Stephen to the Continent for a rest; she feared he might "break down," and be unable to continue writing at his extraordinary rate. By the fall Crane was already asking friends about various health resorts. In mid-September he wrote to the critic George Wyndham for information about Germany:

> What do you know about the Black Forest there? I mean as a health resort? The truth is that Cuba libre just about liberated me from this base blue world. The clockwork is juggling badly.

He was suffering from an abscess in the bowel that made him feel "like hell," and prevented him from riding.

Crane's best work from Brede is a literature of confinement and suffocation, registering his own diminishing hopes. In contrast to the word-counting inflation of the Whilomville idylls, Crane's most intense work of the period is written with extreme concision. He was increasingly divided within himself. While the Whilomville stories looked nostalgically backwards, the better stories probed the ominous future. One can trace in a sequence of eerie works Crane's predictions—his scouting forays, so to speak—regarding his own foreshortened future.

Sometime in the spring, Crane wrote his macabre little

fable of realism called "Manacled." One of his shortest stories, it records the fate of an actor who plays the role of the
hero in a melodrama at a popular theater. The decor of the
theater is remarkably lifelike: "In the first act," the story begins, "there had been a farm scene, wherein real horses had
drunk real water." In one scene the villain puts the hero in
chains, and insults his lover. It is during a performance of
this scene that the actors are suddenly interrupted by cries
of "Fire!" The theater is in flames; the actors flee the stage,
except the chained actor, who is wearing, as it happens,
"real handcuffs on his wrists and real anklets on his ankles."

Crane contrasts the speeding fire engines and the panic
of the crowd—dying on the stairs still clutching their play-
bills—on the one hand with the excruciatingly slow progress of the manacled actor, who "could only take steps four
inches long." Crane pauses, as in *The Monster,* to note the
spectacular play of the fire—"Beautiful flames flashed
above him, some were crimson, some were orange, and here
and there were tongues of purple, blue, green"—and to
note the actor's face as it "turned chalk-color beneath his
skin of manly bronze for the stage."

Crane pursues this nightmare vision as relentlessly as
Poe in the "The Pit and the Pendulum": up these stairs,
down those—"after all, he could fall down stairs." But to no
avail. The closing paragraphs suggest, unmistakably, the
fate of a man dying from tuberculosis; fire and smoke become metaphors for fever and botched lungs. For it is death
by suffocation that Crane imagines, his hero "windless" at
the bottom of the stairs, "with his mouth close to the floor
trying to breathe." In the concluding lines of the story,
Crane projects the "palsy" onto the theater itself:

> The thunder of the fire-lions made the theatre
> have a palsy.
> Suddenly the hero beat his handcuffs against the
> wall, cursing them in a loud wail. Blood started from
> under his fingernails. Soon he began to bite the hot

steel, and blood fell from his blistered mouth. He raved like a wolf.

Peace came to him again. There were charming effects amid the flames. . . . He felt very cool, delightfully cool. . . . "They've left me chained up."

The manacled hands (as Michael Fried has pointed out) have the added significance of the end of a writer's life, his handwriting abruptly curtailed.

But the story has a further theme, and one peculiarly appropriate for the shape of Crane's career. For it is a fable about the blurring of art and life. As the hero lies contemplating the flames, "A curiously calm thought came into his head. 'What a fool I was not to foresee this! I shall have Rogers furnish manacles of papier-mâché tomorrow.'" What Crane had foreseen all his life was, of course, the merging of his art with the shape of his own life, as he tried to live according to his own fictive plots. In a sense, he'd forged the manacles himself, and made a life that in peculiar ways he *could* foresee.

Throughout the spring and summer and part of the fall of 1899, Crane carried in his head another brief and somber story, a sort of sequel to "Manacled." Even before his return from Cuba, Crane was apparently mulling over a story about the burial of a soldier, for Conrad welcomed him back with a letter on January 13: "What have you got in *your* head? You must be full of stuff. I suppose the 'Dead Man' story will have to wait till you unload your new experience"—Crane's war reportage, that is. The story did wait, for nine months or so, before emerging as "The Upturned Face" in early November. It is one of Crane's masterpieces of concentration.

The story is based, according to Stallman, on the burial of Surgeon Gibbs, the doctor whose death Crane had witnessed in Cuba. If that identification is accurate, then "The

Upturned Face" has a private link to *The Monster*, as another narrative of doctors. Illness and health extend even to
the names of Crane's characters during these final months.
Thus, the name of the main (living) character in "The Upturned Face" is Timothy *Lean*, a curious contrast to the
name of the eponymous hero of *The O'Ruddy*, the potboiler
that Crane was hurriedly writing at the same time.

"The Upturned Face," just three pages long, is about
a burial performed under extreme circumstances. The correct performance of the ritual is repeatedly interrupted. One
thinks of Crane's Greek war reportage, which turned on
similar interruptions of ritualized gestures. In this case the
distractions come from three distinct sources: the battle
around the gravediggers, their own faulty memories, and
the mesmerizing presence of the corpse. The story begins
with a staccato exchange, and a shorthand setting of the
scene:

> "What will we do now?" said the adjutant,
> troubled and excited.
> "Bury him," said Timothy Lean.
> The two officers looked down close to their toes
> where lay the body of their comrade. The face was
> chalk-blue; gleaming eyes stared at the sky. Over the
> two upright figures was a windy sound of bullets,
> and on the top of the hill, Lean's prostrate company
> of Spitzbergen infantry was firing measured volleys.
> "Don't you think it would be better—" began the
> adjutant. "We might leave him until to-morrow."
> "No," said Lean, "I can't hold that post an hour
> longer. I've got to fall back, and we've got to bury old
> Bill."
> "Of course," said the adjutant at once. "Your
> men got intrenching tools?"
> Lean shouted back to his little firing line, and
> two men came slowly, one with a pick, one with a
> shovel.

The scene is worked up visually by sharp contrasts between vertical and horizontal: the "upright" officers and the two privates assigned to dig the grave; the "prostrate" infantry and the dead man. Each gesture of the burial is hesitant, halting, as though contact between the officers and the corpse might be somehow contaminating, might blur the distinction between the living and the dead. (One notes in passing the "chalk-blue" face of the corpse; a similar adjective—"chalk-color"—described the dying actor in "Manacled.") The first crisis occurs when the grave is done—"It was not a masterpiece—poor little shallow thing"—and the officers reluctantly place the body in the grave. "Both were particular that their fingers would not feel the corpse." Then they try to recite an appropriate service, and find they don't quite know the text.

> *"O, Father, our friend has sunk in the deep waters of death, but his spirit has leaped toward Thee as the bubble arises from the lips of the drowning. Perceive, we beseech, O, Father, the little flying bubble and—"*

Lean, although husky and ashamed, had suffered no hesitation up to this point, but he stopped with a hopeless feeling and looked at the corpse.

The adjutant moved uneasily. *"And from Thy superb heights—"* he began, and then he, too, came to an end.

"And from Thy superb heights," said Lean.

The adjutant suddenly remembered a phrase in the back part of the Spitzbergen burial service, and he exploited it with the triumphant manner of a man who has recalled everything and can go on.

"O, God, have mercy—"

"O, God, have mercy—" said Lean.

"'Mercy,'" repeated the adjutant in a quick failure.

"'Mercy,'" said Lean. And then he was moved by some violence of feeling, for he turned suddenly

266

upon his two men and tigerishly said: "Throw the dirt in."

Lean's order to fill the grave, putting an end to this Beckett-like dialogue, precipitates the next crisis. The privates cannot bring themselves to throw dirt on the dead man's face. To Lean's relief the first shovelful falls on the man's feet. ("He had felt that perhaps the private might empty the shovel on—on the face.") But then, as though the contamination has occurred anyway one of the privates is shot in the arm, and the two officers are left to complete the ritual. The story turns on Lean's own hesitations, his inability, at critical moments, to "go on." The mood of suffocation is palpable, strengthened by the fear—the gothic fear—of being buried alive.

Crane knew the story was a good one. He wrote his agent on November 4, 1899:

> I am enclosing a double extra special good thing. . . .
> I will not disguise from you that I am wonderfully
> keen on this small bit of 1500 words. It is so good—
> for me—that I would almost sacrifice it to the best
> magazine in England rather than see it appear in
> the best paying magazine.

The word *sacrifice,* here so lightly invoked, soon took on a more ominous meaning in Crane's life.

In Poe's great story "The Masque of the Red Death," a young man rich in friends and courage attempts to elude the horrible illness that threatens his life. He decides to throw a grand party in his magnificent house, and barricade his fears behind its massive walls. The party is to be an elaborate masquerade, filtering among the seven strangely arrayed rooms of the building. Each room and the windows thereof are a different color, but the windows of the last room are scarlet—the color of blood. The invited guests disport themselves according to the young man's carnivalesque directions. But as so often happens at such affairs, an uninvited guest intrudes, despite all precautions, at the stroke of midnight. The figure is tall and gaunt, and dressed in the blood-spattered cerements of the grave. The young man confronts the uninvited guest, dagger in hand. But it is he himself who falls dead upon the carpet, and the other guests find that the grave clothes are empty.

Such is the gothic plot that Stephen Crane proceeded to orchestrate at Brede Place, without attribution to Poe. Ostensibly held to bid farewell to one of the guests at Brede, the great party the Cranes threw at the end of December, to greet the new year and the new century, was really Crane's own valediction, his final curtain call.

"I remember that party as an extraordinary lark," H. G. Wells recalled, "but shot, at the close, with red intimations of a coming tragedy." The invitations were lighthearted. Crane asked each of his guests to contribute a word or a line to the farcical play he had drafted, called "The Ghost." The idea was to bill the play as the collaboration of an imposing list of authors, and so it was, with James, Conrad, Wells, and others participating ("This is a jolly cold world" was Conrad's appropriate contribution). The play itself was silly enough, judging from the text and testimony that have survived. It concerned the divided ghost of Goddard Oxenbridge, who appeared at the stroke of midnight to a group of skeptical tourists. As the local newspaper described it:

> At midnight the company was paralysed by the sudden appearance of the ghost from apparently nowhere, and he commences his weird history, but reminds himself that he can relate it better with soft musical accompaniment, and this is accorded him. He states that in the year 1531 he was sitting in that very same room, consuming six little Brede boys, and washed down his meal with an appropriate quantity of beer. This overcame him, and whilst in a

Stephen Crane in his study, room over the Porch Brede Place. Sep. 1899.

25. *Crane in his red-walled study, above the porch at Brede Place, September 1899. The photograph of Cora in Athens is propped on the desk.*

Past photo taken of Stephen Crane with his dog "Spongie" —

26. *The last photograph of Stephen Crane, Brede Place, 1900. Cora's inscription.*

stupor four courageous Brede men enter, and saw him asunder. . . .

Hence the ghost's division.

The house party began on December 27, and the play was performed the next day, as a sort of Christmas tribute to the townspeople of Brede. On the twenty-ninth a ball was held in the great hall—it ran the length of the house—in Brede Place. The goings-on included dancing till two or three in the morning; breakfast on beer, bacon, and eggs; and continual games of poker.

Soon after the musicians had packed up their instruments, Stephen Crane had a severe hemorrhage of the lungs. The uninvited guest had made his dramatic appearance and claimed his victim. Wells bicycled the seven cold miles to Rye to fetch a doctor, the first of a series of "specialists" whose conflicting diagnoses kept Cora guessing, though Stephen knew the truth. He held out for another four months, dividing his time between his bed and his desk in the red room above the porch. When the worst hemorrhages came, in early April, Cora had to be called home from Paris; in a fit of optimism she'd gone there on a shopping spree. On April 21 Crane composed his will, leaving everything to Cora.

Thus, the divided ghost that haunted Brede Place turned out to be Crane's own. He had split himself in his writing—the idylls of Whilomville yielding to the darker intimations of his own death. He had split himself in his imaginative life—scripting the stories he then tried to live. And he had divided himself in his valiant and increasingly violent battle to keep writing while his body failed. As he headed for the cliffs of Dover, Crane was still hard at work, sketching the final chapters of his last novel. The only immortality he could wish for now was conferred by words.

NOTES

"Brevity," Crane once told Cora, "is an element that enters importantly into all pleasures of life." To avoid cluttering my text with numerals and distracting injunctions to read other things, I have kept scholarly apparatus minimal. Crane's writings are short and easy to track down. Unless another source is given, all quotations from Crane's works are drawn from the readily available Library of America edition: *Stephen Crane: Prose and Poetry*, edited by J. C. Levenson (New York: 1984). Other materials by Crane are taken from *The Works of Stephen Crane*, edited by Fredson Bowers (Charlottesville: The University Press of Virginia, 1969–76), ten volumes, referred to in the Notes, with volume and page number, as "V." Quotations from Crane's letters and correspondents come from *The Correspondence of Stephen Crane*, edited by Stanley Wertheim and Paul Sorrentino (New York: Columbia University Press, 1988), two volumes.

INTRODUCTION *(numbers refer to pages in the text)*

3 Colonel John L. Burleigh, quoted in R. W. Stallman, *Stephen Crane: A Biography*, rev. ed. (New York: Braziller, 1973), p. 181.

4 H. G. Wells, "Stephen Crane from an English Standpoint," in Stephen Crane, *The Red Badge of Courage*, ed. Sculley Bradley, Richmond Croom Beatty, E. Hudson Long (New York: Norton, 1962), p. 205.

4 J. C. Levenson, "Stephen Crane," in *Major Authors of America*, ed. Perry Miller (New York: Harcourt, 1962), vol. 2, p. 385.

5 See Larzer Ziff, "Outstripping the Event: Stephen Crane," in Ziff, *The American 1890's* (New York: Viking, 1966). Of Crane's journalism, Ziff remarks: "Stephen Crane's expectations had a way of outstripping the event . . . [he] developed a set of responses that anticipated the reality" (p. 186).

6 See Miles Orvell, *The Real Thing* (Chapel Hill: University of North Carolina Press, 1989). Orvell argues that Crane's characters take their cues from popular culture, trying to fit their lives to its patterns.

—John Berryman, *Stephen Crane* (New York: Sloane, 1950), p. 97.

8 Thomas Beer, *Stephen Crane* (New York: Alfred A. Knopf, 1923).

—See Stanley Wertheim and Paul Sorrentino, "Thomas Beer: The Clay Feet of Stephen Crane Biography," in *American Literary Realism* 22, no. 3 (1990): pp. 2–16; and John Clendenning, "Thomas Beer's *Stephen Crane*: The Eye of His Imagination," in *Prose Studies* 14, no. 1, (May 1991), pp. 68–80.

9 See Alan Trachtenberg, *The Incorporation of America: Culture and Society in the Gilded Age* (New York: Hill and Wang, 1982), pp. 109, 141, for the generation of the 1890s.

PROLOGUE: JESSIE'S DREAM

13 Jessie Conrad, *Joseph Conrad and His Circle* (New York: Dutton, 1935), p. 74.
14 Joseph Conrad quoted in Stallman, *Stephen Crane*, p. 511.
15 Wells, "Stephen Crane from an English Standpoint," p. 202.
—Conrad, "Stephen Crane: "A Note Without Dates," in *Notes on Life and Letters* (London: J. M. Dent and Sons, 1949), p. 52.
16 Wells quoted in Stallman, *Stephen Crane*, p. 507.
—Barr quoted in Stallman, *Stephen Crane*, p. 512.
18 Jessie Conrad, *Joseph Conrad and His Circle*, p. 75.
19 *Letters of Wallace Stevens*, ed. Holly Stevens (New York: Alfred A. Knopf, 1966), p. 411.

ONE: HOLINESS

21 See, for example, Stallman, *Stephen Crane*, p. 14: "Revolt against the fathers is the common lot of sons, but in Stephen Crane's life it is exemplified more clearly than in any other American writer." Stallman neglects to cite the remarkably similar wording of Stanley Wertheim in his article "Stephen Crane and the Wrath of Jehova," *Literary Review* 7 (1964), p. 501: "The theme of revolt against the father is exemplified more clearly in the life and work of Stephen Crane than in any other American writer."
23 The chronicler was George Hughes, *Days of Power in the Forest Temple* (Boston: John Bent, 1873), p. 37.
25 Cartwright, quoted in Ann Douglas, *The Feminization of American Culture* (New York: Avon, 1977), p. 41. For information on the history of Methodism in the United States, I have relied on Douglas and on Sydney E. Ahlstrom, *A Religious History of the American People* (New Haven: Yale University Press, 1972).
—Harold Frederic, *The Damnation of Theron Ware* (New York: Penguin Books, 1986), p. 3.
26 Invitations and programs for the Peck reunions can be found in the George Peck Papers, Syracuse University Library.
—J. T. Crane, "An Essay on Dancing" (New York: Lane and Scott, 1849), p. 13, quoted in Melvin H. Schoberlin, "Flagon of Despair: Stephen Crane" (unpublished manuscript, Schoberlin Collection, Syracuse University Library), 1–5.
27 Mary Peck, undated letter, George Peck Papers, Syracuse University Library.

—The quoted words on J. T. Crane's style are attributed to the Newark *Journal* and the Boston *Nation*, respectively, and appear in advertisements bound into Crane's *Holiness the Birthright of All God's Children* (New York: Nelson and Phillips, 1874).

28 J. T. Crane, quoted in *Dictionary of American Biography*, s.v. "Crane, Jonathan Townley."

—The quotes are from Hughes, *Days of Power*, pp. 10, 20.

30 A copy of the program for the golden-anniversary celebration is in the George Peck Papers, Syracuse University Library.

—Rev. Anthony Atwood, *The Abiding Comforter* (Philadelphia: A. Wallace, 1874), pp. 40, 70. I am indebted to Melvin Schoberlin for this reference. Schoberlin was aware that Crane's Holiness book was controversial. Schoberlin writes in his "Flagon of Despair": "During 1875 Jonathan Crane was the focal point of unceasing conflict; he was attacked and defended, but he took no part in the battle that threatened to divide the Church" (II–9). Schoberlin suspected a link between the controversy and Crane's professional demotion: "Jonathan Crane was informed that his reappointment [as presiding elder] was impossible. At the Conference of 1876 he was returned to the list of active itinerants and assigned to the First Methodist (old Cross Street) church in Paterson" (II–10). But Schoberlin seems to have been unaware of the precise nature of the Holiness controversy, or of its extent.

31 *Methodist Quarterly Review* (October 1874): pp. 663, 664, 677. The editor's name was D. D. Whedon.

—M. Helen Crane, quoted in Thomas Gullason, ed., *Stephen Crane's Career: Perspectives and Evaluations* (New York: New York University Press, 1972), p. 34.

32 John Leland Peters, *Christian Perfection and American Methodism* (Nashville: Abingdon Press, 1956), p. 174. "Crane's book was written . . . in the midst of controversy. And he frequently says more than he seems to mean. He is in specific protest against what he feels is a disparagement of regeneration which, he holds, brings one into the complete favor of God. Entire sanctification is not, therefore and strictly speaking, a requisite for a barely safe hereafter but a necessity for an abundantly satisfactory here and now" (p. 171).

34 The Newark neighbors are quoted in Stallman, *Stephen Crane*, p. 3.

—Beer, *Stephen Crane*, p. 37.

35 Wilbur Peck, George Peck Papers, Syracuse University Library.

—Port Jervis *Evening Gazette*, May 21, 1878; May 28, 1878; June 13, 1878. Citations from Schoberlin Collection, Syracuse University Library.

36 On Willard, see Barbara L. Epstein, *The Politics of Domesticity: Women, Evangelism, and Temperance in Nineteenth-Century America* (Middletown, Conn.: Wesleyan University Press, 1981), p. 121.

—M. Helen Crane in Asbury Park *Shore News*, July 12, 1889, Schoberlin Collection.

37 Asbury Park *Journal*, in Schoberlin Collection.

—*New Jersey Tribune*, in Schoberlin Collection.

TWO: ACQUIRING A LANGUAGE

40 See Paul Sorrentino, "Newly Discovered Writings of Mary Helen Peck Crane and Agnes Elizabeth Crane," in *Syracuse University Library Associates Courier*, 21 (Spring 1986): p. 127.

42 Edmund Crane, in the Thomas Beer Papers, Yale University Library.
—Beer, *Stephen Crane*, p. 48.

43 Sorrentino, "Newly Discovered Writings," p. 105: "Agnes essentially raised him."

45 Lillian Gilkes, *Cora Crane: A Biography of Mrs. Stephen Crane* (Bloomington: Indiana University Press, 1960), p. 64.
—Edmund Crane, in Thomas Beer Papers, Yale University Library.
—On the history of Methodism in America see Ahlstrom, *A Religious History of the American People*, p. 433.

49 Ernest Smith, quoted in Michael Robertson, "Stephen, a Boy of Lafayette," in *Lafayette Magazine* (Lafayette College, October 1990), pp. 35–36.

52 On Crane writing his name, see Berryman, *Stephen Crane*, p. 73.

THREE: MEAN STREETS

59 Jacob Riis, *How the Other Half Lives* (New York: Dover, 1971), pp. 27–28.

63 Frank Noxon, "The Real Stephen Crane," in Stephen Crane, *Maggie: A Girl of the Streets* (critical edition), ed. Thomas A. Gullason (New York: Norton, 1979), p. 123.
—Willis Fletcher Johnson, "The Launching of Stephen Crane," in Stephen Crane, *Maggie*, ed. Gullason, p. 124.

64 Frank Norris, "Stephen Crane's Stories of Life in the Slums," in Stephen Crane, *Maggie*, ed. Gullason, p. 151.

73 Edith Crane to Thomas Beer, 1922, in Schoberlin Collection, Syracuse University Library.

78 See Stallman, *Stephen Crane*, p. 55, on the Junior Mechanics.
—Asbury Park *Journal*, quoted in Stallman, *Stephen Crane*, p. 55.

FOUR: OMINOUS BABIES

81 Beer, *Stephen Crane*, p. 139.

82 See Conrad, "Introduction" to Beer, *Stephen Crane*, p. 20; and Corwin K. Linson, *My Stephen Crane* (Syracuse: Syracuse University Press, 1958), p. 73.
—Riis, *How the Other Half Lives*, p. 145.

—G. Stanley Hall, "The Contents of Children's Minds" in Hall, *Aspects of Child Life and Education* (Boston: Ginn, 1907), p. 26. In *The Ferment of Realism* (New York: Free Press, 1965), p. 152n, Warner Berthoff links the child-centered works of Crane, Riis, and Hall.

89 Berryman, *Stephen Crane*, p. 70.

92 D. W. Winnicott, "Transitional Objects and Transitional Phenomena" (1953), revised and included in *Playing and Reality* (London: Tavistock, 1971), pp. 3–4.

94 Colvert, *Stephen Crane* (New York: Harcourt Brace Jovanovich, 1984), p. 54; Stallman, *Stephen Crane*, p. 101; Berryman, *Stephen Crane*, p. 69.

95 Winnicott, "Transitional Objects," p. 5.

—Beer, *Stephen Crane*, p. 36.

96 On Crane's need for something to fondle, see Beer, *Stephen Crane*, 106. See also Linson, *My Stephen Crane*, pp. 2–3: "[Crane] smoked cigarettes, or mostly held them in his fingers until they went out. Those nervous fingers were yellowed with holding dead cigarettes."

98 Beer, *Stephen Crane*, p. 49.

—Paul Sorrentino, "Newly Discovered Writings," p. 116n.

100 Sigmund Freud, "Analysis of a Phobia in a Five-Year-Old Boy" (1909), in Freud, *The Sexual Enlightenment of Children* (New York: Collier, 1963), pp. 47–183.

—Linson, *My Stephen Crane*, p. 40.

FIVE: THE PRIVATE WAR

103 See Conrad, "Recollections of Crane and His War Book," in *The Red Badge of Courage*, ed. Bradley, Beatty, Long, p. 212.

104 On the *Century* series, see Linson, *My Stephen Crane*, p. 37; on the city as war, see Linson, *My Stephen Crane*, p. 37.

107 See especially Henry Binder, "The Red Badge of Courage Nobody Knows," in Stephen Crane, *The Red Badge of Courage*, ed. Henry Binder (New York: Norton, 1982); the manuscript passage quoted is on p. 121 of Binder's edition.

108 Daniel Aaron, *The Unwritten War: American Writers and the Civil War* (New York: Oxford University Press, 1973), p. 215.

112 On doubt and verification by wounding, see Elaine Scarry, *The Body in Pain* (New York: Oxford University Press, 1985), especially the section titled "Scenes of Wounding and the Problem of Doubt," pp. 198–221.

113 For death as the violation of privacy see Ralph Ellison, "Stephen Crane and the Mainstream of American Fiction," in *Shadow and Act* (New York: Random House, 1966), pp. 74–88.

117 J. Glenn Gray, *The Warriors: Reflections on Men in Battle* (New York: Harper and Row, 1959; Perennial Library edition, 1973), pp. 127–28.

—For scenes of men bathing in war writings, see Paul Fussell, *The Great*

War and Modern Memory (New York: Oxford University Press, 1975), especially the section titled "Soldiers Bathing," pp. 299–309.

119 James Merrill, "The Country of a Thousand Years of Peace," in Merrill, *From the First Nine: Poems 1946–1976* (New York: Atheneum, 1982), p. 39. In Merrill's poem, the country is literally Switzerland but metaphorically death. The poem is oddly appropriate for Crane's own final days: "Here they all come to die, / Fluent therein as in a fourth tongue. / But for a young man not yet of their race / It was a madness you should lie. . . ."

120 Willa Cather, *The World and the Parish: Articles and Reviews, 1893–1902*, ed. William M. Curtin, 2 vols. (Lincoln: University of Nebraska, 1970), pp. 772, 774, 778.

SIX: LINES

124 For "the big blank," see Frank Lentricchia, "On the Ideologies of Poetic Modernism, 1890–1913," in Sacvan Bercovitch, ed., *Reconstructing American Literary History* (Cambridge: Harvard University Press, 1986), p. 221. Lentricchia's argument is that American imaginative vitality shifted in the 1890s from poetry to philosophy.

—Eliot quoted in Lentricchia, "Poetic Modernism," p. 222. The Robinson poem cited is the early sonnet "Oh for a poet—for a beacon bright."

125 On Crane's poetry and its relation to Methodism, see especially Daniel G. Hoffman, *The Poetry of Stephen Crane* (New York: Columbia University Press, 1956). This line of thought is continued in John Blair's "The Posture of a Bohemian in the Poetry of Stephen Crane," *American Literature*, 61 (1989), which is primarily concerned with " Crane's religious philosophy" (p. 215).

—Gordon quoted in Wertheim and Sorrentino, ed., *The Correspondence of Stephen Crane*, page 89n.

126 Carlin Kindilien, *American Poetry in the Eighteen Nineties* (Providence: Brown University Press, 1956), p. 155.

127 All texts in this chapter are from J. C. Levenson's Library of America edition of Crane's works, though I have restored capitalization to poems from *The Black Riders*. In his own influential edition of Crane's poems, *The Poems of Stephen Crane* (New York: Cooper Square, 1971), Joseph Katz explains vaguely, "It has been considered necessary to provide a text in both upper- and lower-case letters" (p. lxv). Such a practice leads to unnecessary difficulties. For example, since the manuscripts of only five of the poems survive, editors must guess at which words should be capitalized and which not. For example, Katz capitalizes *God* "only when a monotheistic system is operable [*sic*] within a poem."

128 For critics' complaints, see *Stephen Crane: The Critical Heritage*, ed. Richard M. Weatherford (London: Routledge & Kegan Paul, 1973), p. 66.

—The uninspired section of Sandburg's poem subtitled "STEVIE CRANE" runs as follows:

War is kind and we never knew the kindness of war till you came;
Nor the black riders and clashes of spear and shield out of the
sea,
Nor the mumblings and shots that rise from dreams on call.

129 Roy Harvey Pearce, *The Continuity of American Poetry* (Princeton: Princeton University Press, 1961), p. 255. The exact quote is "Crane and Santayana did not yet [at the turn of the century] count for much as poets—nor, I think, should they now."
—Quoted in Hamlin Garland, *Roadside Meetings* (New York: Macmillan, 1930), p. 200.
—See Garland, "Stephen Crane as I Knew Him," *Yale Review* (Apr. 1914; reprinted vol. 75, Autumn 1985), pp. 8–9, and Garland, *Roadside Meetings*, p. 194. The best account of Crane's friendship with Garland is in Donald Pizer, "The Garland-Crane Relationship," *Huntington Library Quarterly* (Nov. 1960), pp. 75–82. For more information on Garland's interest in psychical research, see Katz, ed., *The Poems of Stephen Crane*, p. xxiii.
131 John D. Barry, "A Note on Stephen Crane," *Bookman* 13 (Apr. 1901), reprinted in Weatherford, ed., *Critical Heritage*, p. 81.
—Higginson, from an unsigned review in the *Nation* (Oct. 24, 1895), quoted in Weatherford, ed., *Critical Heritage*, p. 68; and Mark Antony De Wolfe Howe, from a review in the *Atlantic Monthly* (Feb. 1896), reprinted in Weatherford, p. 73. Howells's review appeared in *Harper's Weekly* (Jan. 25, 1896), reprinted in Weatherford, pp. 70–72.
132 Even Daniel Hoffman's claim to have discovered "one instance of direct indebtedness" collapses under close scrutiny. See *The Poetry of Stephen Crane*, p. 205. The "indebtedness" depends on the superficial resemblance of Dickinson's "Two swimmers wrestled on the spar" and Crane's "A man adrift on a slim spar." The image of a man clinging to a spar in the water was a poetic cliché long before Dickinson or Crane wrote.
—Garland, *Roadside Meetings*, p. 194, and "Stephen Crane as I Knew Him," p. 8.
134 On type as lines of battle, see Michael Fried's essay "Stephen Crane's Upturned Faces," in his *Realism, Writing, Disfiguration* (Chicago: University of Chicago Press, 1987). Fried is concerned exclusively with Crane's prose, but his discovery of an obsessive theme of writing in Crane's work has an obvious bearing on Crane's poems. See p. 191, n. 43, on Crane's use of capitalization in *The Black Riders* as a way to distinguish the poems from prose.
135 Two other poems, almost identical in rhetorical structure, show how far Crane could take his obsession with blood and ink. Here are the opening lines:

III

IN THE DESERT
I SAW A CREATURE, NAKED, BESTIAL,
WHO, SQUATTING UPON THE GROUND,
HELD HIS HEART IN HIS HANDS,
AND ATE OF IT.
I SAID, "IS IT GOOD, FRIEND?"

XI

IN A LONELY PLACE
I ENCOUNTERED A SAGE
WHO SAT, ALL STILL,
REGARDING A NEWSPAPER.
HE ACCOSTED ME:
"SIR, WHAT IS THIS?"

The similarity in structure, as well as the theme of ink as blood I have been tracing, invite us to interpret both of these poems as about reading. The wit of both poems lies in the questions. Coming across a man who is eating his heart, we would be more likely to ask, "What are you doing?" and not, as Crane's interlocutor does, "Is it good?" The question is ambiguous of course: he doesn't say, "Does it taste good?" So he may be asking whether the man is pure of heart.

136 William Dana Orcutt, "Frederick Holland Day," in *Publishers' Weekly* (Jan. 6, 1934), pp. 51–52. Day's given name was Fred, not Frederick. For more information on his life and work see Estelle Jussim, *Slave to Beauty* (Boston: Godine, 1981).

137 On Hubbard and other Arts and Crafts ideologues, see T. J. Jackson Lears, *No Place of Grace: Antimodernism and the Transformation of American Culture 1880–1920* (New York: Pantheon, 1981), especially the second chapter, "The Figure of the Artisan: Arts and Crafts Ideology," pp. 59–96.

—Elbert Hubbard, *William Morris* (East Aurora, N.Y.: Roycrofters Press, 1900), p. 19.

138 Stanley Cavell, *The World Viewed, Enlarged Edition* (Cambridge: Harvard University Press, 1979), p. 198.

139 Did Crane know the work of Mallarmé and Yeats? Asked whether he admired Mallarmé, Crane is reported to have answered, "I don't know much about Irish authors." But the reporter is Thomas Beer, who is notoriously unreliable (Beer, *Stephen Crane*, p. 124).

SEVEN: CRANE IN LOVE

142 For the major gallery, one that specialized in American art, see Macbeth Gallery Papers, Archives of American Art, New York City.

145 On sin and thinness, see Linson, *My Stephen Crane*, p. 14.

147 Linson, *My Stephen Crane*, p. 3.

—Robert Bremner, *From the Depths: The Discovery of Poverty in the United States* (New York: New York University Press, 1956), pp. 114–15.

150 Berryman, *Stephen Crane*, p. 122.

150 English reviewer, quoted in Weatherford, ed., *Critical Heritage*, p. 202.

151 Berryman, *Stephen Crane*, p. 123. On the talk of real life, see Weatherford, ed., *Critical Heritage*, p. 214.

153 On the prestige of the sketch, see Doreen Bolger Burke, "Painters and Sculptors in a Decorative Age," in Burke et al., *In Pursuit of Beauty: Americans and the Aesthetic Movement* (New York: The Metropolitan Museum of Art/Rizzoli, 1986), p. 314.

157 Sigmund Freud, "The Most Prevalent Form of Degradation in Erotic Life," in Freud, *Sexuality and the Psychology of Love* (New York: Collier, 1963), p. 62.

164 For Kafka's fantasy, see Elias Canetti, *Kafka's Other Trial*, trans. Christopher Middleton (New York: Schocken, 1974), p. 7.

166 The Columbia University Library has an etiquette manual from Crane's collection, titled *The Complete Bachelor: Manners for Men* (New York: Appleton, 1896). No author is given.

168 On "Flagons of despair," see Hoffman, *The Poetry of Stephen Crane*, p. 118.

EIGHT: DORA

172 This is Stallman's wording of Williams's remark (Stallman, *Stephen Crane*, pp. 233–34). See Andy Logan, *Against the Evidence: The Becker-Rosenthal Affair* (New York: McCall, 1970), p. 106, for a slightly different version.

173 Papers related to magistrate's court proceedings are housed in the Municipal Records of New York City. Though many papers exist for Magistrate Cornell's cases during September of 1896, and several of these involve Officer Becker, there is no record of the Dora Clark case in these archives.

174 Hearst, quoted in Christopher P. Wilson, *The Labor of Words: Literary Professionalism in the Progressive Era* (Athens: University of Georgia Press, 1985), p. 28.

—On studying victims in their haunts see V, vol. 8, p. 938.

175 On bird and bottle suppers see Lewis Erenberg, *Steppin' Out* (Westport, Conn.: Greenwood Press, 1981), pp. 50–56.

176 Stallman, *Stephen Crane*, p. 220.

—Logan hints at a motive for entrapment in *Against the Evidence*: "The September 1896 issue of *Book News* reported that [Crane] was at work on a series of short stories about a Metropolitan police officer. They were not expected to give a favorable picture of men in that line of work" (p. 109).

177 For Becker's background, see Logan, *Against the Evidence*, pp. 105–106.

178 Lawrence, quoted in Stallman, *Stephen Crane*, p. 221.

—On Grant, see *The Brooklyn Daily Eagle* (Oct. 17, 1896), reprinted in R. W. Stallman and E. R. Hagemann, ed., *The New York City Sketches of Stephen Crane* (New York: New York University Press, 1966), pp. 252–54. For a detailed account of the Dora Clark affair, drawing on many newspaper sources, see Olov W. Fryckstedt, "Stephen Crane in the Tenderloin," *Studia Neophilologica* 34 (1962): pp. 135–63.

179 "The Devil's Acre," V, vol. 8, pp. 664–65.

180 At the time of the murder trial it was often said that Becker's abuse of a prostitute had inspired Crane to write *Maggie*, though Crane wrote the book five years before he encountered Becker. Crane was again living according to his fictions. See Logan, *Against The Evidence*, p. 108.

181 See Stallman and Hagemann, ed., *The New York City Sketches*, pp. xi–xii,*n.*, for the Becker connection in *The Great Gatsby*.

NINE: SHIPWRECKS

183 On the land of shipwrecks, see "The Wreck of the 'New Era,'" in V, vol. 8, p. 580.

184 John D. Conway, "The Stephen Crane–Amy Leslie Affair: A Reconsideration," in *Journal of Modern Literature* 7 (1979): 4. The editors of Crane's correspondence speculate that before Crane left New York, Amy Leslie "may have told him . . . that she was pregnant with his child" (*Correspondence*, p. 262). This would help explain the various payments he made to her during the following year. There is no evidence that Amy Leslie bore a child by Crane.

187 Berryman, *Stephen Crane*, pp. 298–304.

—Cora quoted in Gilkes, *Cora Crane*, p. 51.

193 Stallman, *Stephen Crane*, p. 257. Paine quoted in Stallman, *Stephen Crane*, p. 257.

195 Lorenz E. A. Eitner, *Géricault: His Life and Work* (Ithaca: Cornell University Press, 1983), p. 194. Eitner gives close attention to Last Judgment imagery in Géricault's shipwreck painting (pp. 167–68, 192), precisely the same association present in Crane's representation.

198 J. T. Crane, *Arts of Intoxication* (New York: Carlton and Lanahan, 1870), p. 263.

—"The Wreck of the 'New Era,'" in V. vol. 8, pp. 580, 583.

199 "The Ghostly Sphinx," in V, vol. 8, p. 648.

TEN: REAL WAR

203 Davis quoted in Stallman, *Stephen Crane*, p. 268.

204 Crane's reports from Greece are collected in V, vol. 9. For quotations on this page and those immediately following, see pp. 7, 12–15, 19–21, 41. Wertheim and Sorrentino in their commentary to the *Correspondence* note the resemblance between *The Red Badge* and Crane's

Greek reportage: "Crane's dispatches to the New York *Journal* from the combat zone reflect the pattern of enthusiasm, disillusionment, and final reconciliation experienced by Henry Fleming" (p. 283).

208 Sigmund Freud, *The Psychopathology of Everyday Life*, trans. Alan Tyson (New York: Norton, 1965). Henri Bergson, "Laughter," in *Comedy* (New York: Anchor, 1956), p. 79: "The attitudes, gestures and movements of the human body are laughable in exact proportion as that body reminds us of a mere machine."

209 Quotations from Crane's Greek reportage on this page and those immediately following are taken from V, vol. 9, pp. 21–22, 31, 37, 73, 28–29, 34, 53, 54, 56.

210 Scarry, *The Body in Pain*, p. 73.

211 Scarry, *The Body in Pain*, p. 66.

212 Ford Madox Ford, *Portraits from Life* (Chicago: Gateway, 1937), p. 30.

213 Conrad, "Introduction" to Beer, *Stephen Crane*, p. 20.

218 Sigmund Freud, *Beyond the Pleasure Principle*, trans. James Strachey (New York: Norton, 1961), pp. 9–10.

ELEVEN: RAVENSBROOK

221 Ford, *Portraits*, p. 35.

224 Conrad quoted in Stallman, *Stephen Crane*, p. 330.

228 A. J. Liebling, "The Dollars Damned Him," in *Stephen Crane: A Collection of Critical Essays*, ed. Maurice Bassan (Englewood Cliffs, N.J.: Prentice-Hall, 1967), pp. 18–26.

229 Leon Edel, *Henry James: A Life* (New York: Harper & Row, 1985), p. 532.

—Gilkes, *Cora Crane*, p. 21.

230 Hemingway, *Green Hills of Africa* (New York: Scribner's, 1935), p. 23.

233 Cora, notebook in Stephen Crane Collection, Columbia University. Quoted in Gilkes, *Cora Crane*, p. 22.

235 Wallace Stevens, *The Palm at the End of the Mind*, ed. Holly Stevens (New York: Vintage, 1972), p. 46.

237 My discussion of the Swede's "demand for certainty" owes much to the ideas of Stanley Cavell concerning the place of skepticism in daily life. See, for example, *The Claim of Reason* (New York: Oxford, 1979), pp. 329–496.

TWELVE: WIGWAG AND SPY

240 Conrad quoted in Stallman, *Stephen Crane*, p. 347.

244 Crane's Cuban reportage is included in V, vol. 9. For quotations on this page and those immediately following, see pp. 103, 107, 110–112.

245 On Crane as wigwagger, see Stallman, *Stephen Crane*, p. 364.
246 Stallman notes the anticipation, *Stephen Crane*, p. 372. English reporter quoted in Stallman, *Stephen Crane*, p. 371.
247 V, vol. 9, p. 138.
248 See Michael Fried, *Absorption and Theatricality* (Chicago: University of Chicago Press, 1980).
249 For Crane's pen portrait see V, vol. 9, pp. 108–9.
—On Scovel and Thrall, see Joyce Milton, *The Yellow Kids: Foreign Correspondents in the Heyday of Yellow Journalism* (New York: Harper & Row, 1989), p. 251.
250 Crane on Scovel, Scovel on Santiago harbor, quoted in Milton, *The Yellow Kids*, pp. 306–307.
251 Crane as corpse, quoted in Stallman, *Stephen Crane*, p. 373.
—Crane on the church, quoted in Stallman, *Stephen Crane*, p. 400. The reporter is Charles Michelson, quoted in Stallman, *Stephen Crane*, p. 407.
253 Crane on Havana, quoted in Stallman, *Stephen Crane*, p. 413–14.
—For speculations about debts and blackmail, see Milton, *The Yellow Kids*, p. 358.

EPILOGUE: THE DIVIDED GHOST

258 For Crane on the ghost, see V, vol. 4, p. 246.
264 See Fried, "Stephen Crane's Upturned Faces," p. 198: "It is as though Crane . . . figures his own death through that of a surrogate who cannot use his hands (hence cannot write)."
268 Wells quoted in Stallman, *Stephen Crane*, p. 492. Newspaper account quoted in Stallman, *Stephen Crane*, pp. 556–57.

INDEX

A NOTE ABOUT THE AUTHOR

Christopher Benfey was born in 1954 and grew up in Indiana. He attended the Putney School and Guilford College, and has a doctorate in comparative literature from Harvard. The author of two books on Emily Dickinson, he is also a frequent contributor to many magazines and journals, including the *New Republic* and the *New York Review of Books*. His poems have appeared in the *Paris Review, Ploughshares*, and other journals. He has held Guggenheim and Danforth fellowships. He lives in Amherst, Massachusetts, with his wife and son, and teaches American literature at Mount Holyoke College.

A NOTE ON THE TYPE

The text of this book was set in a typeface called Walbaum, named for Justus Erich Walbaum (1768–1839), a typefounder who removed from his beginnings in Goslar to Weimar in 1803. It is likely that he produced this famous type face shortly thereafter, following the designs of the French typefounder, Firmin Didot. His original matrices are still in existence, owned by the Berthold foundry of Berlin. Continuously popular in Germany since its inception, the face was introduced to England by the Monotype Corporation in 1934, and has steadily grown in popularity ever since.

Composition by Graphic Composition, Inc., Athens, Georgia
Printed and bound by Halliday Lithographers,
West Hanover, Massachusetts
Designed by Harry Ford